BARRON'S

ENGLISH THE EASY WAY

SECOND EDITION

By

HARRIET DIAMOND

President
DIAMOND ASSOCIATES
Multi-Faceted Training & Development
Westfield, New Jersey

and

PHYLLIS DUTWIN

Vice President
READING & EDUCATIONAL SERVICES, INC.
East Greenwich, Rhode Island

BARRON'S EDUCATIONAL SERIES, INC.

This book is dedicated to those adults committed to
lifelong learning: the students and their teachers.

ACKNOWLEDGMENTS

We wish to express our appreciation to Walter Hauck, former director of the
New Jersey State Department of Education's Office of High School Completion, for his encouragement and assistance.

Thanks to Harry Linkin, former director of Adult and Continuing Education at
the Union County Regional Adult School, to Wayne Hemingway, former
director of the High School Equivalency Program and Ted Gnagey, former
director of Adult Education at the South Orange-Maplewood Adult School, for
providing the teaching atmospheres which allowed us to work creatively and
develop our material.

Finally, we would like to thank our families for their patience and encouragement.

All inquiries should be addressed to:

Barron's Educational Series, Inc.
250 Wireless Boulevard
Hauppauge, New York 11788

Library of Congress Catalog Card No. 88-6301
International Standard Book No. 0-8120-3347-7

Library of Congress Cataloging in Publication Data

Diamond, Harriet.
  English the easy way.

  1. English language — Grammar — 1950–
2. English language — Usage. I. Dutwin, Phyllis.
II. Title.
PE1112.D47   1988   428.2   88-6301
ISBN 0-8120-3347-7

Portion of material adapted from Russell Baker's "Backwards Wheels the Mind," *The New York Times*, July 1,
1973. © 1973 by The New York Times Company. Reprinted by permission.

Quote from Richard Bach's *Jonathan Livingston Seagull*.
© 1970, Macmillan Publishing Co., Inc. Reprinted by
permission.

Paragraph from *A Civil Tongue* by Edwin Newman. © 1976
by Edwin Newman.

Portions of Chapter 22 adapted from *Writing the Easy Way*
by Harriet Diamond and Phyllis Dutwin.
© 1985 by Barron's Educational Series, Inc.

PRINTED IN THE UNITED STATES OF AMERICA

3456   510   16 15 14

TABLE OF CONTENTS

Introduction

In traditional grammar programs, students are often baffled by the necessity of memorizing numerous definitions of grammatical terminology, none of which has any practical meaning in terms of day-to-day speech and writing. The confusion which results is often detrimental; the student's frustration ultimately overcomes his or her desire to learn.

English The Easy Way is designed to encourage, not frustrate, the student. Written specifically for adult students who want an all-inclusive self-help program in grammar, *English The Easy Way* also serves as an invaluable tool for all English language improvement programs.

Its main feature is a common sense approach to language study. Recognizing that traditional grammar is not easy for everyone to master, *English The Easy Way* emphasizes language structure. Thus, the main purpose of this format is to motivate by showing how much the student already knows about the language.

English The Easy Way builds upon the student's basic understanding in an organized way. Beginning with the basic sentence pattern—performer-action—the book continues until all essential elements are introduced. Ample practice material follows each newly introduced concept. Because of the manner of presentation of the instructional material, *English The Easy Way* lends itself easily either to group or individualized classroom instruction or to independent study.

Effective Use of This Book

Because *English The Easy Way* is a cumulative study, we recommend beginning with Chapter 1 and continuing consecutively. There are two chapters which do not fit into the consecutive pattern of the book, "Spelling" and "Word Usage." Spelling rules can be summarized in one chapter, but they cannot be learned in one lesson. The same is true of word usage. The authors, therefore, recommend that students begin studying these chapters early in their program and continue on a regular basis.

Guard against skimming over instructional material. Skipping instructional material, in order to complete practices quickly, will result in unnecessary errors and time lost. Before attempting a Cumulative Review, the authors recommend reviewing the major concepts presented in the chapters which precede it.

Consistent use of the *Answer Key* is essential to proper study. The authors recommend that students check each practice exercise with the *Answer Key* before going on to the next section. By checking answers after each exercise, students can avoid repeating errors. Cumulative Reviews should be considered tests and should be taken in their entirety before checking answers. Students should note the kinds of errors made in Cumulative Reviews (these answers have been keyed to the applicable review chapters) and return to these appropriate chapters for reinforcement of the correct concepts.

1.
The Simplest Complete Thought

"Twas brillig and the slithy toves
  Did gyre and gimble in the wabe;
All mimsy were the borogroves,
  All the mome raths outgrabe.

"Beware the Jabberwock, my son!
  The jaws that bite, the claws that catch!
Beware the Jubjub bird, and shun
  The frumious Bandersnatch!"
                    —Lewis Carroll
                    "Jabberwocky"

A Word With You . . .

"Jabberwocky," the most famous nonsense poem ever written, can be enjoyed on several levels. Literary detectives have tried to find hidden meanings in the madeup words, while others have been amused by the poet's cleverness with sounds and rhythms.

Although Lewis Carroll never heard of "the flink glopped," it is a phrase he might have approved of—especially in the way it is used in the chapter you are about to read.

What You've Always Known . . .

The flink glopped.

What is the above sentence about? What action is taking place in this sentence? Who is performing this action? You are able to understand the nonsense sentence because you are familiar with that sentence pattern: a person or thing performing an action.

PERFORMER ACTION
        \   /
     (The) flink glopped.

You frequently see this pattern written, and you hear it spoken.

Another clue in this sentence is a clue to time. Is the action past, present, or future? What was the clue? Yes, the *-ed* ending is the clue to time. The action occurred in the past.

Notice the word endings in the following sentences:

> The flin*k* glo*ps*.
> Two flin*ks* glo*p*.

When the performer *(flink)* is *singular,* an *s* is added to the present action. When the performer *(flinks)* is *plural* (more than one), no *s* is added to the present action.

This simple pattern may have *more than one performer:*

> The *flink and his brother glop.*

There may be one performer and *more than one action:*

> The *flink glops* and *glarks.*

There may also be *more than one performer and more than one action:*

> The *flink and his brother glop* and *glark.*

Now, let's examine some real sentences which use the same pattern: a person or thing performing an action and the action. As you read the following sentences, think about who or what is performing the action, what the action is, and when the action occurs (present, past, or future). Next, write in the spaces provided the performer, the action, and the time. The first sentence is done for you.

	PERFORMER	ACTION	*present* *past* *future* TIME
1. The law student completed the difficult exam.	student	completed	past
2. Mrs. Smith sings in the church choir each Sunday.			
3. The plane raced across the sky.			
4. They will speak at the November meeting.			
5. The interviewer listened attentively.			

PERFORMER	ACTION	TIME

6. A cashier always counts the change.

7. Star Cleaners picks up and delivers cleaning.

8. The woman and her children crossed the street.

9. The gardener rakes the leaves and cuts the grass.

10. Diane and Joe dined at the tavern and attended the theater.

PRACTICE

I   **Directions:** Complete the pattern in each of the following sentences by adding either the person or thing performing the action or the action.

1. The children _____ into the street.

2. _____ barked at the mailman.

3. _____ will signal at the light.

4. The choir _____ last Sunday.

5. _____ hesitated in the doorway.

PRACTICE

II   **Directions:** Draw a line from the people or things in the left column to the actions in the right column to make complete sentences.

PERFORMERS	ACTIONS
The jury	travel.
An accident	will attend.
A salesman and his assistant	occurred.
	convened and concurred.
A motorcycle	
We	backfires.

PRACTICE

III **Directions:** Write three sentences of your own using the sentence pattern you have just studied: a person or thing performing an action and an action.

PERFORMER   ACTION

1. _____

2. _____

3. _____

PRACTICE

IV **Directions:** In each of the following sentences one word is underlined. If the underlined word is the person or thing performing the action, blacken the space in column 1. If the underlined word is the action word, blacken the space in column 2.

		1	2
1.	The *manager* shouted at the salesman.	‖	‖
2.	A large delivery *truck* approached the intersection.	‖	‖
3.	We *celebrated* her graduation.	‖	‖
4.	The *mayor* proclaimed a clean-up week.	‖	‖
5.	The members *contributed* large sums of money.	‖	‖
6.	The huge *machine* sputtered menacingly.	‖	‖
7.	A committee *will convene* within the week.	‖	‖
8.	The *union* struck after much negotiation.	‖	‖
9.	The checkbook *balances* for the first time.	‖	‖
10.	A soprano *will sing* this part of the opera.	‖	‖

PRACTICE

V **Directions:** Blacken column 1 if a sentence has one performer and one action; blacken column 2 if a sentence has more than one performer and one action; blacken column 3 if a sentence has one performer and two actions; blacken column 4 if a sentence has more than one performer and two actions.

		1	2	3	4
1.	This candidate addresses the issues.	‖	‖	‖	‖
2.	His opponent evades difficult questions.	‖	‖	‖	‖

<table>
<tr><td></td><td></td><td>1</td><td>2</td><td>3</td><td>4</td></tr>
<tr><td>3.</td><td>Meditation relaxes many people.</td><td>||</td><td>||</td><td>||</td><td>||</td></tr>
<tr><td>4.</td><td>Mr. Valdez proposed several good ideas.</td><td>||</td><td>||</td><td>||</td><td>||</td></tr>
<tr><td>5.</td><td>Six team members shouted at the coach.</td><td>||</td><td>||</td><td>||</td><td>||</td></tr>
<tr><td>6.</td><td>Maria and Julia sold their pottery.</td><td>||</td><td>||</td><td>||</td><td>||</td></tr>
<tr><td>7.</td><td>The electrician and his assistant stopped and rested.</td><td>||</td><td>||</td><td>||</td><td>||</td></tr>
<tr><td>8.</td><td>The audience cheered and applauded.</td><td>||</td><td>||</td><td>||</td><td>||</td></tr>
<tr><td>9.</td><td>Batman always wins.</td><td>||</td><td>||</td><td>||</td><td>||</td></tr>
<tr><td>10.</td><td>I asked a searching question.</td><td>||</td><td>||</td><td>||</td><td>||</td></tr>
</table>

Recognizing Complete and Incomplete Thoughts

You are ready now to add another element to your understanding of complete thoughts.

> *Example:* When you arrive.

The above sentence has a performer *(you)* and an action *(arrive)*; yet, it is not a complete thought. Because the sentence begins with the word *when,* the thought is not complete as it stands.

> Any sentence which begins with words as *when, after, because, as soon as, before,* or *since* needs to have a completing thought.

Possible thought completions for *When you arrive* are:

    a. When you arrive, *relax.*
    b. When you arrive, *call me.*
    c. When you arrive, *I will leave.*

> *Example:* The bustling figure walking hurriedly through the park.

The above sentence has a performer *(figure)*, but the action *(walking)* is incomplete. It would be correct to say the figure *was walking* or the figure *is walking.*

Possible thought completions for *The figure* are:

    a. The bustling figure *is walking hurriedly through the park.*

    b. The bustling figure *was walking hurriedly through the park.*

    c. The bustling figure *walked hurriedly through the park.*

PRACTICE

VI   **Directions:** Blacken the space beneath the number which corresponds to the number of the incomplete sentence in each group. If there is no error, blacken space number 5.

                                        1 2 3 4 5

1 (1) After McCarthy's defeat, he retired from public office. || || || || ||

(2) Bring me a cup of coffee, please.

(3) When Richard called his office.

(4) The two truckers arrived at the delivery depot at the same time.

(5) No error

                                        1 2 3 4 5

2 (1) The man in the blue suit and the lady in the tan coat walking. || || || || ||

(2) The legislature meets daily.

(3) I did not buy enough yarn for the sweater.

(4) A large delivery truck reached the intersection.

(5) No error

                                        1 2 3 4 5

3 (1) The nervous waitress spilled the coffee in the celebrity's lap. || || || || ||

(2) The fumbling, bumbling clown dancing.

(3) The county official faced the angry crowd.

(4) The women in the community organized a boycott against Sam's Market.

(5) No error

                                        1 2 3 4 5

4 (1) A favorite history question involves the causative factors of the Civil War. || || || || ||

(2) Federal spending cuts will cause much discussion.

(3) The winning pitcher threw a fast ball.

(4) Her considerate husband brought a dozen roses for their anniversary.

(5) No error

1 2 3 4 5
|| || || || ||

5 (1) The students studied and reviewed.

(2) Flour, sugar, and three eggs blending.

(3) The book fell suddenly from the shelf.

(4) The mayor proclaimed a clean-up week.

(5) No error

1 2 3 4 5
|| || || || ||

6 (1) Leona working harder than any other lawyer in the firm.

(2) A soprano will sing this part in the opera.

(3) Robert and Chico prepare the finest paella.

(4) The candidate spoke the truth.

(5) No error

1 2 3 4 5
|| || || || ||

7 (1) The man threw away the garbage.

(2) The soldiers walked quietly.

(3) When I have finished dusting and vacuuming and washing, I will relax.

(4) The mayor commended the members of the local Rescue Squad.

(5) No error

Action Words: Special Problems

Many action words undergo simple changes to show changes in time. *For example:*

PRESENT	PAST	ACTION WORDS USED WITH HELPING WORDS, SUCH AS HAS, HAD, HAVE, IS, ETC.
kick	kicked	kicked
plan	planned	planned
laugh	laughed	laughed

The simplest change is the addition of an *-ed* ending.

1. I *kick* the ball 200 yards each time.
2. The tenants' association *planned* a victory party.
3. The overzealous Viking fans *had cheered* before they realized that the Eagle quarterback was really injured.

Many action words use entirely different forms to show these same time changes. *For example:*

PRESENT	PAST	ACTION WORDS USED WITH HELPING WORDS, SUCH AS HAS, HAD, HAVE, IS, ETC.
break	broke	broken

1. Anna never *breaks* a promise.
2. Rosemary *broke* several promises to Anna.
3. Rosemary *has broken* her last promise.

Following is a list of commonly used action words which change their forms to show time changes.

PRESENT	PAST	ACTION WORDS USED WITH HELPING WORDS, SUCH AS HAS, HAD, HAVE, IS, ETC.
begin	began	begun
blow	blew	blown
break	broke	broken
bring	brought	brought
build	built	built
burst	burst	burst
choose	chose	chosen
dive	dived or dove	dived
do	did	done

PRESENT	PAST	ACTION WORDS USED WITH HELPING WORDS, SUCH AS HAS, HAD, HAVE, IS, ETC.
draw	drew	drawn
drink	drank	drunk
drive	drove	driven
eat	ate	eaten
fall	fell	fallen
flee	fled	fled
fly	flew	flown
forbid	forbade	forbidden
freeze	froze	frozen
get	got	gotten or got
give	gave	given
go	went	gone
grow	grew	grown
have, has	had	had
know	knew	known
lay (place)	laid	laid
lead	led	led
leave (depart)	left	left
let (allow)	let	let
lie (recline)	lay	lain
pay	paid	paid
raise (elevate)	raised	raised
ride	rode	ridden
ring	rang	rung
rise (ascend)	rose	risen
run	ran	run
see	saw	seen
set (place)	set	set
shake	shook	shaken
shine	shone, shined	shone, shined
shoot	shot	shot
shrink	shrank, shrunk	shrunk
sing	sang	sung
sit	sat	sat
slay	slew	slain
speak	spoke	spoken
spring	sprang	sprung

PRESENT	PAST	ACTION WORDS USED WITH HELPING WORDS, SUCH AS HAS, HAD, HAVE, IS, ETC.
steal	stole	stolen
sting	stung	stung
swear	swore	sworn
swing	swung	swung
swim	swam	swum
take	took	taken
tear	tore	torn
throw	threw	thrown
wake	waked *or* woke	waked
wear	wore	worn
write	wrote	written

PRACTICE

VII   **Directions:** Blacken the space beneath the number which corresponds to the number of the sentence with the incorrect action word in each group. If there is no error, blacken space number 5.

                                                                                      1 2 3 4 5

1 (1)   Marigolds always have *grown* well in that sunny spot.   ‖ ‖ ‖ ‖ ‖

  (2)   I have *rang* her doorbell several times today.

  (3)   After we had *set* the bowl of flowers on the table, the room looked complete.

  (4)   Having *ridden* for hours, sightseers were ready to check into a motel.

  (5)   No error

                                                                                      1 2 3 4 5

2 (1)   Angela *led* the church choir.   ‖ ‖ ‖ ‖ ‖

  (2)   Last year, Marlene *lead* the church choir.

  (3)   I never *have led* a church choir.

  (4)   Have you ever *led* a church choir?

  (5)   No error

                                                                                      1 2 3 4 5

3 (1)   I *swear* that I told the truth.   ‖ ‖ ‖ ‖ ‖

  (2)   The defendant *swore* to tell the truth.

(3) The plaintiff _swore_ to tell the truth.

(4) All of the witnesses have been _sworn_ in.

(5) No error

	1	2	3	4	5

4 (1) Bobby Riggs has _swung_ many tennis rackets in his time.

(2) Billy Jean King had never _swung_ a tennis racket quite like she did during that decisive game.

(3) I wonder if Bobby Riggs _swings_ a golf club incorrectly?

(4) He _swinged_ a tennis racket fairly well.

(5) No error

	1	2	3	4	5

5 (1) The opinionated Mr. Dobbs never had _run_ for office himself.

(2) Colonel Adams has _run_ for mayor several times.

(3) I have _ran_ for public office once.

(4) Mrs. Diaz plans to _run_ next year.

(5) No error

6 (1) Did you _write_ to Mattie about your promotion?

	1	2	3	4	5

(2) Arthur _wrote_ to her several times.

(3) I had not _written_ before the summer ended.

(4) Mrs. Scott has always _written_ excellent business letters.

(5) No error

	1	2	3	4	5

7 (1) Mother had _threw_ out my favorite old sneakers before I could stop her.

(2) I wouldn't _throw_ out someone else's sneakers.

(3) I saved those sneakers from being _thrown_ out several times.

(4) This time, they were _thrown_ out for the last time.

(5) No error

PRACTICE VIII

Directions: Blacken the space beneath the number which corresponds to the number of the incorrect word in each sentence. If there is no error, blacken space number 5.

1 2 3 4 5
|| || || || ||

1. The injured bird *flew* to the ground, *letting*
$\quad\quad\quad\quad\quad\quad\quad$ 1 $\quad\quad\quad\quad\quad\quad\quad$ 2

   his *broken* wing *lay* at his side. *No error*
   $\quad\quad$ 3 $\quad\quad\quad$ 4 $\quad\quad\quad\quad\quad\quad$ 5

1 2 3 4 5
|| || || || ||

2. Upon seeing the young child *fall* into the
   $\quad\quad\quad\quad\quad\quad\quad\quad\quad\quad\quad$ 1

   lake, Eric *sprung* to his feet, *ran* , and *dived.*
   $\quad\quad\quad\quad$ 2 $\quad\quad\quad\quad\quad\quad$ 3 $\quad\quad\quad$ 4

   No error
   $\quad$ 5

1 2 3 4 5
|| || || || ||

3. Because Teddy had frequently *fallen* asleep
   $\quad\quad\quad\quad\quad\quad\quad\quad\quad\quad\quad\quad$ 1

   on the job, he was not *payed* the full *amount*
   $\quad\quad\quad\quad\quad\quad\quad\quad\quad\quad$ 2 $\quad\quad\quad\quad\quad$ 3

   that had been *written* into his contract.
   $\quad\quad\quad\quad\quad\quad$ 4

   No error
   $\quad$ 5

1 2 3 4 5
|| || || || ||

4. If you *choose* to *rise* within the company, you
   $\quad\quad\quad$ 1 $\quad\quad\quad$ 2

   must raise your level of work. *No error*
   $\quad$ 3 $\quad$ 4 $\quad\quad\quad\quad\quad\quad\quad\quad$ 5

1 2 3 4 5
|| || || || ||

5. The guest *arrived* unexpectedly, *shaked*
   $\quad\quad\quad\quad$ 1 $\quad\quad\quad\quad\quad\quad\quad\quad$ 2

   everyone's hand, *ate*, and *left* as unexpect-
   $\quad\quad\quad\quad\quad\quad$ 3 $\quad\quad\quad$ 4

   edly as he had arrived. *No error*
   $\quad\quad\quad\quad\quad\quad\quad\quad$ 5

6. We *seen* the lights which *shined* in the dis-
   1   2

   tance, and we *began* to *walk* toward them.
                  3   4

   No error
   5

   1 2 3 4 5
   || || || || ||

7. Because I had *forgotten* my driver's license,
                  1

   the policeman *forbidded* me to *drive* any
                  2   3

   farther. *No error*
   4   5

   1 2 3 4 5
   || || || || ||

8. Once their leader had *fallen*, the young sol-
                         1

   diers did not *know* how to continue, so they
                  2

   fleed in many directions and were never
   3

   seen again. *No error*
   4   5

   1 2 3 4 5
   || || || || ||

9. The *armed* man *slayed* the innocent victim,
       1   2

   stole his watch, and *ran* down the alley.
   3   4

   No error
   5

   1 2 3 4 5
   || || || || ||

10. Maxine *waked* me early this morning, and
           1

    I *ate* my eggs, *drunk* my juice, and *left*.
      2   3   4

    No error
    5

    1 2 3 4 5
    || || || || ||

ANSWER KEY

Chapter I

The Simplest Complete Thought

	PERFORMER	ACTION	TIME
1.	student	completed	past
2.	Mrs. Smith	sings	present
3.	plane	raced	past
4.	they	will speak	future
5.	interviewer	listened	past
6.	cashier	counts	present
7.	Star Cleaners	picks up, delivers	present
8.	woman, children	crossed	past
9.	gardener	rakes, cuts	present
10.	Diane, Joe	dined, attended	past

Practice I *Page 3.*

Answers will vary. *Sample* answers:
1. The children *ran* into the street.
2. *The dog* barked at the mailman.
3. *Henry* will signal at the light.
4. The choir *sang* last Sunday.
5. *Susan* hesitated in the doorway.

Practice II *Page 3.*

1. The jury convened and concurred.
2. An accident occurred.
3. A salesman and his assistant travel.
4. A motorcycle backfires.
5. We will attend.

Practice III *Page 4.*

Answers will vary. *Sample* answers:
1. *John cashed* a check at the bank.
2. The *roses bloomed* early this year.
3. My *mother-in-law calls* every Friday.

Practice IV *Page 4.*

	PERFORMER	ACTION
1. (1)	manager	
2. (1)	truck	
3. (2)		celebrated
4. (1)	mayor	
5. (2)		contributed
6. (1)	machine	
7. (2)		will convene
8. (1)	union	
9. (2)		balances
10. (2)		will sing

Practice V *Page 4.*

	PERFORMER	ACTION
1. (1)	candidate	addresses
2. (1)	opponent	evades
3. (1)	meditation	relaxes
4. (1)	Mr. Valdez	proposed
5. (2)	members	shouted
6. (2)	Maria and Julia	sold
7. (4)	electrician and assistant	stopped and rested
8. (3)	audience	cheered and applauded
9. (1)	Batman	wins
10. (1)	I	asked

Practice VI *Page 6.*

Possible Corrections:
1. (3) a. When Richard called his office, the phone rang unanswered.
   b. Richard called his office.
2. (1) a. The man in the blue suit and the lady in the tan coat walk.
   b. The man in the blue suit and the lady in the tan coat, walking along the street, were stopped by a stranger.
3. (2) a. The fumbling, bumbling clown danced.
   b. The fumbling, bumbling clown dancing makes the children laugh.
4. (5) No error
5. (2) a. Blend flour, sugar, and three eggs.
   b. Flour, sugar, and three eggs blending completes the recipe.
6. (1) a. Leona worked harder than any other lawyer in the firm.
   b. Leona, working harder than any other lawyer in the firm, was promoted to Vice President.
7. (5) No error

Practice VII *Page 10.*

1. (2) have *rung*   Use *rung* with the helping word *have*.
2. (2) *led*   *Lead* is present; *led* is past.
3. (5) No error
4. (4) *swung*   *Swinged* is not a word.
5. (3) have *run*   Use *run* with the helping word *have*.
6. (5) No error
7. (1) *thrown*   Use *thrown* with the helping word *had*.

Practice VIII *Page 12.*

1. (5)   No error
2. (2) sprang   *Sprung* is used only with helping words such as *has*, *have* or *had*.
3. (2) paid   *Payed* is not a word.
4. (5)   No error
5. (2) shook   *Shaked* is not a word.
6. (1) saw   *Seen* is used only with helping words such as *has*, *have* or *had*.
7. (2) forbade *Forbidded* is not a word.
8. (3) fled   *Fleed* is not a word.
9. (2) slew   *Slayed* is not a word.
10. (3) drank   *Drunk* is used only with helping words such as *has*, *have* or *had*.

2.

Performer and Action: Understanding Time and Number

Every so often, Mr. Spector called on Vinnie to answer, and that was when English 117 really came to life.

"So I says to Angie . . ."

"No, Vinnie," interjected Mr. Spector, "you didn't 'says' to Angie, you 'said' to him."

"That's right," continued Vinnie, "I *says* to Angie . . ."

"Go on," Mr. Spector replied wearily; "You *says* to Angie . . ."

"That's what I *said*, man," snorted Vinnie. "Can't a guy tell a story without bein' interrupted?"

—Roger Talifiero
Our Little Red Schoolhouse

A Word With You . . .

Mr. Spector's English class was a lively place because the teacher encouraged free and open discussion. At times, however, Mr. Spector's classical training set his teeth on edge when he saw a misspelling or a failure to capitalize.

In this excerpt, his student, Vinnie, was confused about different forms of the action word *to say*. After you read Chapter 2, you should know why Mr. Spector often needed an aspirin after English 117.

Understanding Time

As you learned in Chapter I, actions occur at different times. *For example:*

John walks. *(present)*
John walked. *(past)*
John will walk. *(future)*

PRACTICE

I   **Directions:** Use *work, worked,* or *will work* in each of the following sentences.

1.   Willie Farris _____ overtime last week.

2.   We must _____ a certain number of hours each day.

3.   Four employees _____ overtime next week.

It is easy to determine the time of the action word in a single sentence. When sentences appear in paragraph form, however, the time of each action is more difficult to determine. *The time of all action words in a paragraph must be the same.* The action word in the first sentence sets the time for the paragraph. *For example:*

INCORRECT: John *entered* the library. He *speaks* to the librarian. Finally, John *chooses* a book.

CORRECT: John *entered* the library. He *spoke* to the librarian. Finally, John *chose* a book.

Because *entered* is in the *past, spoke* and *chose* must be in the *past,* too.

PRACTICE

II   **Directions:** For each underlined action word, blacken the space under number 1 if the time is correct and under number 2 if the time is incorrect. Remember that the action word *filed* sets the time for the other action words in the paragraph.

	1	2
The crowd *filed* into the meeting room. The		
chairman *raps* his gavel. An angry murmur 1)	‖	‖
continued in the room. The chairman *will rap* 2)	‖	‖
his gavel a second time. Quiet finally *settles* 3)	‖	‖
over the room. The chairman *began* his re- 4)	‖	‖
port. 5)	‖	‖

Understanding Number

The performer in a sentence may be singular (one) or plural (more than one). A plural performer may be expressed in one word (girls) or in more than one word (Mary, Sue, and Jane).

PRACTICE

III   **Directions:**   In each of the following sentences, underline the performer or performers. Write an *S* over the word if the performer is singular or a *P* if the performer is plural.

S

Example: <u>Mr. Warner</u> knows everyone in town.

1.   The women work well together.

2.   Mr. Smith and his son address the Cub Scouts.

3.   Flour, sugar, and milk complete this recipe.

4.   Connie Martine understands community relations.

5.   Mr. Luchner's grandchildren often visit him.

The performer must agree with the action word in number. Look at the following sentences:

> All of our relatives *comes* to dinner every Sunday.
> Those cars *travels* at top speed.
> The house *stand* on a hill.

The above sentences sound awkward. Look at the same sentences written correctly. What changes have been made?

> All of our relatives *come* to dinner every Sunday.
> Those cars *travel* at top speed.
> The house *stands* on a hill.

As stated above, every performer must agree with its action word in number. If the performer is singular, the action word must be singular. Notice that agreement in the past is easier to achieve than agreement in the present. Although the performer changes in number in each sentence below, the time of the action remains the same—past. *Rode* is the form used to show past. *For example:*

> I *rode* the subway.
> You *rode* the subway.

(He)	David *rode* the subway.
(She)	Pam *rode* the subway.
	Who *rode* the subway?
(We)	David and I *rode* the subway.
	You and Pam *rode* the subway.
(They)	Ellen and Linda *rode* the subway.

In the following sentences, the time is present. Notice that the form of the action word changes for singular and plural performers. You see that an *s* is added to the action word when the performer is *singular*—except when the performer is _I_ or _you_.

> *Example:* The lad*y* rid*es* the subway.
> The lad*ies* rid*e* the subway.

	I *ride* the subway.
	You *ride* the subway.
(He)	David *rides* the subway.
(She)	Pam *rides* the subway.
	Who *rides* the subway?
(We)	David and I *ride* the subway.
	You and Pam *ride* the subway.
(They)	Ellen and Linda *ride* the subway.

PRACTICE
IV   **Directions:** Blacken the space beneath the number which corresponds to the number of the incorrect action word in each group of sentences. If there is no error, blacken space number 5.

1 2 3 4 5
‖ ‖ ‖ ‖ ‖

1.   A shopping trip *makes* me angry. Prices *soar*
1   2

each week. Meat prices *changes* almost daily.
3

Oranges, apples, and bananas *cost* more than
4

ever. A shopper needs more and more money

each week. *No error*
5

| | | 1 | 2 | 3 | 4 | 5 |

2.   Tom *jogs* each morning. Macon and Gary *join*
       1   2

him on Mondays and Thursdays. The Robin-

son twins *likes* jogging too. Jogging now
          3

replaces basketball as the neighborhood pas-
 4

time. *No error*
     5

3.   Each year local artists *participate* in an art
                         1

show. The Community Center *offers* a per-
                       2

fect gallery. One artist *wins* in each of five cat-
               3

egories. The winning artists *displays* their
                   4

works in the Town Hall. *No error*
               5

The above paragraphs had errors in *number*. In the following exercise look for errors in *time* and *number*.

**PRACTICE
V**

Directions: Blacken the space beneath the number which corresponds to the number of the incorrect word in each group of sentences. If there is no error, blacken space number 5.

1.   In the spring the honeysuckle *droops* over the
                           1

hillside. Its sweet *smell hangs* heavily in the
            2   3

air outside. It floats into the room when the

doors *are open. No error*
      4   5

2. A hummingbird *dives* daily in and out of the
    $\overline{}$
    1

    honeysuckle. He *bombs* *past* the doors with
    $\overline{}$ $\overline{}$
    2   3

    his heavy load and *balanced* on a branch of
    $\overline{}$
    4

    the little olive tree. *No error*
    $\overline{}$
    5

                      1 2 3 4 5
                      ‖ ‖ ‖ ‖ ‖

3. A teenage driver *causes* one out of every
    $\overline{}$
    1

    three automobile accidents. Many *accuse*
    $\overline{}$
    2

    teen drivers of not concentrating on the

    road. Three out of six parents *interviewed*
    $\overline{}$
    3

    fears for their children's safety. *No error*
    $\overline{}$ $\overline{}$
    4   5

                      1 2 3 4 5
                      ‖ ‖ ‖ ‖ ‖

4. The farmer and his hired men *gathers* the
    $\overline{}$
    1

    corn. The farmer, along with his hired men,

    harvests the wheat. Neither the corn nor
    $\overline{}$
    2

    the wheat is *neglected.* The farmer's wife and
    $\overline{}$
    3

    daughter *argue* a great deal. *No error*
    $\overline{}$ $\overline{}$
    4   5

ANSWER KEY

Chapter 2

Performer and Action: Understanding Time and Number

Practice I *Page 17.*

1. Willie Farris <u>*worked*</u> overtime last week.
2. We must <u>*work*</u> a certain number of hours each day.
3. Four employees <u>*will work*</u> overtime next week.

Practice II *Page 17.*

Remember *filed* set the time (past) for the other action words in the paragraph. The crowd *filed* into the meeting room.

1. (2)   The chairman <u>*rapped*</u> his gavel. An angry
                1
2. (1)   murmur <u>*continued*</u> in the room. The chairman
                  2
3. (2)   <u>*rapped*</u> his gavel a second time. Quiet
       3
4. (2)   finally <u>*settled*</u> over the room. The chairman
           4
5. (1)   <u>*began*</u> his report.
       5

Practice III *Page 18.*

    P
1. women
          P
2. Mr. Smith and his son
         P
3. Flour, sugar, and milk
      S
4. Connie Martine
     P
5. grandchildren

Practice IV *Page 19.*

1. (3) change   *Change* is the plural form of the action word which agrees in number with the performer, *prices*.

2. (3) like   *Like* is the plural form of the action word which agrees in number with the performer, *twins*.

3. (4) display   *Display* is the plural form of the action word which agrees in number with the performer, *artists*.

Practice V *Page 20.*

1. (5)   No error
2. (4)   balances   All of the action words in the paragraph are in the *present time*.
3. (4)   fear   *Fear* is the plural form of the action word which agrees with *parents*.
4. (1)   gather   *Gather* is the plural form of the action word which agrees with *farmer and his hired men*.

3.

Adding Descriptive Words

Vic: We have to advertise, Charley. No wonder no one comes into our store.

Charley: I hate all those phoney ads where they hit you in the head with one lie after another.

Vic: We don't have to lie. The truth will bring the suckers in.

Charley: This is a fruit store—that's it, a fruit store. What else can we say about it?

Vic: Use your head, Charles, my boy. Our fruit isn't just fruit, it's *delectable* fruit; we've got *golden* bananas, our cherries are *heavenly delicious,* the *sugar-sweet* pears would kill a diabetic.

Charley: I dunno, to me fruit is fruit.

—L. I. Meyers
A Lovely Bunch of Coconuts

A Word With You . . .

Vic and Charley, the owners of Plaza Fruit, appear in a one-act play called *A Lovely Bunch of Coconuts.* As you can see, their personalities are different. Charley lacks romance—to him an apple is an apple. But Vic has the Madison Avenue approach to glamorizing his product.

Actually, what Vic did in this brief slice from the play is to add meaning by the use of descriptive words. You'll learn more about the technique in the next few pages.

Descriptive Words: Adding Meaning

You know that an English sentence must have a person or thing (performer) performing an action. You might say that these words are the core of every sentence. But we don't speak in such simple sentences: *He ran. She jumped.* Other words are added to the core to make a sentence more meaningful and interesting. These words may tell you more about the performer, or they may tell you more about the action. Look at the following example:

PERFORMER   ACTION

The beautiful swan swam quickly.

The performer is *swan* and the action is *swam.* Note the words *the, beautiful,* and *quickly.* These are descriptive words. *The* tells which *swan; beautiful* tells you more about the performer, *swan,* and *quickly* tells you more about *swam,* the action.

PERFORMER   ACTION

The beautiful swan swam quickly.
descriptive words

Now study the two sentences below. Label the performer, action, and descriptive words in each sentence.

A large apple fell suddenly.

The decaying tooth throbbed painfully.

PRACTICE

I   **Directions:**   Complete the pattern in each of the following sentences by adding a descriptive word.

1.   A _____ man entered the store.

2.   _____ music annoys me.

3.   The cat jumped _____.

4.   The _____ book slipped to the floor.

5.   Dolores Bremmer walked _____ from the room.

PRACTICE

II   **Directions:**   Write five sentences of your own. Use descriptive words to tell more about the performer, the action, or both.

1.   _____

2.   _____

3.   _____

4.   _____

5.   _____

PRACTICE
III

Directions: In each of the following sentences, one word is underlined. If the underlined word is the performer, blacken column 1. If the underlined word is the action, blacken column 2. If the underlined word describes the performer, blacken column 3. If the underlined word describes the action, blacken column 4.

1 2 3 4

1. The gooey candy stuck to the seat of the un-suspecting moviegoer's pants. ‖ ‖ ‖ ‖

2. Mr. McCarthy strode away angrily. ‖ ‖ ‖ ‖

3. The sweet old man winked. ‖ ‖ ‖ ‖

4. My friend cooks well. ‖ ‖ ‖ ‖

5. Ricardo gave me a good suggestion. ‖ ‖ ‖ ‖

6. We sat down beneath some trees. ‖ ‖ ‖ ‖

7. Four hungry children arrived for lunch. ‖ ‖ ‖ ‖

8. Northern merchants paid little for raw materials. ‖ ‖ ‖ ‖

9. Rita came directly home after work. ‖ ‖ ‖ ‖

10. A violent storm of controversy raged at our council meeting. ‖ ‖ ‖ ‖

PRACTICE
IV

Directions: The descriptive words in the following sentences have been underlined. In each sentence, draw an arrow from the descriptive word to the word which it describes.
Example: The subway lurched *wildly*.

1. The telephone rang unexpectedly.

2. A heavy rain ruined our picnic.

3. The talented fingers knit the sweater.

4. The speeding truck swerved abruptly.

5. The soft snow fell gently.

PRACTICE
V

Directions: Blacken the space beneath the number which corresponds to the number of the action word in each sentence.

1 2 3 4

1. *Janis Joplin sang emotionally* charged *songs*. ‖ ‖ ‖ ‖
      1   2   3   4

                                                          1 2 3 4

2.   The *rumbling* truck *sped down* the *highway*.   ‖ ‖ ‖ ‖
            1   2   3   4

3.   A *monotonous tapping annoyed* the *students*.   ‖ ‖ ‖ ‖
          1   2   3   4

4.   My foreman, Roy, *bought* beer for *all* the men   ‖ ‖ ‖ ‖
                        1   2

      on the *shift*.
       3   4

5.   The *President of the United States walked*   ‖ ‖ ‖ ‖
                    1   2

      slowly toward the microphone.
       3   4

PRACTICE
   VI   **Directions:** Draw an arrow from each descriptive word to the word which it describes.

1.   Mr. Hudson displays a cheerful disposition.

2.   The dull day passed slowly.

3.   The fast car raced quickly.

4.   The cool, clear water shimmered.

5.   A hungry seagull greedily grabbed the fish.

Descriptive Words: Special Problems

Many words which are used to describe performers must add *-ly* in order to describe actions. *For example:*

> The *nice* woman spoke at the meeting.
> The woman spoke *nicely* at the meeting.

In the above sentences *nice* and *nicely* do two very different jobs. *Nice* describes the performer, *woman*. *Nicely* describes the action *spoke*. You would never say, "The *nicely* woman spoke at the meeting." However, a common error is "The woman spoke *nice.*" You can avoid that common error by recognizing that most words which describe actions end in *-ly.*

- *Well* describes actions, unless referring to a state of health. *Good* never describes an action.
  Examples:

  My neighbor paints *well.*
  My neighbor is a *good* painter.
  I don't feel *well* today.

- *Real* describes a person, place, or thing.
  Examples:

  The shoes were made of *real* leather.
  I prefer *real* butter to imitation.
  His loyalty makes him a *real* friend.

- *Really* describes another descriptive word.
  Examples:

  Many of the events in our history are *really* exciting.
  His story was not *really* believable.
  Jan's shoes were *really* too small.

- *Very* describes another descriptive word.
  Examples:

  The basketball game was *very* exciting.
  The members of this community work *very* well together.
  The guitarist played *very* quickly.

PRACTICE
VII   **Directions:** Choose the word that best completes each sentence and draw an arrow from this word to the word it describes.

1. My brother adds (quick, quickly).

2. That neighbor's (loud, loudly) radio annoys me.

3. He behaved (polite, politely) toward me.

4. The old dog walked (lazy, lazily) down the street.

5. I'll give you a (quick, quickly) call when I need you.

6. He plays the piano too (loud, loudly).

7. I don't like (soft, softly) music.

8. The (delicate, delicately) bird hovered in the sky.

9. Maria (sincere, sincerely) apologized for her error in book-keeping.

10. The dancer balanced (delicate, delicately) on one foot.

11. You have my (sincere, sincerely) apology.

12. Stanley answered (immediate, immediately).

13. This problem requires your (immediate, immediately) attention.

14. Rosemary sings (good, well).

15. A (good, well) singer remains calm.

ANSWER KEY

Chapter 3

Adding Descriptive Words

Page 24.

PERFORMER   ACTION

A large apple fell suddenly.

DESCRIPTIVE WORDS

PERFORMER   ACTION

The decaying tooth throbbed painfully.

DESCRIPTIVE WORD

Practice I *Page 24.*

Answers may vary.
Sample answers:
1. A *tall* man entered the store.
2. *Loud* music annoys me.
3. The cat jumped *suddenly*.
4. The *heavy* book slipped to the floor.
5. Dolores Bremmer walked *quickly* from the room.

Practice II *Page 24.*

Answers may vary.
Sample answers:
The shy girl spoke softly.
The delicate jonquils announced spring.

Practice III *Page 25.*

1. (3) *gooey* describes candy, the performer.
2. (4) *away* describes strode, the action.
3. (2) *winked* is the action.
4. (1) *friend* is the performer.
5. (2) *gave* is the action.
6. (2) *sat* is the action.
7. (1) *children* is the performer.
8. (3) *northern* describes merchants, the performers.
9. (4) *directly* describes came, the action.
10. (3) *violent* describes storm, the performer.

Practice IV *Page 25.*

1. rang   *unexpectedly* describes rang.
2. rain   *heavy* describes rain.
3. fingers   *talented* describes fingers.
4. swerved   *abruptly* describes swerved.
5. snow, fell *soft* describes snow, *gently* describes fell.

Practice V *Page 25.*

1. (2)   sang
2. (2)   sped
3. (3)   annoyed
4. (1)   bought
5. (2)   walked

Practice VI *Page 26.*

1. *cheerful* describes disposition.
2. *dull* describes day, *slowly* describes passed.
3. *fast* describes car, *quickly* describes raced.
4. *cool* describes water, *clear* describes water.
5. *hungry* describes seagull, *greedily* describes grabbed.

Practice VII *Page 27.*

1. My brother adds *quickly*.
2. That neighbor's *loud* radio annoys me.
3. He behaved *politely* toward me.
4. The old dog walked *lazily* down the street.
5. I'll give you a *quick* call when I need you.
6. He plays the piano too *loudly*.
7. I don't like *soft* music.
8. The *delicate* bird hovered in the sky.
9. Maria *sincerely* apologized for her error in bookkeeping.
10. The dancer balanced *delicately* on one foot.
11. You have my *sincere* apology.
12. Stanley answered *immediately*.
13. The problem requires your *immediate* attention.
14. Rosemary sings *well*.
15. A *good* singer remains calm.

4.
Using Descriptive Words Correctly

Maury Wills has described a player as having good running speed. "I knew it was hit good," said Mike Schmidt of the Philadelphia Phillies, "but the ball doesn't carry good in the Astrodome." It carries bad. When James J. Braddock died, there were stories about the fight in which he lost his heavyweight championship to Joe Louis. In the first round Braddock knocked Louis down. Louis got up. Braddock: "I thought if I hit him good, he'll stay down." It did not work out that way. Braddock was a brave man, a light-heavyweight, really, who returned to fighting when he was unemployed and on relief and went on to win the heavyweight championship. He was a longshoreman and uneducated. Tom Seaver of the New York Mets is a college graduate: "Cedeno hit the ball pretty good." Budd Schulberg is a novelist. Said he, after the Ali-Foreman fight, "The fight turned out pretty good."

— Edwin Newman
A Civil Tongue

A Word With You . . .

Obviously, many people's use of *good* isn't their *best* grammar. The notables quoted by Edwin Newman are not alone in their misuse of that common adjective. Remember, no matter how *good* a player you are, you *play well*. This chapter will help you *use* descriptive words *well*.

Descriptive Words: Using Comparison

Many descriptive words follow this pattern:

Mr. Smith built a _tall_ fence.
Mr. Jones built a _taller_ fence.
Mr. White built the _tallest_ fence _of the three._

Why is the fence in sentence 1 described as _tall,_ the fence in sentence 2 described as _taller,_ and the fence in sentence 3 described as _tallest? Tall_ is a descriptive word which describes _fence. Taller_ is a descriptive word which describes and compares _two fences. Tallest_ is a descriptive word which compares _more than two fences._

As you have seen in the above sentences, _-er_ is added to a descriptive word to show a comparison between two people or things; _-est_ is added to a descriptive word to show a comparison among more than two people or things. This is the general rule for comparison of descriptive words. _Study the examples below:_

DESCRIPTION	COMPARISON OF TWO	COMPARISON OF MORE THAN TWO
pretty	prettier	prettiest
small	smaller	smallest
fast	faster	fastest
near	nearer	nearest
soon	sooner	soonest
rude	ruder	rudest
shrewd	shrewder	shrewdest
spicy	spicier	spiciest
green	greener	greenest
stout	stouter	stoutest

Many descriptive words sound awkward when _-er_ or _-est_ is added. These words use _more_ instead of _-er_ and _most_ instead of _-est_ when making a comparison. _Study the examples below:_

DESCRIPTION	COMPARISON OF TWO	COMPARISON OF MORE THAN TWO
beautiful	more beautiful	most beautiful
tenacious	more tenacious	most tenacious
enormous	more enormous	most enormous
quickly	more quickly	most quickly

DESCRIPTION	COMPARISON OF TWO	COMPARISON OF MORE THAN TWO
torrid	more torrid	most torrid
valuable	more valuable	most valuable
legible	more legible	most legible
difficult	more difficult	most difficult
wonderful	more wonderful	most wonderful
sympathetic	more sympathetic	most sympathetic

Some descriptive words have entirely different forms to express different degrees of comparison. *Study the examples below:*

DESCRIPTION	COMPARISON OF TWO	COMPARISON OF MORE THAN TWO
good	better	best
bad	worse	worst

PRACTICE

I   **Directions:** Complete the pattern in each of the following sentences by adding the *proper form* of one of the descriptive words below.

boring   magnificent   long   high   good

1. This is the _____ meeting I've ever attended.
2. We chose the _____ day of the summer for our office picnic.
3. Mr. Valdez is one of the _____ people I know.
4. Ricky works _____ than anyone else in the plant.
5. Our plants grew _____ this year than last year.

PRACTICE

II   **Directions:** Blacken the space beneath the number which corresponds to the number of the incorrect sentence in each group.

	1	2	3
	‖	‖	‖

1 1) This week's show was more funnier than last week's show.

2) A tiny, delicate bird flew quietly away.

3) That loud noise is very irritating.

		1	2	3

2 1) The nervous woman seemed very impatient.

2) Only close relatives visited the very old man.

3) John received the job because he was the efficientest competitor.

		1	2	3

3 1) Seven of the candidates competed vigorously for the local mayoralty.

2) This dinner is the most delicious I've ever had.

3) Willie is the better basketball player of the three.

		1	2	3

4 1) Harry Truman read continually.

2) Of the two, Freddie runs quicker.

3) The delightful aroma drifted across the room.

		1	2	3

5 1) Ed suggests a better solution.

2) This coffee pot makes the baddest coffee I've ever had.

3) He handled the bus more skillfully than any other driver.

		1	2	3

6 1) The worst damage occurred in the rear.

2) Of the two books, I like this one most.

3) This is the shortest of the three books.

		1	2	3

7 1) I like Indian sand paintings better than modern art.

2) When I buy meat, I always choose the best quality.

3) I chose the evergreen because it is the beautifulest of the three.

		1	2	3

8 1) Navaho art work is more elaborate than Pueblo art work.

2) The morning trains are slower than the afternoon trains.

3) This horse wins frequentlyer than any other.

1	2	3
‖	‖	‖

9 1) We liked this movie more better than any other.

2) Our team was the best in the league.

3) Colonel Eden was a better officer than anyone else in the brigade.

1	2	3
‖	‖	‖

10 1) He lost his composure during the worse battle of the war.

2) The science teacher carefully explained that this was the best technique.

3) The record showed that their team was stronger than any other in the conference.

ANSWER KEY

Chapter 4

Using Descriptive Words Correctly

Practice I *Page 32.*

Answers may vary.
  Sample answers:
1. longest
   most boring
   best
2. best
   most magnificent
3. most boring
   most magnificent
   best
4. better
   longer
5. higher
   better

Practice II *Page 32.*

1. (1) This week's show was *funnier* than last week's show. Do not use *more* with a descriptive word that ends in *-er*.
2. (3) John received the job because he was the *most efficient* competitor. Use *most* rather than *-est* with *efficient*.
3. (3) Willie is the *best* basketball player of the three. Use *best* when comparing three or more.
4. (2) Of the two, Freddie runs *more quickly*. Quickly describes run; therefore, *more quickly* compares how *two* people run.
5. (2) This coffee pot makes the *worst* coffee I've ever had. *Worst* is the form of *bad* used when comparing three or more.
6. (2) Of the two books, I like this one *more*. Use *more* to compare two items.
7. (3) I chose the evergreen because it is the *most beautiful* of the three. Use *most* rather than *-est* with *beautiful*.
8. (3) This horse wins *more frequently* than any other. Use *more* with *frequently* rather than *-er*.
9. (1) We liked this movie *better* than any other. Do not use *more* with better.
10. (1) He lost his composure during the *worst* battle of the war. *Worst* is the form of *bad* used when comparing three or more.

5.

Adding Descriptive Phrases

"I spoke to Jerry at the office party about his need to get more education," said Mr. Grogan.

"You mean that there was an office party just to consider Jerry's lack of education," Mrs. Grogan sweetly replied. "Maybe Jerry should ask you to go back to school if you use sentences like that."

Mrs. Grogan ducked as the pillow came sailing at her head. Lions don't like to have their tails tugged.

—Les Camhi
V.I.P. at I.B.M.

A Word With You . . .

Mrs. Grogan was having some fun at her husband's expense because he had been tarred with his own brush. Instead of coming across as the friendly vice-president who points out a weakness to his employee, he had the tables turned on him by the clever Mrs. Grogan who spotted an error in her husband's sentence structure.

Do you see the mistake? In Chapter 5 you will learn how to avoid it.

Descriptive Phrases: Adding Meaning

You have just been working with descriptive words which help to make the sentence more meaningful and interesting. Frequently, one descriptive word is not enough. We need a group of words (a phrase) to expand the meaning.

Example: The coffee cup fell *on the floor.*

Before you look for descriptive phrases, you must be sure that you understand the core of the sentence. Ask yourself these questions:

1. What is the action word in the sentence?
Fell.
2. What is performing the action?
Cup.
3. What do *the* and *coffee* describe?
Cup.
4. Finally, what does *on the floor* describe?
Fell.

Example: *Jaws*, the movie *at our local theater*, terrifies audiences.

1. What is the action word in the sentence?
Terrifies.
2. Who or what is performing the action?
Jaws.
3. What does *movie* describe?
Jaws.
4. Finally, what does *at our local theater* describe?
Movie.

PRACTICE

I   **Directions:**   Each of the sentences below contains at least one descriptive phrase. Draw an arrow from each descriptive phrase to the word it describes. The first one is done for you.

1.   The company solved its financial problems through efficiency techniques.

2.   The fire in the fireplace crackled into the night.

3.   The dentist's ultrasonic cleaner sped along the surfaces of his patient's teeth.

4.   Shrubbery grew around the house.

5.   A contestant with a soprano voice won the talent competition.

6. During the training session, the recruits crawled <u>under the fence.</u>

7. A lonely figure waited <u>on the bridge.</u>

8. Everyone <u>except him</u> cheered.

9. The dealer divided the cards <u>among the four players.</u>

10. An argument raged <u>between the two teams.</u>

PRACTICE II

Directions: These words frequently begin descriptive phrases. Choose from among them to complete the following sentences. More than one answer may be correct.

of	at	between	after	under	on
in	from	through	beside	over	before
to	into	around	except	off	along
for	among	by	alongside	up	with

1. A brief summary of World War I is _____ the first chapter.

2. A large crowd walked _____ the stairs in the historic building.

3. Surprised by the house owner's return, the intruder hurried _____ the door.

4. The unseasoned traveler put his hand _____ his pocket in search of the proper coin.

5. The book _____ the top shelf belongs _____ Ada.

6. _____ more peaceful methods had failed, the government seized control of the newspapers and radio stations.

7. Combined _____ the bank's inter-office banking service is their policy of all-day, all-night depositing.

8. In dull winter weather, African violets will bloom _____ 100 watt grow lights.

9. Sitting _____ me was a man who laughed and clapped loudly.

10. The unfortunate children were scattered _____ many homes.

Descriptive Phrases: Correct Placement

A descriptive phrase should be placed next to the word which it describes. Misplacement of a descriptive phrase results in confused meaning. *For example:*

> The congressman made an unfavorable comment at a White House reception *about rising prices.*

The reception was not *about rising prices;* the congressman's comment was *about rising prices.* The sentence should read:

> The congressman made an unfavorable comment *about rising prices* at a White House reception.

PRACTICE III

Directions: The underlined descriptive phrase in each of the following sentences is correctly placed. Draw an arrow from each descriptive phrase to the word which it describes. The first one is done for you.

1. The American way <u>of life</u> changes constantly.

2. The price of fuel increased <u>through the 1970's.</u>

3. This course <u>of action</u> is intolerable.

4. The prosecutor spoke <u>to Steve.</u>

5. John Canady writes <u>about art.</u>

6. Several angry commuters walked <u>to the bus stop.</u>

7. Representatives <u>of the different factions</u> spoke.

8. The actors dine <u>after the show.</u>

9.   The panelist <u>at the end</u> of the table spoke decisively.

10.   Mr. Simmons spoke <u>at length</u>.

Notice that each descriptive phrase is next to the word which it describes. In the following exercise, each descriptive phrase is incorrectly placed.

PRACTICE

IV   **Directions:** On the line provided, rewrite each sentence so that each descriptive phrase is next to the word which it describes.

1.   The man ran down the stairs in a blue coat.

_____

2.   That gentleman often walks to the corner in the trenchcoat.

_____

3.   Tom did not see across the street the accident.

_____

4.   Show Ella in the baggy pants the clown.

_____

5.   That boy runs around the track in the sweatsuit each day.

_____

6.   The dog belongs to that child with the brown spots.

_____

All of the above sentences had simple placement errors. Each incorrectly placed phrase began with a clue word such as: of, in, to, at, from, with, across, etc.

PRACTICE

V   **Directions:** One sentence in each group has a placement error in it. Blacken the space beneath the number which corresponds to the number of the incorrect sentence.

			1	2	3
1	1)	The man in the tweed suit ran toward the departing bus.	‖	‖	‖
	2)	A woman in a raincoat hailed a passing taxi.			
	3)	The man in the drawer found his handkerchief.			

			1	2	3
2	1)	The grateful veteran relaxed after years of battle in his living room.	‖	‖	‖

2) The battery in my car died.

3) The woman on the park bench smiled warmly.

	1	2	3
	‖	‖	‖

3 1) Cher sang as she sauntered across the stage.

2) Magic Johnson will play in next Tuesday's game.

3) Mrs. Smith hung on the wall her favorite painting.

	1	2	3
	‖	‖	‖

4 1) The car drove 7,000 miles in the driveway.

2) The new sports car in the parking lot was stolen.

3) The man in the moon winked at the astronauts.

	1	2	3
	‖	‖	‖

5 1) The registration desk was located in the gymnasium.

2) Voter registration took place at three o'clock.

3) The voters on the table completed the forms.

Frequently, a descriptive phrase separates the performer and the action. You must remember that *the action agrees in number with the performer. For example:*

The *man walks* slowly.
The *man* in the blue coat *walks* slowly.
The *man* in the blue boots *walks* slowly.

Notice that the action word remains *walks* in each sentence. The number of that word is not affected by any word in the descriptive phrase. The action word, *walks*, agrees with *man* in each sentence. It does not, for example, change to agree with *boots*.

PRACTICE VI

Directions: For each sentence below, blacken the space under column 1 if the performer and action agree. If the performer and action do not agree, blacken the space under column 2.

		1	2
1.	Russell Baker writes excellent satire.	‖	‖
2.	The girl in the blue overalls builds skyscrapers.	‖	‖
3.	The clouds in the sky drifts by.	‖	‖
4.	The problem of too many cooks create chaos.	‖	‖

		1	2
5.	One of the men in our office works late every night.	‖	‖
6.	The latest machine in the line features a self-cleaning device.	‖	‖
7.	Some of the most unusual animals lives at the Bronx Zoo.	‖	‖
8.	The rollers in her hair detracts from her beauty.	‖	‖
9.	One out of three employees stays with the company after the first year.	‖	‖
10.	A catalog of publications arrive at our office monthly.	‖	‖

ANSWER KEY

Chapter 5

Adding Descriptive Phrases

Practice I *Page 37.*

1. *through efficiency techniques* describes solved.
2. *in the fireplace* describes fire.
    into the night describes crackled.
3. *along the surfaces* describes sped.
4. *around the house* describes grew.
5. *with a soprano voice* describes contestant.
6. *under the fence* describes crawled.
7. *on the bridge* describes waited.
8. *except him* describes everyone.
9. *among the four players* describes divided.
10. *between the two teams* describes raged.

Practice II *Page 38.*

Answers will vary.
  Sample answers:
1. in, after, before
2. up
3. through, to, from
4. into
5. on, to
6. After, Before
7. with
8. under
9. beside
10. among

Practice III *Page 39.*

1. *of life* describes way.
2. *through the 1970's* describes increased.
3. *of action* describes course.
4. *to Steve* describes spoke.
5. *about art* describes writes.
6. *to the bus stop* describes walked.
7. *of the different factions* describes representatives.
8. *after the show* describes dine.
9. *at the end* describes panelist; *of the table* describes end.
10. *at length* describes spoke.

Practice IV *Page 40.*

1. The man in a blue coat ran down the stairs.
2. That gentleman in the trenchcoat often walks to the corner.
3. Tom did not see the accident across the street.
4. Show Ella the clown in the baggy pants.
5. That boy in the sweatsuit runs around the track each day.
6. The dog with the brown spots belongs to that child.

Practice V *Page 40.*

1. (3) The man found his handkerchief in the drawer.
2. (1) The grateful veteran relaxed in his living room after years of battle.
3. (3) Mrs. Smith hung her favorite painting on the wall.
4. (1) The car in the driveway drove 7,000 miles.
5. (3) The voters completed the forms on the table.

Practice VI *Page 41.*

The descriptive phrases in these sentences have been set off with parentheses so that you can clearly see the *performer* and *action* in each sentence.

1. (1) Russell Baker writes
2. (1) girl (in the blue overalls) builds
3. (2) clouds (in the sky) drift
4. (2) problem (of too many cooks) creates
5. (1) one (of the men in our office) works
6. (1) machine (in the line) features
7. (2) some (of the most unusual animals) live
8. (2) rollers (in her hair) detract
9. (1) one (out of three employees) stays
10. (2) catalogue (of publications) arrives

6.
Cumulative Review

This review covers:

- Performer and Action: Agreement in Number
- Action Words: Agreement in Time
- Correct Use of Descriptive Words

—After completing the Cumulative Review exercises, evaluate your ability using the SUMMARY OF RESULTS chart on page 51. Acceptable scores for each practice are given.

—To learn your weaknesses, find the question numbers you answered incorrectly on the SKILLS ANALYSIS table. The table will show which of your skills need improvement and the necessary chapters to review.

PRACTICE

I   **Directions:**   Blacken the space beneath the number which corresponds to the number of the error in each sentence. If there is no error, blacken space number 5.

1. The delegate and *his* alternate *votes* at *each*
                        1   2   3

   monthly meeting. *No error*
      4   5

   1 2 3 4 5

2. If a person *maintains* a *good* historical per-
                   1   2

   spective, he *understands* the present and
                    3

   predicted the future. *No error*
      4   5

   1 2 3 4 5

3. Although I *cannot see* you, I can *hear* you *good.*
                   1   2   3   4

   No error
    5

   1 2 3 4 5

4. The *plumbers* union, along with *several* other
   1   2

   unions in the area, *choose* not to *work* on
                        3   4

   Saturdays. *No error*
              5

   1 2 3 4 5

5. We *spent* a perfect day at the beach because
       1

   the ocean was *real* calm and the sun *wasn't too*
                  2   3   4

   hot. *No error*
        5

   1 2 3 4 5

6. Before anyone *makes* a decision, he *weighs*
                  1   2

   all of the alternatives and *chose* the *best.*
                                3   4

   No error
   5

   1 2 3 4 5

7. Because *she* *enjoys* the exercise, Patricia,
            1   2

   along with several of her friends, *skates*
    3   4

   every Friday evening. *No error*
                         5

   1 2 3 4 5

8. Because *less* money is available, we are *faced*
            1   2

   with the problem of providing *better* educa-
                                  3

   tion at *lower* cost. *No error*
           4   5

   1 2 3 4 5

                                                                1 2 3 4 5

9. The *more* they *grapple* with the problem, || || || || ||
           1   2

   the *less* the members of the legislature
          3

   understands it. *No error*
       4   5

                                                                 1 2 3 4 5

10. Of *all* the *downtown* merchants, I *like* Mr. || || || || ||
         1   2   3

   Mitchell *more*. *No error*
            4   5

PRACTICE II

Directions: Blacken the space beneath the number which corresponds to the number of the error in each sentence. If there is no error, blacken space number 5.

                                                                  1 2 3 4 5

1. The electrician and his assistant *always shuts* || || || || ||
                                        1   2

   off the electricity *before* beginning *work*.
                           3   4

   No error
     5

                                                                 1 2 3 4 5

2. The late Louis Braille, *inventor* of the Braille || || || || ||
                                   1

   alphabet, *pioneered* in his own right and
                  2

   contributes to *aids* for the handicapped.
         3   4

   No error
     5

                                                                 1 2 3 4 5

3. As food prices continue to *rise*, more and || || || || ||
                                 1

   more people turn to farming and *most* of
     2   3

   them *enjoy* it. *No error*
           4   5

4.
1 2 3 4 5
‖ ‖ ‖ ‖ ‖

Some of the finest modern artists cannot

sketch *accurate* nor *reproduce* a likeness
  1   2   3

well. *No error*
 4   5

5.
1 2 3 4 5
‖ ‖ ‖ ‖ ‖

Robert Pace *designed* a unique method of
          1

piano instruction which *combines* *classical,*
            2   3

romantic, and contemporary music. *No error*
  4   5

6.
1 2 3 4 5
‖ ‖ ‖ ‖ ‖

During the *recent* blackout, *many* refrigera-
       1   2

tors *defrosted* and the food *spoils.* *No error*
     3   4   5

7.
1 2 3 4 5
‖ ‖ ‖ ‖ ‖

Maria and her *best* friend, Lucy, *goes* to *adult*
           1   2   3

school twice each week and *study* together.
                    4

No error
  5

8.
1 2 3 4 5
‖ ‖ ‖ ‖ ‖

The tools *in* the storage chest *accomplishes*
       1   2

most of the *necessary* tasks. *No error*
  3   4   5

9.
1 2 3 4 5
‖ ‖ ‖ ‖ ‖

The *tiles* in the bathroom *shows* *signs* of *wear.*
   1   2   3   4

No error
  5

10. Of all the people I _know_, Manuel _works_ _most_
       <u>   </u>   <u>   </u> <u>   </u>
          1   2   3

   efficient. _No error_
   <u>   </u> <u>   </u>
       4   5

   1 2 3 4 5
   ‖ ‖ ‖ ‖ ‖

PRACTICE III

Directions: Blacken the space beneath the number which corresponds to the number of the error in each sentence. If there is no error, blacken space number 5.

1. Martin and his brother _walks_ to _work_ _each_
                           <u>   </u>   <u>   </u> <u>   </u>
                              1   2   3

   morning and _take_ the bus home each evening.
               <u>   </u>
                  4

   No error
   <u>   </u>
       5

   1 2 3 4 5
   ‖ ‖ ‖ ‖ ‖

2. _One_ of those packages _belong_ to the _tall_ man
   <u>   </u>   <u>   </u>   <u>   </u>
     1   2   3

   at the end of the _long_ line. _No error_
                     <u>   </u>   <u>   </u>
                        4   5

   1 2 3 4 5
   ‖ ‖ ‖ ‖ ‖

3. A book of food _stamps_ _fell_ _onto_ the counter
                  <u>   </u> <u>   </u> <u>   </u>
                     1   2   3

   in the supermarket and several people

   reached for it. _No error_
   <u>   </u>   <u>   </u>
       4   5

   1 2 3 4 5
   ‖ ‖ ‖ ‖ ‖

4. The superintendent and his wife _argues_
                                   <u>   </u>
                                      1

   frequently and the neighbors _listen_
   <u>   </u>   <u>   </u>
       2   3

   attentively. _No error_
   <u>   </u> <u>   </u>
        4   5

   1 2 3 4 5
   ‖ ‖ ‖ ‖ ‖

5. The team *played* *clumsy* and, therefore, *lost*
    ₁   ₂   ₃
    the *game*. *No error*
    ₄   ₅

1	2	3	4	5
‖	‖	‖	‖	‖

6. Perry *enters* the *crowded* movie theater, *buys*
    ₁   ₂   ₃
    popcorn, and *looked* for a seat. *No error*
    ₄   ₅

1	2	3	4	5
‖	‖	‖	‖	‖

7. Don't *rise* your hand at the meeting unless
    ₁
    you *plan* to *speak* in *favor* of the proposal.
    ₂   ₃   ₄
    No error
    ₅

1	2	3	4	5
‖	‖	‖	‖	‖

8. *Please* *bring* the *tape* recorder with you and
    ₁   ₂   ₃
    tape the evening's *discussion*. *No error*
    ₄   ₅

1	2	3	4	5
‖	‖	‖	‖	‖

9. A carton of eggs *smash* on the floor at *least*
    ₁   ₂
    once a week in *that* store. *No error*
    ₃   ₄   ₅

1	2	3	4	5
‖	‖	‖	‖	‖

10. The radio and the TV *play* so *loud* that I have
    ₁   ₂
    trouble *reading*. *No error*
    ₄   ₅

1	2	3	4	5
‖	‖	‖	‖	‖

11. I would not *have* *rang* your doorbell if I didn't
    ₁   ₂
    have an *important* message. *No error*
    ₃   ₄   ₅

1	2	3	4	5
‖	‖	‖	‖	‖

12. Mr. Ricardi *played* basketball *so* *good* that
                  1   2 3

the men *asked* him to be the center on the
       4

neighborhood team. *No error*
             5

1 2 3 4 5
‖ ‖ ‖ ‖ ‖

13. Several doses of that medicine *makes* me *feel*
                       1   2

tired and *react* *slowly*. *No error*
        3   4   5

1 2 3 4 5
‖ ‖ ‖ ‖ ‖

14. Buddy *listens* to instructions *attentively*, but
       1   2

cannot *remember* them *clear*. *No error*
        3   4   5

1 2 3 4 5
‖ ‖ ‖ ‖ ‖

15. One of the women *on* the bus *talk* *incessantly*
               1   2   3

and *annoys* the driver. *No error*
    4   5

1 2 3 4 5
‖ ‖ ‖ ‖ ‖

SUMMARY OF RESULTS

After reviewing the Answer Key on page 53, chart your scores below for each practice exercise

Practice Number	Your Number Right	Your Number Wrong (Including Omissions)	Acceptable Score
I			7 correct
II			7 correct
III			11 correct

SKILLS ANALYSIS

To discover your weak areas, locate the question numbers you got wrong and circle them on this Skills Analysis chart. Refer back to those chapters where you got questions wrong.

Skill	Question Number	Chapter Reference
Practice I		*See Chapter*
Performer and Action: Agreement in Number	1, 4, 9	2
Action Words: Agreement in Time	2, 6	2
Correct Use of Descriptive Words	3, 5	3
Correct Use of Descriptive Words: Comparison	10	4
Practice II		
Performer and Action: Agreement in Number	1, 7, 8, 9	2
Action Words: Agreement in Time	2, 6	2
Correct Use of Descriptive Words	4, 10	2
Practice III		
Performer and Action: Agreement in Number	1, 2, 4, 9, 13, 15	2
Correct Use of Descriptive Words	5, 10, 12, 14	3
Performer and Action: Agreement in Time	6	2
Action Words: Special Problems	7, 11	1

ANSWER KEY

Chapter 6

Cumulative Review

Practice I *Page 45.*

1. (2) *Vote* agrees with the plural performer, *The delegate and his alternate.*
2. (4) *Predicts* agrees in time with the action words, *maintains* and *understands.*
3. (4) *Well* describes the action word, *hear.*
4. (3) *Chooses* agrees with the singular performer, *union.*
5. (2) *Really* describes the descriptive word, *calm.*
6. (3) *Chooses* agrees in time with the action words *makes* and *weighs.*
7. (5) No error
8. (5) No error
9. (4) *Understand* agrees in number with the plural performer, *members.*
10. (4) Use *most* to compare three or more groups of people, as indicated in, "Of *all* the downtown *merchants . . ."*

Practice II *Page 47.*

1. (2) *Shut* agrees with the plural performer, *the electrician and his assistant.*
2. (3) *Contributed* agrees in time with the action word, *pioneered.*
3. (5) No error
4. (2) *Accurately* describes the action word, *sketch.*
5. (5) No error
6. (4) *Spoiled* agrees in time with the action word, *defrosted.*
7. (2) *Go* agrees with the plural performer, *Maria and her best friend, Lucy.*
8. (2) *Accomplish* agrees with the plural performer, *tools.*
9. (2) *Show* agrees with the plural performer, *tiles.*
10. (4) *Efficiently* describes the action word, *works.*

Practice III *Page 49.*

1. (1) *Walk* agrees with the plural performer, *Martin and his brother.*
2. (2) *Belongs* agrees with the singular performer, *one (of those packages* describes one).
3. (5) No error
4. (1) *Argue* agrees with the plural performer, *superintendent and his wife.*
5. (2) *Clumsily* describes the action, *played.* Clumsy would describe a person or thing.
6. (4) *Looks* agrees in time with *enters* and *buys.*
7. (1) *Raise* means *lift;* rise means get up.
8. (5) No error
9. (1) *Smashes* agrees with the singular performer, *carton.*
10. (2) *Loudly* describes the action, *play.* Loud would describe a person or thing.
11. (2) *Rung* is used with the helping word, *have.*
12. (3) *Well* describes the action, *played.* Good would describe a person or thing.
13. (1) *Make* agrees with the plural performer, *doses.*
14. (4) *Clearly* describes the action, *remember.* Clear would describe a person or thing.
15. (2) *Talks* agrees with the singular performer, *one.*

7.
Linking Words

"The murderer is . . ."

"Yes, yes," exclaimed Colonel Van Raalte, speaking for everyone in the living room. "Tell us who it is."

Detective Ling went on: "The murderer is . . . a real villain."

"We don't need any genius of a Chinese detective to tell us that," sneered the Colonel. "You might just twist that sentence around and tell us that 'the real villain is . . . a murderer.' It makes just as much sense—or stupidity!"

Patience, my friend, patience," said Ling. "Before the evening is much older, I will point my finger in the direction of the killer."

—Stillwell Kee
The Inscrutable Detective Ling

A Word With You . . .

The murderer is a villain.
A villain is the murderer.
Colonel Van Raalte was right in that he didn't learn anything from Detective Ling's statement.
You, however, are going to learn what a *linking word* is, why certain sentences can be reversed without changing their meanings —and you might even discover who killed Mrs. Van Raalte.

The Flink Is Pretty: the Subject is *Being*, not *Doing*.

You have been working with the simplest complete thought: a performer and an action. *For example:*

PERFORMER   ACTION

The huge Boeing 747 swerved unexpectedly.

Another simple, complete thought in the English language is one in which a person or thing is *being* something rather than *doing* something. *For example:*

The Boeing 747 is huge.

As you see, the word *Boeing 747* in this sentence cannot be called the performer since it is not performing any action (swerving, flying, landing, departing). It is actually being described (huge). *Huge* describes *Boeing 747. Is* links the descriptive word *huge* to the subject *Boeing 747*. The subject is the word which the sentence is about.

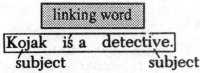

The word *is* is not an action word; it is a *linking word*. Study these examples of linking words:

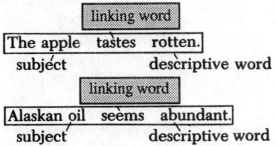

Sometimes *is* links the subject with another word which equals the subject. *For example:*

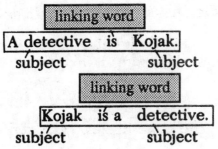

It is interesting to note that whenever the word linked with the subject *equals* the subject, the sentence can be reversed without changing its meaning. The reversed sentences may sound awkward; however, the meaning remains clear. *For example:*

A detective is Kojak.
subject   subject

Kojak is a detective.
subject   subject

linking word

Gerald Ford was the United States' first non-elected president.

subject   subject

linking word

The United States' first non-elected president was Gerald Ford.

subject   subject

linking word

The Statue of Liberty is a remarkable sight.

subject   subject

linking word

A remarkable sight is the Statue of Liberty.

subject   subject

Linking Words

appear	remain	become	seem
feel	smell	grow	sound
look	taste	be	is
are	am	was	were

PRACTICE

I   **Directions:** Complete each sentence using the correct form of a **linking** word from the above list. Several words may be appropriate. **Choose one.**

1. After the Knick game, the players _____ tired.

2. The labor representative _____ angry during the extensive negotiations.

3. The late Dwight Eisenhower _____ once a general.

4. The watchman _____ restless.

5. During the tennis match, the women never _____ exhausted.

PRACTICE

II   **Directions:** Locate the subject in each sentence, and label it. Then underline the linking word which connects the subject and the **descriptive** word. Draw an arrow from the descriptive word to the subject.

subject

Example: An extensive renovation <u>seems</u> wasteful.

1. The entire class felt more ambitious after the coffee-break.

2. The rose bushes in the park are breathtaking.

3. Seven noisy children suddenly grew still.

4. Theodore Roosevelt had been President of the United States for eight years.

5. The smoke in the kitchen became unbearable.

PRACTICE III

Directions: Each of the sentences below contains either an action word or a linking word. If the sentence contains an action word, blacken the space beneath column 1. If the sentence contains a linking word, blacken the space beneath column 2.

		1	2
1.	The snowmobile raced down the hill.	‖	‖
2.	The tone of the meeting became threatening.	‖	‖
3.	That candidate was our favorite.	‖	‖
4.	We eat only organic foods.	‖	‖
5.	Our day at the lake was pleasant.	‖	‖
6.	Maximum individual choice is the democratic ideal.	‖	‖
7.	Alvin Toffler, author of *Future Shock,* conjures up a bleak picture of the future.	‖	‖
8.	People turn to a variety of experts.	‖	‖
9.	The situation appeared uncomfortable.	‖	‖
10.	Most people do not consider their own lives as typical of particular life styles.	‖	‖
11.	It was I at the door.	‖	‖

Use the descriptive word correctly in the *Subject-linking Word-Descriptive Word* pattern. Never use a descriptive word which ends in *-ly* to describe the subject of the sentence. Descriptive words which end in *-ly* are reserved for describing actions.

CORRECT: The child *is* adorable. (linking word)
INCORRECT: The child is adorably.

CORRECT: She *speaks* too softly. (action)
INCORRECT: She speaks too soft.

PRACTICE

IV   **Directions:** Blacken the space beneath the number which corresponds to the number of the incorrect sentence in each group. If all the sentences in a group are correct, blacken space number 5.

1
1) The delicate bird is graceful.
2) The graceful bird seems delicate.
3) The bird is graceful and delicate.
4) The bird flies graceful.
5) No error

1 2 3 4 5
‖ ‖ ‖ ‖ ‖

2
1) Mr. Jackson plays piano loud.
2) Mr. Jackson's piano is loud.
3) Mr. Jackson, along with his piano, is loud.
4) Mr. Jackson plays piano loudly.
5) No error

1 2 3 4 5
‖ ‖ ‖ ‖ ‖

3
1) Floyd reads quickly.
2) Angelo is the quickest sorter in the mailroom.
3) Floyd reads more quick than Harvey.
4) Alex seems very quick.
5) No error

1 2 3 4 5
‖ ‖ ‖ ‖ ‖

4
1) Annemarie seems nicely.
2) Carmen seems nice.
3) Annemarie seems nicer than Cathy.
4) Raymond's nice sister is Georgia.
5) No error

1 2 3 4 5
‖ ‖ ‖ ‖ ‖

	1	2	3	4	5
	‖	‖	‖	‖	‖

5 1) Good butter tastes sweet.

2) Taste the good butter.

3) The butter tastes well.

4) This butter tastes good!

5) No error

	1	2	3	4	5
	‖	‖	‖	‖	‖

6 1) Rudy feels badly about the argument.

2) That dress looks bad on Vera.

3) That was a bad choice.

4) Since she had the flu, Carla has felt bad.

5) No error

Subject and Linking Word: Agreement in Number

You have already studied agreement of performer and action in number. The same concept applies to the subject and the linking word. For example, look at the following incorrect sentences:

1. *All* of our relatives *is* coming to dinner.
2. Those *cars appears* fast.
3. The *house are* on a hill.

Of course, these sentences sound awkward. Look at the same sentences written correctly. What changes have been made?

1. *All* of our relatives *are* coming to dinner.
2. Those *cars appear* fast.
3. The *house is* on a hill.

You see that a singular subject needs a singular linking word, and a plural subject needs a plural linking word.

Every linking word must agree with its subject in time and number. Notice that agreement in the past tense is easier to achieve than agreement in the present. For example:

Linking word: *appear*

Present Time, Singular and Plural

I appear nervous.
You appear confident.

(He)   David appears belligerent.
(She)   Pam appears calm.
(It)   The dog appears ill.
        Who appears contented?
(We)   Michael and I appear relaxed.
(You)   You and Marcel appear tired.
(They) Ellen and Linda appear friendly.

Linking word: *appear*

Past Time, Singular and Plural

        I appeared nervous.
        You appeared confident.
(He)   David appeared belligerent.
(She)   Pam appeared calm.
(It)   The dog appeared ill.
        Who appeared contented?
(We)   Michael and I appeared relaxed.
(You)   You and Marcel appeared tired.
(They) Ellen and Linda appeared friendly.

Linking word: *be*

Be is a difficult word to understand. *Be* is used when preceded by *to, will, can, could, would,* or *should. Examples:*

        The policeman wants *to be* helpful.
        Next time, I *will be* more thoughtful.
        Crowded supermarkets *can be* annoying.
        This *could be* one chance in a lifetime.
        The supervisor *would be* grateful if you could work late.
        World peace *should be* everyone's goal.

Other forms of *be* are used in sentences which do not have the helping words *to, will, can, could, would,* or *should.* You already are familiar with these forms: *am, is, are, was, were.* The following lists show you the proper use of these words.

Linking word: *be*

        Present Time, Singular and Plural
        I am a nurse.
        You are a policeman.
(He)   David is a crossing guard.

(She)   Pam is a teacher.
(It)   The dog is a Collie.
        Who is that lady?
(We)   Bill and I are co-chairmen.
(You)   You and your brother are partners.
        Who are those ladies?
(They) Ellen and Linda are sisters.

Linking word: *be*

Past Time, Singular and Plural

        I was a nurse.
        You were a policeman.
(He)   David was a crossing guard.
(She)   Pam was a teacher.
(It)   The dog was a Collie.
        Who was that lady?
(We)   Bill and I were co-chairmen.
(You)   You and your brother were partners.
        Who were those ladies?
(They) Ellen and Linda were sisters.

PRACTICE
V   **Directions:** Use *is, are, was,* or *were* in each of the following sentences.

1. Fritz _____ always late.
2. The Murphys _____ home from their vacation.
3. The woman and her child _____ in the park.
4. The books _____ interesting.
5. He _____ a member of the group when it was first formed.

PRACTICE
VI   **Directions:** Use the *correct form* of one of the following linking words to complete each of the following sentences. Use at least one form of each word.

        be   grow   become   appear   feel

1. The soldiers _____ weary after the long march.
2. The crowd _____ angry.
3. The child quickly _____ tired of his new toy.

4.   Mr. and Mrs. Smith _____ elated after winning the lottery.

5.   The football players _____ traded.

PRACTICE
VII   **Directions:** Blacken the space beneath the number which corresponds to the number of the error in each passage. If there is no error, blacken space number 5.

1.   Ecology *is* *emerging* into an exact science. At
              1   2

                            1 2 3 4 5
                            ‖ ‖ ‖ ‖ ‖

last, the function of waste products *are* *being*
                                   3   4

discovered. *No error*
                  5

2.   Glass, plastic, and paper finally *has been*
                                  1

                            1 2 3 4 5
                            ‖ ‖ ‖ ‖ ‖

recognized as reusable and *are* being recy-
               2   3

cled. *No error*
              5

3.   Now, as their multiple functions *are* gradu-
                                   1

                            1 2 3 4 5
                            ‖ ‖ ‖ ‖ ‖

ally *being* *studied*, their importance *is* more
             2   3   4

apparent than ever before. *No error*
                             5

4.   Finally, man's *belief* that his own actions, at
                      1

                            1 2 3 4 5
                            ‖ ‖ ‖ ‖ ‖

least in part, *control* his destiny *are* *being*
                    2   3   4

justified. *No error*
               5

5.   Each local ecology group through its efforts,

$$\begin{array}{ccccc} 1 & 2 & 3 & 4 & 5 \\ \| & \| & \| & \| & \| \end{array}$$

have been instrumental, in recent years, in
  1   2

identifying and *solving* solid waste prob-
    3   4

lems. *No error*
       5

6.   The chairman of one local organization

$$\begin{array}{ccccc} 1 & 2 & 3 & 4 & 5 \\ \| & \| & \| & \| & \| \end{array}$$

believes that the advent of recycling waste
  1

products *are* just beginning. The same *is* true
     2   3

of non-polluting detergents, which *may* per-
                             4

haps be even more important. *No error*
                           5

The Missing Link(ing word)

Often, a linking word is combined with another word. In combining, the initial letters of the linking word are dropped and replaced by an apostrophe.

Example: *There is* one answer to that question.
                There's one answer to that question.

                There is = there's

Common missing link(ing word) combinations:

he is = he's	*He's* the most forward-looking senator.
she is = she's	*She's* the strongest voice in Congress.
we are = we're	*We're* eager to hear your proposal.
you are = you're	*You're* one of the few people I trust.
they are = they're	*They're* determined to interfere.
here is = here's	*Here's* your hat.
it is = it's	*It's* an active committee.

NOTE: *Its* without the apostrophe means possession.

Example: The committee concluded *its* hearing.

Missing link combinations with *not:*

is not = isn't	Destruction *isn't* my idea of fun.
are not = aren't	The striking workers *aren't* going to settle for less pay.
were not = weren't	Lou and Toby *weren't* on the train.
was not = wasn't	I *wasn't* prepared for the crowd at the bus stop.

PRACTICE
VIII

Directions: In each of the following sentences, there is an underlined phrase. Make a missing link combination from each underlined phrase and write it on the line provided.

Example: If it is convenient for Lucy, the bowling team will meet at 6 P.M.
it's

1. They are the best approaches to the problem. _____

2. If you can understand management-labor relations, you are a better businessman than I. _____

3. Agreement is not as important as understanding. _____

4. We did not realize that the job action had ended. _____

5. Here is the name of an excellent mechanic. _____

6. The legislators were not expecting such a strong consumer lobby. _____

7. He is the least competent programmer in the company.

    _____

8. There is only one best product in each line of merchandise.

    _____

ANSWER KEY

Chapter 7

Linking Words

Practice I *Page 56.*

Answers may vary.
  Sample answers:
1. appeared, felt, looked
2. seemed, became, grew
3. was
4. became, grew, is, was
5. were, seemed

Practice II *Page 56.*

1. The entire class *felt* more ambitious after the coffee-break. [subject]
2. The rose bushes in the park *are* breathtaking. [subject]
3. Seven noisy children suddenly *grew* still. [subject]
4. Theodore Roosevelt *had been* president of the United States for eight years. [subject]
5. The smoke in the kitchen *became* unbearable. [subject]

Practice III *Page 57.*

1. (1) raced
2. (2) became
3. (2) was
4. (1) eat
5. (2) was
6. (2) is
7. (1) conjures
8. (1) turn
9. (2) appeared
10. (1) consider
11. (2) was

Practice IV *Page 58.*

1. (4) The bird flies gracefully.
2. (1) Mr. Jackson plays piano loudly.
3. (3) Floyd reads more quickly than Harvey.
4. (1) Annemarie seems nice.
5. (3) The butter tastes good.
6. (1) Rudy feels bad about the argument.

Practice V *Page 61.*

Answers may vary.
  Sample answers:
1. is, was
2. are, were
3. are, were
4. are, were
5. was

Practice VI *Page 61.*

Answers may vary.
  Sample answers:
1. were, grew, became, appeared, felt, are, become, grow, appear, feel
2. was, grew, became, appeared, appears, becomes, grows, is
3. grew, became, is, grows, becomes
4. were, appeared, felt, are, appear, feel
5. were, are

Practice VII *Page 62.*

                     subject   **linking word**

1. (3) At last, the function (of waste products) *is* being discovered.

       Is agrees in number with the singular subject, *function.*

                   subject   **linking word**

2. (1) Glass, plastic, and paper finally *have been* recognized as reusable.

       Have been agrees in number with the plural subjects, *glass, plastic, and paper.*

3. (5) No error

                       subject   **linking word**

4. (3) Finally, man's belief (that his own actions at least in part, control his destiny) *is* being justified . . .

       Is agrees in number with the singular subject, *belief.*

                           subject   **linking word**

5. (1) Each local ecology group (through its efforts,) *has been* instrumental . . .

       Has been agrees in number with the singular subject, *group.*

                    subject

6. (2) The chairman of one local organization believes that the advent (of recycling waste prod-

                  linking word

ucts) *is* just beginning.

       Is agrees in number with the singular word, *advent.*

Practice VIII *Page 64.*

1. They're
2. you're
3. isn't
4. didn't
5. Here's
6. Weren't
7. He's
8. There's

8.
Agreement: Special Problems

Each of the veterinary surgeons gathered around Ruffian knew *his* job. *Neither* the doctors *nor* Mr. Janney *was* willing to give up on the magnificent filly, but despite *everyone's* desire to do *his* best, it became necessary to put the horse to sleep.

—Murray Bromberg
The Great Match Race

A Word With You . . .

The scene from the book took place in the early hours of Monday morning, July 7, 1975, as the veterinarians tried to save the life of a great horse whose leg had been shattered.

Our chief interest, however, is in the italicized words:
each—his
neither . . . nor—was
everyone's—his
Some people might not see the reason for using these word combinations. Their relationships will be made clear in the following pages.

You know that an action word must *agree* with its performer in number, and with the sentence or paragraph in time. *For example:*

The jury *enters* the courtroom. A hush *falls* over the crowd. The judge *asks* for the verdict.

You know that a linking word must agree with its subject in number and with the sentence or paragraph in time. *For example:*

Court *is* in session. Please *remain* silent.
The defendant *seems* apprehensive. The prosecutor *appears* angry.

Rules Concerning Special Problems of Agreement

- *Each*

  Each is singular when it is the performer or subject of the sentence. *Example:*

Performer	Action

  <u>*Each*</u> *shows* promise.

PRACTICE

I **Directions:** Underline either the singular or plural action word or linking word that correctly completes each sentence.

1. Each (gives, give) a lecture.
2. Each of the teachers (gives, give) a lecture.
3. They each (gives, give) a lecture.
4. Each (is, are) a good candidate.

- *Either-Or*

  When using *either-or*, you are choosing *one* or the *other*. The action or linking word is *singular* if the performer or subject closest to it is singular.

  Example: <u>*Either*</u> Tom <u>*or*</u> Bill drives to school.

Drives agrees with the singular performer, *Bill.*
The action or linking word is *plural* if the performer or subject closest to it is plural.

  Example: <u>*Either*</u> Tom <u>*or*</u> his friends drive to school.

Drive agrees with the plural performer, *friends.*

PRACTICE

II **Directions:** Underline either the singular or plural linking word that correctly completes each sentence.

1. Either the coach or the captain (is, are) late.
2. Either the coach or the players (is, are) late.
3. Either the players or the coach (is, are) late.
4. Either these players or those players (is, are) late.

- *Any*

  Any is singular. It is used when a choice involves *three* or more. *Either* is used for a choice between *two.*

  Example: <u>*Any*</u> of the *three* movies suits me.

PRACTICE
III   **Directions:** Underline either the singular or plural action or linking word that correctly completes each sentence.

1.   Any of the sandwiches (is, are) fine.
2.   Any of the four records (sounds, sound) good.
3.   (Any, either) of the three books (serves, serve) well.

- *Here and There*
  In sentences which begin with *here* or *there*, the action or linking word must agree with the performer or subject. *Here* and *there* are never performers or subjects.
  Example: Here (is, are) my coat.
  (WHAT is here? COAT. COAT is the SUBJECT.) *Coat* is singular; therefore the singular linking word *is* correctly completes the sentence.

PRACTICE
IV   **Directions:** Locate the performer or subject in each sentence. Underline the action or linking word that correctly completes each sentence.

1.   There (is, are) my boots.
2.   There (is, are) two sides to the argument.
3.   Here (goes, go) my last chance.
4.   There (is, are) no way out.

- *Who and That*
  You are familiar with the following sentence structures:

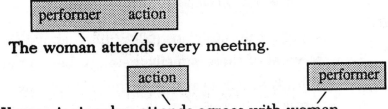

The woman attends every meeting.

Woman is singular; attends agrees with woman.

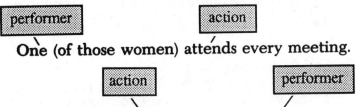

One (of those women) attends every meeting.

One is singular: *attends* agrees with *one.*

The following example is significantly different from the above.

> *One* (of those women) *who* ATTEND every meeting seldom
> SPEAKS.

Ready?

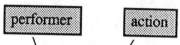

"One seldom speaks" is the *core* of the sentence. *One* is singular: *speaks* agrees with *one*.

"Of those women who attend every meeting" describes or tells more about, *one*.

Who might be singular or plural. How do we decide? We look at the word to which *who* refers. In this case that word is *women*. *Women* is plural; therefore, *who* is plural. Within the descriptive group of words, "of those women who attend every meeting," *attend* must agree with *who*. *Who* is plural; *attend* agrees with *who*.

This rule also applies to *that*.

Examples: The *ruler belongs* to me.
One (of those rulers) belongs to me.
One (of those rulers) *that* ARE on the desk BELONGS to me.

PRACTICE
V   **Directions:** Underline either the singular or plural action or linking word which correctly completes each sentence.

1. One of the musicians (plays, play) above the others.
2. Several of those pencils (belongs, belong) in this container.
3. John Kennedy was one of those leaders who (has, have) charisma.
4. One of those underdeveloped nations that (counts, count) upon outside sources for food will inevitably be disappointed.
5. One of those vocations that (has, have) always appealed to me (is, are) radio announcing.

• *Surprisingly Singular Subjects*
Some words seem to refer to more than one person. In fact, they do not. They are singular. These include:

Everybody	means every *single* body.
Somebody	means some *one* body.
Anybody	means any *one* body.
None	means no *one*.
Everyone	means every *one*.

- *Some Plural Subjects*

  Six words which take plural action or linking words are:

  all   few   several   both   many   some

PRACTICE VI

Directions: Underline the action word that correctly completes each sentence.

1. Everybody (hear, hears) a different drummer.
2. Somebody (call, calls) our office at 5:05 each day.
3. Anybody who (want, wants) to can join our cooperative supermarket.
4. None of the scout leaders (shirk, shirks) his responsibility.

REVIEW EXERCISES

PRACTICE VII

Directions: Underline the action or linking word which agrees with the performer or subject in each of the following sentences.

Example: The coat (is, are) too large.

1. The books (is, are) on the shelf.
2. Each (selects, select) his own menu.
3. Each of the students (is, are) registered for ten weeks.
4. Any of the six choices (is, are) suitable.
5. Everybody (does, do) his job.
6. This kind of movie (is, are) boring.
7. Those kinds of flowers (seems, seem) delicate.
8. None of the candidates (speaks, speak) well.
9. There (was, were) several good items on the menu.
10. Neither the meats nor the vegetables (is, are) fresh.
11. Either the children or the babysitter (drinks, drink) the milk.
12. He (doesn't, don't) speak well.

13. She is one of those women who never (says, say) **what they mean.**

14. One of those tractors (is, are) broken.

PRACTICE VIII

Directions: If the action or linking word in each sentence agrees with the subject, blacken the space under column 1. If the action or linking word does not agree with the subject, blacken the space under column 2.

		1	2
1.	There were two planes outside the hangar.	‖	‖
2.	Macaroni or potatoes go with this dinner.	‖	‖
3.	Any of these dips are great with crackers.	‖	‖
4.	Ten minutes of my time is all that I can offer.	‖	‖
5.	Don't she know your address?	‖	‖
6.	My son or my daughter are coming for me.	‖	‖
7.	There's two overseas routes to Europe.	‖	‖
8.	One of the most recent discoveries are in regard to aging.	‖	‖
9.	Doesn't any famous politician ever arrive on time?	‖	‖
10.	Here's Joanna's friends.	‖	‖
11.	One of those library books is lost.	‖	‖
12.	Either the coach or the players argue with the manager every week.	‖	‖
13.	Margaret Mead is one of those people who says what she means.	‖	‖

PRACTICE IX

Directions: Blacken the space beneath the number which corresponds to the number of the incorrect sentence in each group. If there is no error, blacken space number 5.

		1	2	3	4	5
1	1) Each of the projects is interesting.	‖	‖	‖	‖	‖
	2) There's my two favorite magazines.					
	3) Here's the best seat in the house.					
	4) Any of those concerts would please me.					
	5) No error					

1 2 3 4 5

2
1) Neither of us is really qualified for that job.
2) Those kinds of personalities are most difficult to live with.
3) Everybody shirks their responsibility occasionally.
4) Dr. Margaret Mead is one of the most interesting people I know about.
5) No error

1 2 3 4 5

3
1) Any of those arrangements is a suitable centerpiece.
2) Either Mr. Hanns or his assistants write the weekly reports.
3) The men each take a turn nailing the paneling.
4) Either of the two plants enhances that corner.
5) No error

1 2 3 4 5

4
1) The Jones sisters are among those people who always have time to listen.
2) One of those books is mine.
3) Each of those buildings have to be painted.
4) Here are my choices.
5) No error

1 2 3 4 5

5
1) Don't he ever get to work on time?
2) One of these records belongs to the library.
3) There's the only gifted writer I know.
4) Carmen is one of those people who speak constantly.
5) No error

1 2 3 4 5

6
1) Every day seems busier than the day before.
2) Either the stewardesses or their captain make the necessary announcements.
3) Neither the lemons nor the oranges were fresh.
4) Several of his poems are very good.
5) No error

1 2 3 4 5
|| || || || ||

7 1) Any of these coats or dresses suits you well.

    2) Here's the most authoritative book about the Civil War.

    3) Doesn't he seem right for the job?

    4) Each participant is expected to follow the rules.

    5) No error

1 2 3 4 5
|| || || || ||

8 1) They each sings in the community choir.

    2) There's no time to waste.

    3) Colonel Adams or Major Niles is planning to attend.

    4) Here's the last of those tapes you ordered.

    5) No error

1 2 3 4 5
|| || || || ||

9 1) Doesn't he ever take a day off?

    2) Each of my children visits during the holidays.

    3) Any of these shirts are a bargain.

    4) Either the grass or the shrubs need tending.

    5) No error

1 2 3 4 5
|| || || || ||

10 1) Any one of those mountain trails is the same as the others.

    2) Don't Angie look pretty?

    3) Four days is long enough for this type of project.

    4) One of the biggest problems is a lack of honesty.

    5) No error

ANSWER KEY

Chapter 8

Agreement: Special Problems

Practice I *Page 68.*

1. Each *gives*   *Gives* agrees with the singular performer, *each.*
2. Each *gives*   *Gives* agrees with the singular performer, *each.*
3. They *give*   *Give* agrees with the plural performer, *they.*
4. Each *is*   *Is* agrees with the singular subject, *each.*

Practice II *Page 68.*

1. captain *is*   *Is* agrees with the singular subject, *captain.*
2. players *are*   *Are* agrees with the plural subject, *players.*
3. coach *is*   *Is* agrees with the singular subject, *coach.*
4. players *are*   *Are* agrees with the plural subject, *players.*

Practice III *Page 69.*

              [Linking Word]

1. Any (of the sandwiches) *is* fine.
   Is agrees with the singular subject, *any.*

              [Linking Word]

2. Any (of the four records) *sounds* good.
   Sounds agrees with the singular subject, *any.*

              [Action Word]

3. Any (of the three books) *serves* well.
   Serves agrees with the singular performer, *any.*

Practice IV *Page 69.*

1. There *are* my boots.
   Are agrees with the plural subjects *boots.*
2. There *are* two sides to the argument.
   Are agrees with the plural subject *sides.*
3. Here *goes* my last chance.
   Goes agrees with the singular performer *chance.*
4. There *is* no way out.
   Is agrees with the singular subject *way.*

Practice V *Page 70.*

1. One of the musicians *plays* . . .
   Plays agrees with the singular subject *One.*
2. Several of those pencils *belong* . . .
   Belong agrees with the plural subject *several.*
3. John Kennedy was one of those leaders who *have* charisma.
   Have agrees with its subject *who*, which refers to the plural word *leaders.*
4. One of those underdeveloped nations that *count* . . .
   Count agrees with its subject *that*, which refers to the plural word *nations.*

5. One of those vocations that *have* . . . always appealed to me *is* . . .
   Have agrees with its subject *that*, which refers to the plural word *vocations; is* agrees with the singular subject *One*.

Practice VI *Page 71.*

1. Everybody *hears* a different drummer.
2. Somebody *calls* our office at 5:05 each day.
3. Anybody who *wants* to can join our cooperative supermarket.
4. None of the scout leaders *shirks* his responsibility.

The performer in each sentence is singular and requires a singular action word.

REVIEW

Practice VII *Page 71.*

The correct action or linking word in each sentence is underlined twice.
The subject in each sentence is underlined once.
1. The books are on the shelf.
2. Each selects his own menu.
3. Each (of the students) is registered for ten weeks.
4. Any (of the six choices) is suitable.
5. Everybody does his job.
6. This kind (of movie) is boring.
7. Those kinds (of flowers) seem delicate.
8. None (of the candidates) speaks well.
9. There were several good items on the menu.
10. Neither the meats nor the vegetables are fresh.
11. Either the children or the babysitter drinks the milk.
12. He doesn't speak well.
13. She is one of those women who never say what they mean.
14. One (of those tractors) is broken.

Practice VIII *Page 72.*

1. (1) planes were there — *Were* agrees with the plural subject, *planes.*
2. (1) potatoes go — *Go* agrees with the plural subject, *potatoes.*
3. (2) any (of these dips) is — *Is* agrees with the singular subject, *any.*
4. (1) ten minutes (as a *unit* of time) is — *Is* agrees with the singular subject, *ten minutes.*
5. (2) doesn't she know — *Doesn't* agrees with the singular performer, *she.*
6. (2) my daughter is — *Is* agrees with the singular subject, *daughter.*
7. (2) two routes are there — *Are* agrees with the plural subject, *routes.*
8. (2) one (of the most recent discoveries) is — *Is* agrees with the singular subject, *one.*
9. (1) doesn't any famous politician ever arrive — *Doesn't* agrees with the singular performer, *any.*
10. (2) Joanna's friends are here — *Are* agrees with the plural subject, *friends.*
11. (1) One (of those library books) is — *Is* agrees with the singular subject, *one.*
12. (1) players argue — *Argue* agrees with the plural performer, *players.*
13. (2) people who say what they mean. — *Say* agrees with the plural performer, *who.*
    They agrees with the plural performer, *who.*
    Mean agrees with *they.*

Practice IX *Page 72.*

1. (2) There *are* my two favorite magazines.

 The plural linking word *are* agrees with the plural subject, *magazines.*

2. (3) Everybody shirks *his* responsibility occasionally.

 The singular word *his* agrees with the singular performer, *everybody.*

3. (5) No error

4. (3) Each of those buildings *has* to be painted.

 The singular action word *has* agrees with the singular performer, *each.*

5. (1) *Doesn't* he ever get to work on time?

 The singular helping word *does* (not) agrees with the singular performer, *he.*

6. (2) Either the stewardesses or their captain *makes* the necessary announcements.

 The action word *makes* is singular because the performer which is closest to it, *captain,* is singular.

7. (5) No error

8. (1) They each *sing* in the community choir.

 The plural action word, *sing,* agrees with the plural performer, *they.*

9. (3) Any of these shirts *is* a bargain.

 The singular linking word *is* agrees with the singular subject, *any.*

10. (2) *Doesn't* Angie look pretty?

 The singular helping word *does* (not) agrees with the singular subject, *Angie.*

9.
Time: Special Problems

Eddie's father insisted that he pay attention. If Dad was going to give up a half hour of Archie Bunker in order to help Eddie with his homework, he wanted to make sure that Eddie was all ears.

"Now, there are the *present perfect*, the *past perfect*, and the *future perfect*," explained Eddie's father. "Why can't you understand that?"

"Well, nobody's perfect, Dad," quipped Eddie.

"Okay, wise guy," his father said. "Just listen to this example of the *future perfect tense:* 'By next week, you *will have discovered* a decrease in your allowance.' "

—Carol Lehrer
Tenting Out in the Suburbs

A Word With You . . .

It might not be cricket to cut a youngster's allowance because he had trouble with tenses (time), but Eddie's father seemed to know what he was doing in grammar, as well as in child-rearing.

The hapless Eddie was not concentrating—but you will, we are sure. Fortunately, you won't have to grapple with the "perfect" terms.

You know that sentences express time:

Present Action	-	I commute to work each day.
Past Action	-	I commuted to work each day.
Future Action	-	I will commute to work each day.

Occasionally, time is more complicated than the simple expression of past or future.

• Sometimes an action which began in the past continues into the present.

Examples: I *have commuted* to work for six years.

Marie *has commuted* to work for five years.

The addition of the helping word *have* or *has* expresses the idea of an action which began in the past, but is continuing into the present. In the above examples, the helping words, *have* and *has,* are in the present and the action word, *commuted,* is in the past.

Common Misuses of Has and Have

a. I *commuted* to work for six years and I am tired of commuting.
b. I *commuted* to work for six years and I have been tired of commuting.

The only correct use of the helping word have in these examples is:

I *have commuted* to work for six years and I am tired of commuting.

PRACTICE

I Directions: Blacken the space beneath the number which corresponds to the number of the incorrect sentence in each group.

1   2   3   4

1 1) I have lived in this community for ten years.   ‖ ‖ ‖ ‖
   2) Ellen has been climbing trees since she was six years old.
   3) Eric was the last in line since he began school.
   4) Liz and Paula have known each other for six years.

1   2   3   4

2 1) You and she have worked together for years.   ‖ ‖ ‖ ‖
   2) Shirley has spoken highly of you always.
   3) Andrea did not visit us for the past several days.
   4) Wendy and Karen have babysat for us since we moved here.

• Sometimes a past action has occurred before another past action.

> *Example:* I *had commuted* for two hours each way before I *moved* to the city.

The addition of the helping word *had* shows that the commuting occurred in the past *before* the moving occurred.

Common Misuses of Had

a. I *had commuted* two hours each way before I *had moved* to the city.

b. I *commuted* two hours each way before I *had moved* to the city.

The only correct use of the helping word *had* in this sentence is:

> I *had commuted* two hours each way before I *moved* to the city.

PRACTICE

II   **Directions:** Blacken the space beneath the number which corresponds to the number of the incorrect sentence in each group.

1 2 3 4
‖ ‖ ‖ ‖

1   1) John Milton had become immortalized before Ernest Hemingway was born.

2) Jean had driven fifteen miles before she had realized that she was going north instead of south.

3) Prior to our purchasing a new one, our old refrigerator had needed repair every six to eight weeks.

4) Since environmental care has become a public concern, paper and glass recycling are common in many communities.

1 2 3 4
‖ ‖ ‖ ‖

2   1) If I had known I could have a paying job, I never would have volunteered my services.

2) If you had planned a thorough outline earlier, you would not be so rushed to complete your report now.

3) I had suffered the pain of a sore throat for three days before I had called a doctor.

4) After we had bought the large oak table, we saw the glaring imperfection in it.

• Sometimes a future action can occur before another future action.

> *Example:* I *will have commuted* four million miles by the time I retire.

The addition of the helping word *have* shows that the commuting will be completed before the retiring.

Common Misuses of Will Have

a. I *will have commuted* four million miles by the time I *will have retired.*

b. I *will commute* four million miles by the time I *will have retired.*

The only correct use of *will have* in this sentence is:

> I *will have commuted* four million miles by the time I *retire.*

PRACTICE

III   **Directions:** Blacken the space beneath the number which corresponds to the number of the incorrect sentence in each group.

                                                        1 2 3 4
                                                        ‖ ‖ ‖ ‖
1 1) By the time your plane lands in Cleveland, I will have left for Colorado.

2) By the time you call for me, I will have typed our report.

3) Before they leave, Mary and Agnes will have instructed the children to go to bed at nine.

4) Martin will complete high school by the time his brother begins.

                                                        1 2 3 4
                                                        ‖ ‖ ‖ ‖
2 1) Jeannie will have graduated from high school before David enters.

2) By next summer, I will retire from public office.

3) By this time next week, I will have seen Paris.

4) The meeting will have adjourned before you leave your office.

- When two actions occur simultaneously, their time must be the same.

  Example: As the curtain *rises*, the audience *applauds*.

  As the curtain *rose*, the audience *applauded*.

Common Errors Regarding Simultaneous Actions

   a. As the curtain *rose* to reveal the elaborate set, the enthusiastic audience *had applauded*.

   b. As the curtain *had risen* to reveal the elaborate set, the enthusiastic audience *applauded*.

In sentences a and b, the audience applauded *as* the curtain rose. Since both actions occurred *at the same time*, neither action word should be accompanied by *had*.

PRACTICE

   IV   **Directions:** Blacken the space beneath the number which corresponds to the number of the incorrect sentence in each group.

			1 2 3 4
1	1)	As the class filed out of the room, David noticed the trampled book on the floor.	‖ ‖ ‖ ‖
	2)	When the power failed, all of our food was ruined.	
	3)	As soon as you finish rereading the *Pathfinders*, please call me.	
	4)	As the fish bit the worm, he had realized his error.	

			1 2 3 4
2	1)	As we began our trip in our brand new convertible, gray clouds hovered threateningly above.	‖ ‖ ‖ ‖
	2)	When the automobile industry's strike ended, our car was delivered.	
	3)	When I lifted the papers, I had found Ellen's missing glasses.	
	4)	As soon as you gave me your requirements, I shipped the order.	

- Linking words express time, also. *Has, have,* and *had* are used with linking words in order to clarify time.

  Examples: Tom *has been* irritable all morning.

  Tom *had been* irritable before he received his promotion.

Tom *will have been* president for two years, by the time he retires.

PRACTICE

V   Directions: Blacken the space beneath the number which corresponds to the number of the incorrect sentence in each group.

1 2 3 4 5
‖ ‖ ‖ ‖ ‖

1   1)   I have felt tired since my illness.

2)   Jules always has been a good sport.

3)   Before she began working full-time, Erica seemed more relaxed.

4)   By the time this very long documentary ends, I will have grown bored.

1 2 3 4 5
‖ ‖ ‖ ‖ ‖

2   1)   The amplifier had sounded distorted for several hours before it stopped working.

2)   The court claimed that the children had been neglected.

3)   For the past three days, your socks have been in the same place on the floor.

4)   As I looked across the room at the woman who bore an uncanny resemblance to me, I had felt as though I were looking into a mirror.

REVIEW EXERCISES

PRACTICE

VI   Directions: Blacken the space beneath the number which corresponds to the number of the incorrect sentence. If there is no error, blacken space number 5.

1 2 3 4 5
‖ ‖ ‖ ‖ ‖

1   1)   Lady Bird Johnson had shown an interest in conservation long before she became the First Lady.

2)   The CIA had overstepped its bounds long before Watergate publicized its far-reaching arm.

3)   As I spoke, I realized my error.

4)   Prior to the election, the candidate promised law and order.

5)   No error

1 2 3 4 5

2
1) I am teaching for twenty years.
2) Betty Friedan has been a pioneer in the women's movement.
3) The Thompsons have owned the drug store since 1947.
4) Before he spoke, he had carefully prepared his speech.
5) No error

1 2 3 4 5

3
1) In 1974, Richard Nixon resigned.
2) John had changed jobs. Then the family followed him.
3) During this decade, elections have been less exciting each year.
4) We had seen Laura last night.
5) No error

1 2 3 4 5

4
1) As the car pulled to the curb, a man jumped out.
2) Before the phone stopped ringing, Mary had answered it.
3) Before the music had stopped, a shot rang out.
4) When you arrive, we will begin the discussion.
5) No error

1 2 3 4 5

5
1) By 1995, the price of gas will have risen to over two dollars per gallon.
2) Before the doorbell rang, Ida seemed nervous.
3) Because he had known the temper of the crowd, he spoke calmly and clearly.
4) By the time the repairman arrives, I will have left.
5) No error

                                                    1 2 3 4 5
6 1) By this time tomorrow, I will have taken the test.   ‖ ‖ ‖ ‖ ‖

2) If you studied, you might have known the answer.

3) The historian carefully studied his subject.

4) Before boarding the plane, Tom had expressed a fear of flying.

5) No error

                                                    1 2 3 4 5
7 1) These sentences have been difficult.   ‖ ‖ ‖ ‖ ‖

2) Last week, they would have been impossible.

3) By next week, you will have mastered the problem.

4) Before he passed the test, the man studied for many hours.

5) No error

PRACTICE
VII   **Directions:** Blacken the space beneath the number which corresponds to the correct rewriting of the underlined portion of the sentence. Choice 1 is always the same as the underlined portion and is sometimes the right answer.

                                                    1 2 3 4 5
1.   I signed the letter several days after I <u>wrote</u>   ‖ ‖ ‖ ‖ ‖
      it.

      1) I wrote it.
      2) I writed it.
      3) it was written.
      4) I had written it.
      5) I have written it.

                                                    1 2 3 4 5
2.   By the time the sun comes out, the pool <u>will</u>   ‖ ‖ ‖ ‖ ‖
      <u>close</u> for the day.

      1) will close
      2) will have closed
      3) has closed
      4) will be closed
      5) would close

3. The telephone rang as my guest entered the room.

       1) rang as my guest entered
       2) rang as my guest had entered
       3) had rung as my guest entered
       4) had rung as my guest had entered
       5) rang as my guest has entered

4. Since I began to study music appreciation, I had enjoyed Beethoven.

       1) had enjoyed
       2) always had enjoyed
       3) have enjoyed
       4) will enjoy
       5) enjoy

5. On this, his anniversary, Simpson was with the bank for forty years.

       1) was with the bank
       2) had been with the bank
       3) is with the bank
       4) has been with the bank
       5) will be with the bank

6. I received a ticket because I parked in a no parking zone.

       1) received a ticket because I parked
       2) received a ticket because I had parked
       3) had received a ticket because I parked
       4) had received a ticket because I had parked
       5) received a ticket because parking

7. If you arrive after 10, the kitchen <u>will have closed</u>.

    1) will have closed.

    2) closes.

    3) will close.

    4) should close.

    5) has closed.

8. As soon as the bell rings, the horses <u>will begin</u> to run.

    1) will begin

    2) shall begin

    3) have begun

    4) began

    5) begin

9. He <u>made the appointment</u> before he consulted me.

    1) made the appointment

    2) made that appointment

    3) had made the appointment

    4) has made the appointment

    5) have made the appointment

10. I <u>was unusually busy</u> for the past two weeks.

    1) was unusually busy

    2) will have been unusually busy

    3) am unusually busy

    4) have been unusually busy

    5) had been unusually busy

PRACTICE
VIII

Directions: Blacken the space beneath the number which corresponds to the number of the error in each sentence. If there is no error, blacken space number 5.

1. We *had traveled* extensively *before* we *had* bought our summer home. *No error*
   (1) (2) (3) (4) (5)

   1 2 3 4 5
   ‖ ‖ ‖ ‖ ‖

2. We *traveled* in Europe and Asia *before* we *went* to *South* America. *No error*
   (1) (2) (3) (4) (5)

   1 2 3 4 5
   ‖ ‖ ‖ ‖ ‖

3. For the past year, *however,* we *were inclined* to stay home. *No error*
   (1) (2) (3) (4) (5)

   1 2 3 4 5
   ‖ ‖ ‖ ‖ ‖

4. Travel *became* so expensive over the *past* few years that we *can* no longer *afford* it. *No error*
   (1) (2) (3) (4) (5)

   1 2 3 4 5
   ‖ ‖ ‖ ‖ ‖

5. Perhaps *by the time* our children *are grown,* *we will have decided* to *travel* again. *No error*
   (1) (2) (3) (4) (5)

   1 2 3 4 5
   ‖ ‖ ‖ ‖ ‖

1 2 3 4 5

6. As soon as they *become* independent of us, ‖ ‖ ‖ ‖ ‖
    —————
    1

    we will have become independent of them.
    —— —— ————
    2   3   4

    No error
    ————
    5

1 2 3 4 5

7. During the *past several* years, the children's ‖ ‖ ‖ ‖ ‖
    ———— ——————
    1   2

    increasing activities *hampered* our inde-
    —————————   ——————
    3   4

    pendence. *No error*
              ————————
              5

1 2 3 4 5

8. Before we *started* a family, we *did not travel* ‖ ‖ ‖ ‖ ‖
    —————   ——————————
    1   2

    as much as we *should have*. *No error*
                  —————— ———— ————————
                  3   4   5

ANSWER KEY

Chapter 9

Time: Special Problems

Practice I *Page 79.*

1. (3) Eric *has been* the last in line since he began school.
   The addition of the helping word *has* expresses the idea of an action which began in the past but is continuing into the present.
2. (3) Andrea *has not visited* us for the past several days.
   See explanation above.

Practice II *Page 80.*

1. (2) Jean *had driven* fifteen miles before she *realized* that she was going north instead of south.
   When a sentence contains two past actions, the action which occurred first is accompanied by the helping word *had*.
2. (3) I *had suffered* the pain of a sore throat for three days before I *called* a doctor.
   See explanation above.

Practice III *Page 81.*

1. (4) Martin *will have completed* high school by the time his brother *begins.*
   When a sentence contains two future actions, the action which will occur first is accompanied by the helping words *will have.*
2. (2) By next summer, I *will have retired* from public office.
   See explanation above.

Practice IV *Page 82.*

1. (4) As the fish *bit* the worm, he *realized* his error.
   When two actions occur simultaneously, their forms must be the same. Omit *had* before *realized.*
2. (3) When I *lifted* the papers, I *found* Ellen's missing glasses.
   See explanation above. Omit *had* before *found.*

Practice V *Page 83.*

1. (3) Before she *had begun* working full-time, Erica seemed more relaxed.
   Addition of the helping word *had* shows the *begun* occurred in the past before *seemed.*
2. (4) As I looked across the room at the woman who bore an uncanny resemblance to me, I *felt* as though I were looking into a mirror.
   Eliminate *had* before *felt. Looked* and *felt* are simultaneous actions.

REVIEW

Practice VI *Page 83.*

1. (4) Prior to the election, the candidate *had promised* law and order.
   The addition of the helping word *had* shows that the promising occurred in the past *before* the election.
2. (1) I *have been teaching* for twenty years.
   The helping words *have been* show that the teaching began in the past and continues into the present.
3. (4) We *saw* Laura last night.
   Eliminate the helping word *had* since the seeing did not occur in the past before another action.

4. (3) Before the music stopped, a shot *had rung* out.

The helping word *had* shows that *rung* occurred in the past before the music stopped.

5. (2) Before the doorbell rang, Ida *had seemed* nervous.

The helping word *had* shows that *seemed* occurred before the doorbell rang.

6. (2) If you *had studied*, you might have known the answer.

The helping word *had* shows that *studied* began in the past before the knowing.

7. (4) Before he passed the test, the man *had studied* for many hours.

The helping word *had* shows that *studied* began in the past before *passed*.

Practice VII *Page 85.*

1. (4) I signed the letter several days after *I had written it.*

The helping word *had* shows that the writing occurred in the past *before* the signing.

2. (2) By the time the sun comes out, the pool *will have closed* for the day.

The helping words *will have* show that the closing will be completed *before* the sun comes out.

3. (1) The telephone *rang as my guest entered* the room.

Since both actions occurred at *the same time*, the same form (past) is used for both action words.

4. (3) Since I began to study music appreciation, I *have enjoyed* Beethoven.

The helping word *have* shows that *enjoyed* began in the past and is continuing into the present.

5. (4) On this, his anniversary, Simpson *has been with the bank* for forty years.

The helping word *has* shows that Simpson *has been* with the bank in the past and is continuing into the present.

6. (2) I *received a ticket because I had parked* in a no parking zone.

The helping word *had* shows that the parking occurred in the past *before* the receiving.

7. (1) If you arrive after 10, the kitchen *will have closed*.

The helping words *will have* show that the closing will be completed *before* the arrival.

8. (5) As soon as the bell rings, the horses *begin* to run.

Since both actions occur at the *same time*, the *same form* (present) is used for both action words.

9. (3) He *had made the appointment* before he consulted me.

The helping word *had* shows that the appointment was made *before* the consulting took place.

10. (4) I *have been unusually busy* for the past two weeks.

The helping word *have* shows that I *have been* busy in the past and am continuing into the present.

Practice VIII *Page 88.*

1. (3) We had traveled extensively before we *bought* our summer home.
2. (1) We *had traveled* in Europe and Asia before we went to South America.
3. (2) For the past year, however, we *have been* inclined to stay home.
4. (1) Travel *has become* so expensive over the past few years that we can no longer afford it.
5. (5) No error
6. (3) As soon as they become independent of us, we *will become* independent of them.
7. (4) During the past several years, the children's increasing activities *have hampered* our independence.
8. (2) Before we started a family, we *had not traveled* as much as we should have.

10.

Pronouns

Years ago when I was just out of graduate school and thought I could remake society by cleaning up slovenly grammar in the media, I sent some naive letters to the networks. Johnny Carson's quiz show should be called "*Whom* Do You Trust?" not "*Who* Do You Trust?" Arthur Godfrey should ask his Talent Scouts, "*Whom* did you bring to the show?" instead of "*Who* . . . ?" and the ABC situation comedy should be "My Sister and *I*" not "My Sister and *Me*."

The networks never made any changes, and now I sing "Ain't Misbehavin' " just like every other former purist.

—Bob Kassell
Surrounded By Assassins

A Word With You . . .

The picture of critic Bob Kassell beating his head against the networks in order to get them to use pronouns properly is an amusing one. There is a serious side to it, however, for students of language. Why, for example, are some people more comfortable while using the incorrect form of the language?

You might not find the answer to that question in Chapter 10—but you will learn why "I gave the books to Joe and *her*," "It is *I*," "Just between Edith and *me*," and "It is *we* players who must protest" all illustrate correct pronoun usage.

Pronouns are used as performers/subjects or as words which receive action. *For example:*

performer	performer pronoun
Lloyd ran home.	Hé ran home.

subject	subject pronoun
Lloyd is pleasant.	Hé is pleasant.

performer	receives action

Elána gave a bright smile to Tóm.

performer

pronoun which receives action

Eláná gave a bright smile to hím.

performer

receives action

Máríá gave Toḿ an icy stare.

performer

pronoun which receives action

Máríá gave hiḿ an icy stare.

PERFORMER/SUBJECT PRONOUNS	PRONOUNS WHICH RECEIVE ACTION
I	me
you	you
he	him
she	her
it	it
we	us
they	them
who	whom

PRACTICE

I **Directions:** Complete each sentence using a pronoun from the above list. More than one choice may be correct.

1. _____ won the election.

2. _____ campaigned all week.

3. The National Organization for Women gave the citation to _____.

4. The student hitchhiker got a lift from _____.

5. _____ was responsible for legislation providing consumer protection?

6. For _____ did the witness testify?

• PRONOUN CLUE 1:

Don't be confused by *who* and *whom*. As you can see in the preceding list, *who* is a subject/performer and *whom* is a pronoun which receives action.

If: *He* painted the house.
Then: *Who* painted the house?
If: The phone call is for *him*.
Then: For *whom* is the phone call?

PRACTICE

II   Directions: Underline the pronoun which correctly completes each sentence.

Example: (*Who* - Whom) rang the doorbell?

Clue: *He* rang the doorbell.

1.   (Who - Whom) did you call?
2.   (Who - Whom) answered your letter?
3.   (Who - Whom) will help with this project?
4.   *Consumer Reports* cites manufacturers from (who - whom) we can expect quality products.
5.   Alice Cooper is the singer (who - whom) Tony likes best.

• **PRONOUN CLUE 2:**

Don't be confused by more than one subject.

If: He won the election.
Then: Macon and *he* won the election.

Because it is incorrect to say:
   Him won the election.

It is equally incorrect to say:
   Macon and *him* won the election.

PRACTICE

III   Directions: Underline the pronoun which correctly completes each sentence.

1.   Mr. Jones and (he, him) ran the fair.
2.   (They, Them) and their father went fishing.
3.   My friend and (I, me) are planning a camping trip.
4.   (She, her) and (he, him) were delegates to the convention.
5.   The Walters and (we, us) go to the shore each summer.
6.   (Who, whom), along with Susan, will work on this committee?

• **PRONOUN CLUE 3:**

Don't be confused by more than one word receiving the action.

If: I gave the present to *her.*
Then: I gave the present to Tom and *her.*

Because it is incorrect to say:
   I gave the present to *she.*

It is equally incorrect to say:
   I gave the present to Tom and *she.*

PRACTICE

IV   **Directions:** Underline the pronoun which correctly completes each sentence.

1. When the plans for the new community center are completed, call Mr. Faldez and (I, me).

2. The supermarket manager gave discount coupons to Olga and (she, her).

3. When they question you about the accident, tell Paul and (they, them) the truth.

4. Will you be speaking to Hiroko and (he, him)?

5. The MacDonalds sent regards to Joanna and (we, us).

• **PRONOUN CLUE 4:**

Don't be confused by a condensed thought.

If: Elmer runs more quickly *than I do.*
Then: Elmer runs more quickly *than I.*

Because it is incorrect to say:
    Elmer runs more quickly *than me do.*

It is equally incorrect to say:
    Elmer runs more quickly *than me.*

PRACTICE

V   **Directions:** Underline the pronoun which correctly completes each sentence.

1. Mary is a better cook than (I, me).

2. I sew better than (she, her).

3. You don't feel as sorry as (he, him).

4. The Ortegas are better swimmers than (we, us).

5. Their neighbors don't argue as often as (they, them).

• **PRONOUN CLUE 5:**

A sentence in which a linking word is connecting the subject to a word which means the same thing as the subject, is reversible.

If: Carl is the mayor.
Then: The mayor is Carl.
If: He is the mayor.
Then: The mayor is *he.*

Because it is incorrect to say:
> *Him* is the mayor.

It is equally incorrect to say:
> The mayor is *him*.

PRACTICE

VI   **Directions:**   Underline the pronoun which correctly completes each sentence.

1.   My secretary is (she, her).
2.   The winner of the contest was (he, him).
3.   (Who, whom) seems most likely to get the promotion?
4.   The culprits were (they, them).
5.   The person who called you was (I, me).
6.   If there is a couple who enjoys dancing, it is (we, us).

• **PRONOUN CLUE 6:**

Certain pronouns—*my, your, his, her, its, our, their*—may be used as descriptive words.

> *Example:*   I like the *red* hat.
> I like *his* hat.

Descriptive pronouns are never a problem in the above context. However, errors tend to be made in sentences such as the following:

INCORRECT: I do not like *him* smoking.
CORRECT: I do not like *his* smoking.

INCORRECT: Of course I approve of *you* jogging.
CORRECT: Of course I approve of *your* jogging.

PRACTICE

VII   **Directions:**   Underline the pronoun which correctly completes each sentence.

1.   Tom is very proud of (him, his) swimming.
2.   I don't like (you, your) calling me at the office.
3.   The professor was glad to hear about (me, my) writing a story.
4.   We wondered (who's, whose) contribution to medicine was greatest?
5.   I don't like (them, their) refusing to take BHA and BHT out of foods.

• **PRONOUN CLUE 7:**

Words such as *to, from, between, except, among* are followed by pronouns which receive action (p. 93).

For example:

1. Between you and *me*, I don't enjoy cooking.
2. The package is for *her*.
3. Please divide the workload among *them*.
4. Everyone, except *us*, is attending the meeting.

PRACTICE VIII

Directions: Underline the pronoun which correctly completes each sentence.

1. From (who, whom) did you learn that myth about not eating before swimming?
2. Many secrets have passed between you and (he, him).
3. The personnel director gave notices to John and (they, them).
4. Everyone, except (she, her), plans to take the test.
5. The host and his friends divided the four bottles of beer among (they, them).

• **PRONOUN CLUE 8:**

A pronoun must agree in number with the word to which it refers.

For example:

1. One of the men in the back of the room could not project *his* voice.

   His refers to *one*. Both words are singular.
2. All of those women left *their* coats after the rally.

   Their refers to *all*. Both words are plural.

PRACTICE IX

Directions: Select the word which correctly completes each sentence.

1. Everyone must decide for (himself, themselves).
2. Each of the painters worked (his, their) best.
3. They each performed to the best of (his, their) ability.
4. All of the members brought (his, their) wives.

PRACTICE X

REVIEW EXERCISES

Directions: Blacken the space beneath the number which corresponds to the number of the incorrect word in each sentence. If there is no error, blacken space number 5

1. *He* and *his* brother strenuously object to *me*
   1   2   3

   smoking. *No error*
   4   5

   1 2 3 4 5

2. Although *she* is interesting and *she's* witty, I
            1   2

   don't think that *she* is the right girl for *my*
            3   4

   friend. *No error*
         5

   1 2 3 4 5

3. Sam finds *my* singing offensive, but *he* enjoys
          1   2

   me playing *the* piano. *No error*
   3   4   5

   1 2 3 4 5

4. The man *who* you called is out and *his* assist-
       1   2

   ant insists *that he* will not return again today.
           3   4

   No error
   5

   1 2 3 4 5

5. If you are wondering *who* it was *who* called
               1   2

   you earlier in the week, it was *him. No error*
   3   4   5

   1 2 3 4 5

6. Although *he* plays tennis better than *I* do,
         1   2

   I play chess better than *him. No error*
   3   4   5

   1 2 3 4 5

                                                    1 2 3 4 5
                                                    ‖ ‖ ‖ ‖ ‖

7. Would *you* please buy tickets for the basket-
         ‾‾
          1

    ball game *for* *him* and *I?* *No error*
              ‾‾‾ ‾‾‾   ‾‾ ‾‾‾‾‾‾‾‾
               2   3   4   5

                                                    1 2 3 4 5
                                                    ‖ ‖ ‖ ‖ ‖

8. *He* invited Jim and *she* to join *his* car pool
    ‾‾   ‾‾‾   ‾‾‾
     1   2   3

    that day. *No error*
    ‾‾‾‾   ‾‾‾‾‾‾‾‾
      4   5

                                                    1 2 3 4 5
                                                    ‖ ‖ ‖ ‖ ‖

9. Don wanted *us,* John and *I,* to help *him* build
              ‾‾‾   ‾‾   ‾‾‾
               1   2   3

    his new garage. *No error*
    ‾‾‾   ‾‾‾‾‾‾‾‾
     4   5

                                                    1 2 3 4 5
                                                    ‖ ‖ ‖ ‖ ‖

10. Jane and *me* invited *our* husbands and *them*
            ‾‾‾   ‾‾‾   ‾‾‾‾
             1   2   3

    to join *our* physical fitness class. *No error*
            ‾‾‾   ‾‾‾‾‾‾‾‾
             4   5

PRACTICE
XI   **Directions:** Blacken the space beneath the number which corresponds
            to the number of the incorrect sentence in each group. If there is no error,
            blacken space number 5.

                                                    1 2 3 4 5
                                                    ‖ ‖ ‖ ‖ ‖

1 1) Them and us play gin rummy each Wednesday.

    2) Please write to the folks and me while you're away.

    3) The friendliest person on the street is he.

    4) I did not give the information about the adverse
       effects of food additives to him.

    5) No error

                                                    1 2 3 4 5
                                                    ‖ ‖ ‖ ‖ ‖

2 1) Who told you that oil drilling equipment does not
       cause pollution?

    2) Rita is a more knowledgeable gardener than me.

    3) For whom did you buy that impractical gift?

    4) The person responsible for creating the Equal
       Rights Amendment is she.

    5) No error

3

	1	2	3	4	5
	‖	‖	‖	‖	‖

1) In the bright light, Theresa and I could see their faces clearly.

2) Either she or I am working late.

3) A package just arrived, and it is marked for either him or her.

4) The person who gave the lecture did not speak well.

5) No error

4

	1	2	3	4	5
	‖	‖	‖	‖	‖

1) Since they went to Marriage Encounter, Simon fights more fairly than she.

2) In 1954, Roberto and me saw Stan Musial hit five home runs in one game.

3) Arthur and he claim to have seen several UFO's.

4) At whose request do I announce the slate?

5) No error

5

	1	2	3	4	5
	‖	‖	‖	‖	‖

1) Who's going to pay for education if all funding legislation is defeated?

2) Please call Henry and I as soon as you know the election returns.

3) Do you really approve of his playing football?

4) Arlene will always be younger than I.

5) No error

6

	1	2	3	4	5
	‖	‖	‖	‖	‖

1) Who called?

2) After you've repaired the sink, give the tools to John and him.

3) Mike and me will carry the steel beam.

4) In case you didn't know, the new mayor is he.

5) No error

<table>
<tr><td></td><td></td><td></td><td>1   2   3   4   5</td></tr>
</table>

7 1) We hope the new police commissioner will be as ‖ ‖ ‖ ‖ ‖
friendly as him.

    2) The Jensens and they organize a block party each
year to raise money for the Fresh Air Fund.

    3) Who do you think will run his campaign?

    4) Give responsible jobs to Kate and her because they
have had the most experience.

    5) No error

1   2   3   4   5

8 1) Daniel and I exchange information with them about ‖ ‖ ‖ ‖ ‖
the Bermuda Triangle.

    2) I have always worked harder than he.

    3) If you don't do the job, who will?

    4) He really shouldn't have objected to me leaving
since my work had been finished.

    5) No error

1   2   3   4   5

9 1) I was very pleased with them for thinking of me ‖ ‖ ‖ ‖ ‖
when they decided to expand their company.

    2) If it is his turn, then allow him to take it.

    3) Davis has always been more punctual than us.

    4) The Boss is one of those musicians who are full of
surprises.

    5) No error

1   2   3   4   5

10 1) Give me your word that you and he will comply ‖ ‖ ‖ ‖ ‖
with our terms.

    2) Jean and I completed the forms and left them at the
main desk.

    3) If I can find you and her, I will give you his instruc-
tions.

    4) According to a survey among writers, one of the
finest authors of the century is Saul Bellow.

    5) No error

ANSWER KEY

Chapter 10

Pronouns

Practice I *Page 93.*

Answers will vary.
Sample answers:
1. I, You, He, She, We, They
2. I, You, He, She, We, They
3. him, her, you, them
4. him, me, you, her, us, them
5. Who
6. whom

Practice II *Page 94.*

For explanations of these answers,
see *Pronoun Clue 1.*
1. *Whom* did you call?
2. *Who* answered?
3. *Who* will help?
4. from *whom*
5. *whom* Tony likes

Practice III *Page 94.*

For explanations of these answers,
see *Pronoun Clue 2.*
1. *he* ran
2. *They* went
3. My friend and *I* are
4. *She, he* were
5. *we* go
6. *Who* will work

Practice IV *Page 95.*

For explanations of these answers,
see *Pronoun Clue 3.*
1. call *me*
2. gave to *her*
3. Tell *them*
4. speaking to *him*
5. sent to *us*

Practice V *Page 95.*

For explanations of these answers,
see *Pronoun Clue 4.*
1. than *I* (am)
2. than *she* (sews)
3. as *he* (feels)
4. than *we* (are)
5. as *they* (argue)

Practice VI *Page 96.*

For explanations of these answers,
see *Pronoun Clue 5.*
1. *she* (is my secretary)
2. *he* (was the winner)
3. *who* (seems)
4. *they* (were the culprits)
5. *I* (was the person)
6. *we* (are it)

Practice VII *Page 96.*

For explanations of these answers,
see *Pronoun Clue 6.*
1. *his* swimming
2. *your* calling
3. *my* writing
4. *whose* contribution
5. *their* refusing

Practice VIII *Page 97.*

For explanations of these answers,
see *Pronoun Clue 7.*
1. from *whom*
2. between you and *him*
3. to John and *them*
4. except *her*
5. among *them*

Practice IX *Page 97.*

For explanations of these answers,
see *Pronoun Clue 8.*
1. *himself* refers to everyone (singular).
2. *his* refers to each (singular).
3. *their* refers to they (plural).
4. *their* refers to all (plural).

Practice X *Page 98.*

1. (3) *my* smoking	See Pronoun Clue 6.
2. (5) No error	
3. (3) *my* playing	See Pronoun Clue 6.
4. (1) *whom*	See Pronoun Clues 3 and 7.
5. (4) *he* was it	See Pronoun Clue 5.
6. (4) *he* (plays)	See Pronoun Clue 8.
7. (4) for *me*	See Pronoun Clues 3 and 7.
8. (2) he invited *her*	See Pronoun Clue 3.
9. (2) Don wanted *me*	See Pronoun Clue 3.
10. (1) *I* invited	See Pronoun Clue 2.

Practice XI *Page 99.*

1. (1) *They* and *we* play gin rummy each Wednesday.
2. (2) Rita is a more knowledgeable gardner than *I* (am).
3. (5) No error
4. (2) In 1954, Roberto and *I* saw Stan Musial hit five home runs in one game.
5. (2) Please call Henry and *me* as soon as you know the election returns.
6. (3) Mike and *I* will carry the steel beam.
7. (1) We hope the new police commissioner will be as friendly as *he* (is).
8. (4) He really shouldn't have objected to *my* leaving since my work had been finished.
9. (3) Davis has always been more punctual than *we* (have been).
10. (5) No error

11.

Cumulative Review

This review covers the following concepts which have been included in the preceding chapters:

- Agreement in Time and Number
- Correct Use of Descriptive Words and Phrases
- Recognizing Complete and Incomplete Thoughts
- Special Problems in Agreement
- Special Problems in Time
- Correct Use of Pronouns

After completing the Cumulative Review exercises, evaluate your ability using the SUMMARY OF RESULTS chart on page 112. Acceptable scores for each practice are given.

To learn your weaknesses, find the question numbers you answered incorrectly on the SKILLS ANALYSIS table. The table will show which of your skills need improvement and the necessary chapters to review.

PRACTICE

I   Directions: Blacken the space beneath the number which corresponds to the number of the incorrect word in each sentence. If there is no error, blacken space number 5.

                                                     1 2 3 4 5

1.   The *angry* man *ran* *hurriedly* into the   ‖ ‖ ‖ ‖ ‖
             1   2   3

       crowded room and shouted *loud* at the
                                     4

       guest. *No error*
                5

                                            1 2 3 4 5

2.   Airman Donald G. Farrell *grimaced* as *he*   ‖ ‖ ‖ ‖ ‖
                                    1   2

       squeezed into the simulated space cabin
        3

       which was to be his home for seven days.
           4

       No error.
        5

3. *What* *is* the *social* implications of the *small*
      1 2   3   4

   car? *No error*
          5

   1 2 3 4 5

4. Although Jan *worked* all day, she *did* not *feel*
                 1   2   3

   good. *No error*
     4   5

   1 2 3 4 5

5. There again, I must *insist* that I *do* not like
                  1   2

   you smoking in *my* home. *No error*
     3   4   5

   1 2 3 4 5

6. Just between *we* two, I *believe* Jim did not
               1   2

   write the contract *properly*. *No error*
     3   4   5

   1 2 3 4 5

7. Without *fail*, Carlo and *she* *attend* *monthly*
         1   2   3   4

   board of education meetings. *No error*
                        5

   1 2 3 4 5

8. Neither the congressman *nor* the people
                        1

   whom he *represents* *approves* of this bill.
     2   3   4

   No error
     5

                                                    1 2 3 4 5
                                                    || || || || ||

9.   *Somehow* a misunderstanding about *this*
          1   2

      situation *has developed* between you and
                        3

      me. *No error*
       4   5

PRACTICE

II   **Directions:** Blacken the space beneath the number which corresponds to the number of the incorrect sentence in each group. If there is no error, blacken space number 5.

                                                    1 2 3 4 5
                                                    || || || || ||

1 1) Mark and Eloise gave gifts to Bill and her.

    2) A waiting room crowded with impatient patients were common at Dr. Rizzo's.

    3) George Samason is one man whom I trust.

    4) Every one of those boxes represents a large investment.

    5) No error

                                                    1 2 3 4 5
                                                    || || || || ||

2 1) Is this the man who you gave the information to?

    2) Mrs. Stover is one of those teachers who relish new ideas.

    3) If anyone can be unfailingly stubborn, it is she.

    4) The L.A. Dodgers and their manager are in the dugout.

    5) No error

                                                    1 2 3 4 5
                                                    || || || || ||

3 1) All of our energy should be directed toward maintaining a clean environment.

    2) Please remind all of the members of your organization to vote for Alex and him.

    3) There was several short stories in the magazine, but the last was by far the best one.

    4) Whoever calls the radio station within three minutes with the name of the third vice president of the United States will win the contest.

    5) No error

1 2 3 4 5
|| || || || ||

4

1) There goes Chester Kallow and his wife, Olga, to their weekly bowling game.

2) Mrs. Jana, along with her teacher's aide, initiates a new science project each week.

3) There are no correct or incorrect answers when speaking of the interpretations of dreams.

4) If the inflation continues and the political scandal goes on, we are headed for hard times.

5) No error

1 2 3 4 5
|| || || || ||

5

1) When you can't find the solution to a problem and help is not forthcoming and you don't know where to turn.

2) Of all the recipes for quiche, this is the quickest.

3) The musician who lives in the downstairs apartment plays ragtime piano loudly.

4) The cold, icy wind cut through the cabin walls and made sleeping uncomfortable.

5) No error

1 2 3 4 5
|| || || || ||

6

1) The young boy and his companion spent the afternoon pretending that the pond was a lake and that they were explorers.

2) Neither the merchants nor their customers approve of the town ordinance to close at 6 P.M.

3) Kicking and splashing, the dog finished his bath.

4) Before signing the order, on the telephone the salesman finished his conversation.

5) No error

1 2 3 4 5
|| || || || ||

7

1) Of all the women in the race, Amelia runs quickest.

2) Everyone in our group believes that the organization must collect dues in order to sustain itself.

3) Please hire whomever you think is best suited for this exacting job.

4) Do you agree that whoever speaks last will make the most lasting impression upon the audience?

5) No error

8

1 2 3 4 5
|| || || || ||

1) The rising price of food, coupled with the current recession, makes it impossible for an average family to obtain even the slightest luxury.

2) Although she enjoys fishing, Theresa, becoming dizzy because of the motion of the sea and increasingly nauseated by the smell of the fish.

3) Any of the three dresses is suitable for this occasion.

4) Here is the file which you requested.

5) No error

PRACTICE

III   **Directions:** Blacken the space beneath the number which corresponds to the correct rewriting of the underlined portion of the sentence. Choice 1 is always the same as the underlined portion and is sometimes the right answer.

1 2 3 4 5
|| || || || ||

1.   The shy girl stood hesitantly in the doorway before she entered the crowded bar.

1) stood hesitantly

2) standed hesitantly

3) has stood hesitantly

4) had stood hesitantly

5) stands hesitantly

1 2 3 4 5
|| || || || ||

2.   Either the grass or the shrubs need cutting weekly.

1) Either the grass or the shrubs need

2) Either the grass or the shrubs needs

3) Either the shrubs or the grass need

4) Either the grass or the shrubs needing

5) Either the shrubs or the grass needing

1 2 3 4 5
|| || || || ||

3.   Here's my mother and father.

1) Here's

2) Here is

3) Here are

4) Here was

5) Here were

1 2 3 4 5
|| || || || ||

4.   Last week I <u>went to the boringest party</u>.

   1) went to the boringest party.

   2) went to the most boringest party.

   3) went to the more boring party.

   4) had gone to the most boring party.

   5) went to the most boring party.

1 2 3 4 5
|| || || || ||

5.   David performed the difficult experiment <u>more precisely than any student</u> in the class.

   1) more precisely than any student

   2) most precisely than any student

   3) more precise than any student

   4) more precisely than any other student

   5) more precise than any other student

PRACTICE

IV   **Directions:** Blacken the space beneath the number that corresponds to the number of the incorrect sentence in each group. If all sentences are correct, blacken the space beneath number 5.

1 2 3 4 5
|| || || || ||

1 1) Neither Mrs. Jones nor any of her children were at the school play.

   2) Each of the three entries in the 4-H contest has merit.

   3) Any one of those sandwich meats is an excellent choice for lunch.

   4) That painting hangs in my mother's hallway of which I am proud.

   5) No error

1 2 3 4 5
|| || || || ||

2 1) That lecturer, about whom I've told you, has agreed to speak at our meeting.

   2) Any of the four candidates would serve well.

   3) Neither the child nor his father want to take the responsibility for walking the dog.

   4) The cheese in the refrigerator is no longer fresh.

   5) No error

3

1 2 3 4 5
‖ ‖ ‖ ‖ ‖

1) This excellent thesis surpasses all others and presented the facts most coherently.

2) He is a terrible golfer, but the most tenacious would-be sportsman I know.

3) If you are wondering who left the book in your mailbox, it was I.

4) When you visit Yosemite Park, please take a deep breath for Marty and me.

5) No error

4

1 2 3 4 5
‖ ‖ ‖ ‖ ‖

1) Isaac Asimov, Frank Herbert, and Robert Heinlein write good science fiction.

2) All of the twelve contestants are talented.

3) The tall, handsome man, wearing a plaid jacket and striped pants, stepping snappily off the curb.

4) An English garden, filled with a variety of colors and strains, is an enchanting sight.

5) No error

5

1 2 3 4 5
‖ ‖ ‖ ‖ ‖

1) Tom and she frequently read the same books.

2) If you don't see us, leave.

3) In addition to being rude, he is the most stubborn man I know.

4) How can you expect everyone to do his best when you place them under constant pressure?

5) No error

6

1 2 3 4 5
‖ ‖ ‖ ‖ ‖

1) This is the worst project I've ever been involved in.

2) According to a spokesman for the members, they each gave their own opinions at the meeting.

3) The stapler belongs to that woman on the table.

4) Of the two methods of bidding, I like this one better.

5) No error

1 2 3 4 5

7 1) None of our group is ready for the meet.
2) There's several avenues of approach open to us.
3) The gymnast performed the difficult exercise so well that he received a near-perfect score.
4) I do not.
5) No error

1 2 3 4 5

8 1) Of the two airplanes, the D.C. 10 ascends quicker.
2) No one understands the situation better than he.
3) Maria and I climbed a street which wound around like a spiral staircase.
4) Neither Sheila nor I was particularly pleased with the color of the paint.
5) No error

1 2 3 4 5

9 1) I, myself, completed the difficult job.
2) Before they completed the building, the contractors discovered that the heating system was insufficient.
3) The Jacksons and the Walters take day trips together each summer and visit each other frequently in the winter.
4) This is the liveliest color combination of all.
5) No error

1 2 3 4 5

10 1) Henry and Will have been living in their parents' house for eight years.
2) When I was a child, my family went to the beach every summer.
3) Please check the calendar to see if you are available on the 20th.
4) If you arrive at the theater earlier than me, please buy my ticket.
5) No error

SUMMARY OF RESULTS

After reviewing the Answer Key on page 113, chart your scores below for each practice exercise.

Practice Number	Your Number Right	Your Number Wrong (Including Omissions)	Acceptable Score
I			7 correct
II			6 correct
III			4 correct
IV			8 correct

SKILLS ANALYSIS

To discover your weak areas, locate the question numbers you got wrong and circle them on this Skills Analysis chart. Refer back to these chapters where you got questions wrong.

Skill	Question Number	Chapter Reference
Practice I Correct Use of Descriptive Words	1, 4	*See Chapter* 3
Agreement of Subject and Action or Linking Word in Number	2, 7	2 and 7
Correct Use of Pronouns	5, 6	10
Agreement: Special Problems	3, 8	8
Practice II Agreement: Special Problems	3, 4	8
Correct Use of Pronouns	2	10

Skill	Question Number	Chapter Reference
		See Chapter
Complete and Incomplete Thoughts	5, 8	1
Agreement of Subject and Linking Word	1	7
Correct Use of Descriptive Phrases	6	5
Correct Use of Descriptive Words	7	3
Practice III Time: Special Problems	1	9
Agreement: Special Problems	2, 3	8
Correct Use of Descriptive Words	4, 5	4
Practice IV Correct Use of Descriptive Phrases	1, 6	5
Agreement: Special Problems	2, 7	8
Action Words: Agreement in Time	3	2
Complete and Incomplete Thoughts	4	1
Correct Use of Descriptive Words	8	4
Time: Special Problems	9	9
Correct Use of Pronouns	5, 10	10

ANSWER KEY

Chapter 11

Cumulative Review

Practice I *Page 104.*

1. (4) *loudly* describes shouted.
2. (5) No error

3. (2) *Are* agrees with the plural subject, *implications.*
4. (4) *Well* describes a state of health.

5. (3) *Your* describes smoking.
6. (1) Use *us* after between.
7. (5) No error

8. (4) *Approve* agrees with the plural performer, *people*.
9. (5) No error

Practice II *Page 106.*

1. (2) A waiting room (crowded with impatient patients) *was*. *Was* agrees with the singular subject, *room*.
2. (1) *whom* you gave the information to (to whom). Use whom after *to*.
3. (3) Several short stories *were* there. *Were* agrees with the plural preformer, *stories*.
4. (1) Chester Kallow and his wife, Olga, *go*. *Go* agrees with the plural performer, *Chester Kallow and his wife*.
5. (1) Incomplete thought. Possible thought completion: When you can't find the solution to a problem, and help is not forthcoming, and you don't know where to turn, *call me*.
6. (4) Before signing the order, the salesman finished his conversation on the telephone. *On the telephone* describes conversation and should be placed after it.
7. (1) runs most *quickly*. Descriptive words ending in *-ly* describe actions; therefore, the correct form is *most quickly*.
8. (2) Incomplete thought. Possible thought completion: Although she enjoys fishing, Theresa, becoming dizzy because of the motion of the sea and the smell of the fish, *asked to return to shore*.

Practice III *Page 108.*

1. (4) *Stood* occurred *before* entered, so you must use the helping word *had* with *stood*.
2. (1) *Need* agrees with the closest performer, *shrubs*, which is plural.
3. (3) *Are* agrees with the plural subject, mother and father.
4. (5) *Most boring.* Do not add *-er* or *-est* to a descriptive word ending in *-ing;* use *more* or *most*.
5. (4) *Any other* (He did not perform more precisely than himself.)

Practice IV *Page 109.*

1. (4) That painting, of which I am proud, hangs in my mother's hallway. *Of which I am proud* describes painting, not hallway.
2. (3) Neither the child nor his father *wants* to take the responsibility for walking the dog. In an either/or neither/nor construction, the action or linking word agrees in number with the closest performer or subject.
3. (1) This excellent thesis surpasses all others and *presents* the facts most coherently. *Presents* should have the same form as *surpasses*.
4. (3) Incomplete thought. Possible thought completion: The tall, handsome man, wearing a plaid jacket and striped pants, and stepping snappily off the curb, *tripped*.
5. (4) How can you expect everyone to do his best when you place *him* under constant pressure? Because *everyone* is singular and *his* is singular, use *him* rather than *them* to balance the sentence.
6. (3) The stapler on the table belongs to that woman. *On the table* describes stapler and should be next to it.
7. (2) There are several avenues of approach open to us. *Are* must agree with the plural subject, *avenues*.
8. (1) Of the two airplanes, the D.C. 10 ascends *more quickly*. Descriptive words ending in *-ly* describe actions; therefore the correct form is *more quickly*.
9. (2) Before they *completed* the building, the contractors *had discovered* that the heating system was insufficient. *Discovered* occurred *before completed*, so you must use the helping word *had* with *discovered*.
10. (4) If you arrive at the theater earlier than *I* (do), please buy my ticket. Since you would not say, If you arrive earlier than *me do*, you do not say, If you arrive earlier than *me*.

12.

Balanced Sentences

One of the things that used to irritate me in my junior high English classes was the corrections some teachers made in the margins of my compositions. I didn't mind when they wrote "sp." and circled the misspelled word on the line, or "cap." to indicate that I had written "french" with a small "f."

What got me all riled up, however, were the mysterious jottings such as "awk." and "frag." And one term I had a former C.I.A. agent as a teacher, and he used secret codes, it seemed to me. His favorite was a couple of parallel lines in the margin— and his cryptic explanation to my query was "lack of parallelism." I never got to know what he meant, and, at the time, couldn't see that anything was wrong with "I like swimming, hunting, and to fish."

—Paul Allen
Trouble Deaf Heaven

A Word With You . . .

Paul Allen's teacher did a good job in spotting the error in "I like swimming, hunting, and to fish" but he failed to show his students why it was incorrect. The parallel slash marks in the margins were no substitute for a lesson explaining the need for balance in sentence structure.

You will find that the mystery is removed from that topic in the following pages and why in Paul Allen's latest book we can find a sentence such as, "*Listening* to Beverly Sills, *looking* at a Rembrandt, and *sipping* Chivas Regal all give me goose pimples."

Understanding Correct Sentence Structure

Sentences which are correctly and effectively written are sentences which are balanced. *A balanced sentence is one in which related actions, descriptions, or ideas are presented in the same form.* The following sentences are not balanced. Why not?

1.   He liked swimming and *to dive.*
2.   Mrs. Thompson is pleasant and *has intelligence.*
3.   Tennis is both stimulating and *makes me exhausted.*
4.   Gary is not only a good carpenter *but a fine electrician also.*

In sentence 1 the related actions are not expressed in the same form. One action word ends with *ing;* the other action takes on entirely different form, using *to.* Now, you must choose which form you prefer. Either one would be correct, but the same form must be used for both action words.

He liked swimming and diving.

or

He liked to swim and to dive.

In sentence 2, what are the two terms which describe Mrs. Thompson? _____ and _____. You've probably chosen *pleasant* and *has intelligence.* The sentence would be balanced if *has intelligence* were replaced by one word. *Pleasant* is a descriptive word, describing Mrs. Thompson. What descriptive word means *has intelligence?* In other words, how do you change the form of *has intelligence* to balance with *pleasant?*

Mrs. Thompson is pleasant and *intelligent.*

In sentence 3, what are the two terms which describe tennis? _____ _____ and _____. You've probably chosen *stimulating* and *makes me exhausted.* The sentence would be balanced if *makes me exhausted* were replaced by one word. *Stimulating* is a descriptive word, describing tennis. What descriptive word means *makes me exhausted?* In other words, how do you change the form of *makes me exhausted* to balance with *stimulating?*

Tennis is both stimulating and *exhausting.*

In sentence 4, Gary is two things. He is a *good carpenter* and a *fine electrician.* What two phrases relate carpenter to electrician? _____ and _____. You've probably chosen *not only* and *but.* The relationship is shown, however, by *not only* and *but also.* Just as *not only* comes immediately before *a good carpenter,* so must *but also* come immediately before *a fine electrician.*

Gary is not only a good carpenter *but also a fine electrician.*

Look at a few more examples:

INCORRECT: I like to walk in the rain, to sing in the shower, and stamping in puddles.

CORRECT: I like to walk in the rain, to sing in the shower, and to stamp in puddles.

INCORRECT: The eagle has majesty, strength, and is graceful.

CORRECT: The eagle has majesty, strength, and grace.

PRACTICE

I **Directions:** Blacken the space beneath the number which corresponds to the number of the word or phrase that correctly completes each sentence.

```
                                                    1  2  3  4
                                                    ||  ||  ||  ||
```

1. The long-time servant was faithful and
    1) honestly.
    2) with honesty.
    3) honest.
    4) honesty.

```
                                                    1  2  3  4
                                                    ||  ||  ||  ||
```

2. Please write your evaluation carefully, truthfully, and
    1) concise.
    2) concisely.
    3) with concision.
    4) be concise.

```
                                                    1  2  3  4
                                                    ||  ||  ||  ||
```

3. The advertisement said that at the "Y" Camps our children would learn to swim, play tennis, row boats, and
    1) how to get along with others.
    2) getting along with others.
    3) friendship.
    4) get along with others.

4. Henry is not only a good doctor

        1 2 3 4
        ‖ ‖ ‖ ‖

        1) but also an excellent friend.
        2) but he is also an excellent friend.
        3) but he is an excellent friend also.
        4) but is also an excellent friend.

5. If you want this job,

        1 2 3 4
        ‖ ‖ ‖ ‖

        1) you must be prompt.
        2) one must be prompt.
        3) they must be prompt.
        4) you must have been prompt.

6. This book is a monument to its author and

        1 2 3 4
        ‖ ‖ ‖ ‖

        1) it pays tribute to its subject.
        2) a tribute to its subject.
        3) it tributes its subject.
        4) pays tribute to its subject.

7. This weekend Arthur will fence in the back yard, mow the lawn, and

        1 2 3 4
        ‖ ‖ ‖ ‖

        1) paints the house.
        2) he plans to paint the house.
        3) paint the house.
        4) will be painting the house.

8. The teen-age boy's mother insisted that he hang up his clothes and

        1 2 3 4
        ‖ ‖ ‖ ‖

        1) make his bed.
        2) he should make his bed.
        3) why doesn't he make his bed.
        4) to make his bed.

9. The tennis game was invigorating and

  1) excitement.

  2) had excitement.

  3) excited.

  4) exciting.

1	2	3	4
‖	‖	‖	‖

PRACTICE II

Directions: Blacken the space beneath the number which corresponds to the number of the incorrect word or group of words in each paragraph. If there is no error, blacken space number 5.

1. Soft drinks *satisfy* the appetite, *offer* abso-
      1   2

lutely nothing toward building health, *taking*
              3

up valuable space, and particularly *crowd* out
             4

milk needed for growth and normal bone and

teeth structure. *No error*
       5

1	2	3	4	5
‖	‖	‖	‖	‖

2. Personal health educators would be people

who know the basic facts of *nutrition,*
             1

food buying, *cooking,* physical fitness,
  2   3

how to motivate people, and interviewing.
     4

No error
 5

1	2	3	4	5
‖	‖	‖	‖	‖

3. Doctors *are doing* very little health education.
     1

They *are not oriented or trained* to be health
        2

1	2	3	4	5
‖	‖	‖	‖	‖

educators, *cannot make money* dispensing
$$\overline{3}$$

health education, and *there is no interest* in
$$\overline{4}$$

being health educators. *No error*
$$\overline{5}$$

PRACTICE
III   Directions: Balance each of the following sentences by rewriting them in the spaces provided.

1.   The winner's attitude toward the loser was conciliatory yet not with condescension.

    _____

    _____

2.   Mrs. Smith is conservative not only in business but also politically.

    _____

    _____

3.   The judge asked the defendant to swear to tell the truth and if he would cite the evidence.

    _____

    _____

4.   I cannot abide congested subways or elevators with crowds in them.

    _____

    _____

5. This project is to be a benefit to the neighborhood and it will credit the sponsors.

   _____

   _____

6. Math, reading, and to write are my favorite subjects.

   _____

   _____

7. The professor lectured on anthropology, and he was outlining the child-rearing habits of the Polynesians.

   _____

   _____

8. I splashed cold water on my face and looking into the mirror.

   _____

   _____

9. The rain splashes onto the walk and soaked into the ground.

   _____

   _____

10. Outside the wind rustled the leaves in the trees, while inside the children sleep quietly.

    _____

    _____

PRACTICE

IV **Directions:** In each of the following groups of sentences, one sentence contains an error in either agreement, placement of a descriptive phrase, or balance. Blacken the space beneath the number which corresponds to the number of the incorrect sentence in each group.

1 2 3
‖ ‖ ‖

1 1) After killing his victim, the assassin out of the window jumped.

2) Harry S. Truman enjoyed reading not only fiction but also nonfiction.

3) The labor negotiations were deadlocked.

1 2 3
‖ ‖ ‖

2 1) Many people believe in stronger consumer protection and better consumer information.

2) Walking quickly down the street, I lost my balance.

3) I enjoy knitting and to crochet.

1 2 3
‖ ‖ ‖

3 1) Don't automation deprive many of jobs?

2) Neither the supervisor nor the assemblymen report directly to the president.

3) While reading a dull book, I was interrupted.

1 2 3
‖ ‖ ‖

4 1) A true Yoga must have discipline and concentration.

2) The attainment of freedom and achieving national security were their goals.

3) None of the representatives is lying.

1 2 3
‖ ‖ ‖

5 1) Although the system has defects, it still functions well.

2) I not only endorse his candidacy, but also urge it.

3) The mayor divided among his largest contributors the best municipal positions.

1 2 3
‖ ‖ ‖

6 1) The reasons for shortening the working day is logical.

2) Dashing home from work, the busy woman prepared a menu in her mind.

3) Clouds hang heavily in the sky, signaling rain.

			1	2	3
7	1)	While talking on the telephone, the painting on the kitchen wall caught my eye.	‖	‖	‖
	2)	In the summer, the rosebushes climb along the side of the house.			
	3)	My feelings were hurt, so I cried a little.			

			1	2	3
8	1)	Spring is enjoyable, pretty, and fragrant.	‖	‖	‖
	2)	A duck swam across the lake and dived under the water.			
	3)	Many people in the wealthiest nation in the world are destitute, malnourished, and don't have jobs.			

			1	2	3
9	1)	Before ending their dispute, the doorbell interrupted the two women.	‖	‖	‖
	2)	They each pass the dish to their right.			
	3)	Several ladies in the class play tennis.			

			1	2	3
10	1)	Bacon and eggs is my favorite breakfast.	‖	‖	‖
	2)	Each of the topics on the agenda sound interesting.			
	3)	Tea and toast is a common cure-all.			

ANSWER KEY

Chapter 12

Balanced Sentences

Practice I *Page 117.*

1. (3) *honest* agrees with faithful.
2. (2) *concisely* agrees with carefully and truthfully.
3. (4) *get (along with others)* agrees with swim, play, and row.
4. (1) Henry is two things: *a good doctor, an excellent friend. Not only* precedes *a good doctor,* and *but also* precedes *an excellent friend.*
5. (1) *you* agrees with you.
6. (2) *a tribute* agrees with a monument.
7. (3) *paint* agrees with fence and mow.
8. (1) *make* agrees with hang.
9. (4) *exciting* agrees with *invigorating.*

Practice II *Page 119.*

1. (3) *take* agrees with satisfy, offer, and crowd.
2. (4) *motivation* agrees with nutrition, buying, cooking and interviewing.
3. (4) *are not interested* agrees with are doing, are not oriented or trained, and cannot make.

Practice III *Page 120.*

(Note: Although there is more than one way of rewriting these sentences to make them balanced, the following answers indicate and explain one possible way.)

1. The winner's attitude toward the loser was conciliatory yet not condescending. *Yet not condescending* agrees with conciliatory.
2. Mrs. Smith is conservative not only in business but also in politics. *In politics* agrees with in business.
3. The judge asked the defendant to swear to tell the truth and to cite the evidence. *To cite the evidence* agrees with to swear to tell the truth.
4. I cannot abide congested subways or crowded elevators. *Crowded elevators* agrees with congested subways.
5. This project is to be a benefit to the neighborhood and a credit to the sponsors. *A credit to the sponsors* agrees with a benefit to the neighborhood.
6. Math, reading, and writing are my favorite subjects. *Writing* agrees with math and reading.
7. The professor lectured on anthropology, and he outlined the child-rearing habits of the Polynesians. *Outlined* agrees with lectured.
8. I splashed cold water on my face and looked into the mirror. *Looked* agrees with splashed.
9. The rain splashes onto the walk and soaks into the ground. *Soaks* agrees with splashes.
10. Outside, the wind rustled the leaves in the trees, while inside the children slept quietly. *Slept* agrees with rustled.

Practice IV *Page 121.*

1. (1) After killing his victim, the assassin *jumped out of the window.*
2. (3) I enjoy *knitting* and *crocheting.*
3. (1) *Doesn't automation* deprive many of jobs?
4. (2) The attainment of freedom and *achievement* of national security were their goals.
5. (3) The mayor divided the *best municipal positions among his largest cortributors..*
6. (1) The *reasons* for shortening the working day *are* logical.
7. (1) While talking on the telephone, *I noticed* the painting on the kitchen wall.
8. (3) Many people in the wealthiest nation in the world are destitute, malnourished, and *jobless.*
9. (1) Before ending their dispute, *the two women were interrupted* by the doorbell.
10. (2) *Each* of the topics on the agenda *sounds* interesting.

13.

Punctuation

To punctuate or not to punctuate that is the question is it better in the long run to omit the periods and question marks of English sentences or to include them against a large number of misunderstandings by using them we end all misinterpretation all the problems and confusion that the reader faces this is a result to be greatly valued

Adaptation of a monologue in
William Shakespeare's
Hamlet, Act III, Scene 1

A Word With You . . .

Hamlet pondered the question "To be or not to be." To punctuate or not to punctuate is not open to question. In order to write clearly and meaningfully, we must punctuate. Standard rules of punctuation help all of us gain the same meaning from written material. In this chapter, we review with you some of the more common rules of punctuation.

End Marks

Punctuation is simply a way of keeping ideas straight. The most commonly used forms of punctuation are end marks which are used at the ends of sentences. These include the period (.), the question mark (?), and the exclamation mark (!) Read the following paragraph to see the confusion that results from not using end marks.

Paragraph I:

Preheat oven to 375° in a medium saucepan, melt 3 tablespoons butter stir in flour, salt, and pepper add milk and cook, stirring constantly, until thickened add mushrooms and parsley cook noodles as package directs.

Now place end marks where necessary in order to clarify the recipe.

Consider the following paragraph and place the proper end mark above each number.

Paragraph 2:

We have always considered heartbeat and breathing the basic

signs of life__Legally and medically, their absence indicates
        1

death__But heartbeat and breathing are controlled by the
     2

brain__Is a patient still alive when these functions occur only
     3

through the use of a machine__A clinical decision to turn off
                         4

the machines is either a recognition that life is over or a form

of murder__Many will agree with the former, but an equal
        5

number will cry, "Murder__"
                      6

Turn to the answer key on page 136 to see if you've punctuated correctly.

Commas

The comma is the most difficult form of punctuation because of its varied uses. After studying the comma style sheet, do Practice I to determine where your comma strengths and weaknesses lie.

COMMA STYLE SHEET

RULES	EXAMPLES
1. Commas are used to separate items in a series.	Check the tires, the oil, and the battery.
	Racing car drivers like long, low, streamlined cars.
2. Commas are used to separate words or groups of words that interrupt the flow of the sentence.	Jimmy Doolittle, Air Force squadron leader during WW II, was admired by those who flew with him.

3. The words *therefore, however, nevertheless, inasmuch as,* are set off by commas when they interrupt a complete thought.

Chow mein, if you must know, is my favorite food.

Unfortunately for Herbert Hoover, however, he became president a year before the crash of 1929.

Can we, therefore, call environmentalists over-cautious?

4. An introductory word or group of words is separated from the complete thought by a comma.

Before the New Deal, laissez-faire economics was practiced.

Before Roosevelt introduced the New Deal, laissez-faire economics was practiced.

5. Commas are used to separate two complete thoughts which are joined by a connecting word such as *and, or, but,* or *for.*

The office building will be torn down, and a parking lot will replace it.

6. A comma always separates the day from the year, and a comma separates the year from the rest of the sentence.

His son graduated on June 14, 1972, from New York University.

7. Separate a direct quotation from the rest of the sentence by using commas.

"I cannot attend," he said.

The master of ceremonies shouted, "Attention, ladies and gentlemen!"

"I can understand how you feel," he said, "but please try to see it my way."

8. A comma is used to separate the name of a city from the name of a state or country.

Madeline Manning Jackson is from Cleveland, Ohio.

Paul Martin will be stationed in Paris, France.

9. A comma is used after the salutation in a friendly letter.

Dear Tom,

A comma is used after the closing in a friendly letter, as well as in a business letter.

Sincerely,
Harvey

Common Comma Errors

Frequently, commas are included where they should not be. Following are two common examples.

1. A comma is *not* used to separate two actions if the sentence has one performer.

INCORRECT: *I returned* to the library, and *left* the unread book.

CORRECT: *I returned* to the library and *left* the unread book.

2. When a sentence begins with a complete thought followed by an incomplete thought, a comma is not used.

INCORRECT: The party became lively, when John arrived.

CORRECT: The party became lively when John arrived.

PRACTICE

I   Directions: Insert the missing commas in the sentences below.

1. The "Day in the City" tour included visits to the Metropolitan Museum the Museum of Natural History the Planetarium and Central Park Zoo.

2. The local theater group presented *Death of a Salesman* on June 14 1954.

3. The company transferred my brother from Cleveland Ohio to New York City.

4. After escaping from his pursuers the innocent victim ran breathlessly into the room and he collapsed into a chair.

5. Dear Joe

    We arrived in Phoenix Arizona on July 10 and we were fortunate to find pleasant accommodations. We will come home in January 1976. Feed the cat.

    Love

    Mother

6. Pélé the soccer star brought renewed interest to an old sport.

7. After reading the newspaper Terence Morgan decided to write to his congressman.

8. Will stood up when Mrs. Sullivan the mayor's wife entered the room.

9. "Please bring your camera to the game" said Juan.

10. "I would like to" Mitchell replied "but I can't afford the film."

PRACTICE

II   Directions: Blacken the space beneath the number which corresponds to the number of the incorrectly punctuated sentence in each group. If there is no error, blacken space number 5.

			1	2	3	4	5

1   1) Before eating breakfast, Tom ran two miles.   ‖ ‖ ‖ ‖ ‖

2) Tom ran two miles before eating breakfast.

3) Tom's brother jogs, before eating breakfast.

4) Before any physical activity, John eats breakfast.

5) No error

2   1) Because he was late John missed most of the lecture.   ‖ ‖ ‖ ‖ ‖

2) Professor Simmons always begins on time.

3) John often misses the opening remarks because he is late.

4) Whenever he is late, he copies my notes.

5) No error

			1	2	3	4	5
3	1)	Hubert Humphrey, as well as Adlai Stevenson accepted the Democratic nomination but lost the election.	‖	‖	‖	‖	‖
	2)	Jimmy Carter ran for a second term as President of the U.S. in 1968 but did not win.					
	3)	When I attend the lectures, I bring a notebook, a pencil, my eyeglasses, and a *People* magazine.					
	4)	Each morning the sun rises, and each evening it sets.					
	5)	No error					

			1	2	3	4	5
4	1)	Teddy, along with his friends, enjoys stripping cars.	‖	‖	‖	‖	‖
	2)	The local Memorial Day Committee plans many exciting events for this summer and the Committee will continue to function each summer.					
	3)	I cannot drive when the roads are icy.					
	4)	Ricky was elated because he won the car.					
	5)	No error					

			1	2	3	4	5
5	1)	Because she had overslept, Rosa was late for work.	‖	‖	‖	‖	‖
	2)	*The Save Your Life Diet* by David Reuben, M.D., helps you lose weight and put new vitality in your life.					
	3)	The recipe calls for baking soda, eggs, flour, sugar and milk.					
	4)	I cannot smile when I am angry.					
	5)	No error					

PRACTICE

III Directions: Blacken the space beneath the number that corresponds to the number of each error in the passage below.

		1	2	3	4
For example, another story that appeared in		‖	‖	‖	‖
$\overline{1}$					

the *Herald* on April 20, 1967 states, "Many
$\quad\overline{2}\qquad\overline{3}\qquad\overline{4}$

home economists report that mothers over-

feed their children and allow improper foods."

The story says serious future effects can re-
                                            $\overline{5}$

sult from such habits. Many children are

fed more than necessary and they have many
$\overline{6}$ $\overline{7}$

unnecessary sweets on their menus. These

children may develop future incurable dis-
                              $\overline{8}$

eases.

5 6 7 8
|| || || ||

These same parents will donate generous

sums, of money for research for cures for these
     $\overline{9}$

diseases. But on the other hand, they don't
                              $\overline{10}$

realize that their overindulgence, spoiling,
                                      $\overline{11}$

and doting are not in their children's best
                                          $\overline{12}$

interests.

9 10 11 12
|| || || ||

Semicolons

The semicolon is a strong mark of punctuation. It signals the end of a thought. Unlike a period, it is used in the middle of a sentence because it connects two complete thoughts which are closely related.

> *Examples:* The world acclaimed the Great Houdini's feats of escape. He earned the world's praise.
>
> The world acclaimed the Great Houdini's feats of escape; he earned the world's praise.

The semicolon can also be used to separate two complete and related thoughts that would otherwise be separated by, *and, but, or, nor, for, so.*

> *Examples:* The world acclaimed the Great Houdini's feats of escape, and he earned the world's praise.
>
> The world acclaimed the Great Houdini's feats of escape; he earned the world's praise.

PRACTICE

IV   **Directions:** Each of the following sentences is missing either a comma or a semicolon. If the sentence is missing a comma, blacken the space in column 1. If there is a missing semicolon, blacken the space in column 2.

		1	2
1.	In 1871, Kate O'Leary's cow kicked over a lamp_the City of Chicago burned to the ground.	‖	‖
2.	We accepted the inivitation_but we cancelled because of illness.	‖	‖
3.	Our backs were weak_but our spirit was strong.	‖	‖
4.	The Louisiana Purchase enlarged America by about 140 percent in area_fifteen states were later carved from it.	‖	‖
5.	Lemmings travel toward the sea_and they eat everything that is available on the way.	‖	‖
6.	Dr. Toselli, our physician, was delayed at the hospital_my husband left.	‖	‖
7.	An ancient temple in Mexico was cut out of a mountain_and water was the natural stone-cutting tool used by its builders.	‖	‖
8.	Please walk in_don't run.	‖	‖
9.	Julius Caesar knew that it would be dangerous to transport an army across rough waters_but it was the only way he could learn more about Britain.	‖	‖
10.	I am working late tonight_don't expect me for dinner.	‖	‖

Occasionally, one or both of two complete and related thoughts will contain commas.

> *Example:* John, my older brother, is not a very good pool player; but even though he never wins, he enjoys the game.

Notice that in this type of sentence, in order to avoid confusion, a semicolon is used to separate the two complete thoughts even though a connecting word is present. *Study these examples:*

> Although Jane is five years old, she has never been swimming; and, personally, I think that is a shame.

> When you are ready, please call me; and I, although occupied, will meet you at once.

The following large connecting words are always preceded by a semicolon and followed by a comma when connecting two complete thoughts:

> therefore
> nevertheless
> however
> inasmuch as

For example:

> I don't like the terms of the contract; therefore, I will not sign it.

PRACTICE

    V   **Directions:** Blacken the space beneath the number which corresponds to the number of the incorrect sentence in each group. If there is no error, blacken space number 5.

		1	2	3	4	5
1	1) We, therefore, cannot accept your terms.	‖	‖	‖	‖	‖
	2) The first universities began as scholastic guilds, and arose gradually and with great difficulty.					
	3) The contract is unfair; therefore, we cannot sign it.					
	4) The day was very hot; we cooled ourselves in the park.					
	5) No error					

1 2 3 4 5

2 1) I had wanted to attend, nevertheless, other commitments prevented my doing so.

2) You look, however, as though you like this bargain.

3) The aristocratic Watusi are towering African men with fine features, and they are also remarkable athletes.

4) My friend, Jane Smith, whom you met last week, arrived today; and, in spite of her long trip, she was eager to see the town.

5) No error

1 2 3 4 5

3 1) I went home after work; John went to the game.

2) The town plans to demolish the old buildings, and to replace them with new structures.

3) The painters plan to remove all of the old paint, and they are going to repaint the entire house.

4) Our neighbors, the Wilsons, went on their first camping trip; they loved it.

5) No error

1 2 3 4 5

4 1) The ancient people adapted their construction methods to the quality of their stone, and they used the forces of nature that were available.

2) The Watusi is a gentleman farmer, and his specialty is cattle.

3) I worked on the project all day; however, I was not successful.

4) My checkbook balance, however, will not support that purchase.

5) No error

1 2 3 4 5

‖ ‖ ‖ ‖ ‖

5 1) Joe was late; therefore, he missed the essence of the lecture.

2) I cannot smile when I'm angry, and I'm not smiling today.

3) James Beckwourth was the son of a black Revolutionary War soldier, nevertheless, James was known to the Crow Indians as the brave Medicine Calf.

4) When the science demonstration began, the children became quiet; when the demonstration became exciting, the children became noisy.

5) No error

ANSWER KEY

Chapter 13

Punctuation

End Marks

Introductory Paragraph 1 *Page 125.*

Preheat oven to 375°. In a medium saucepan, melt 3 tablespoons butter. Stir in flour, salt, and pepper. Add milk and cook, stirring constantly, until thickened. Add mushrooms and parsley. Cook noodles as package directs.

Introductory Paragraph 2 *Page 126.*

We have always considered heartbeat and breathing the basic signs of life. Legally and medically, their absence indicates death. But heartbeat and breathing are controlled by the brain. Is a patient still alive when these functions occur only through the use of a machine? A clinical decision to turn off the machines is either a recognition that life is over or a form of murder. Many will agree with the former, but an equal number will cry, "Murder!"

Commas

Practice I *Page 128.*

1. The "Day in the City" tour included visits to the Metropolitan Museum, the Museum of Natural History, the Planetarium, and the Central Park Zoo.
2. The local theater group presented *Death of A Salesman* on June 14, 1954.
3. The company transferred my brother from Cleveland, Ohio to New York City.
4. After escaping from his pursuers, the innocent victim ran breathlessly into the room, and he collapsed into a chair.
5. Dear Joe,
   We arrived in Phoenix, Arizona on July 10, and we were fortunate to find pleasant accommodations. We will come home in January, 1976. Feed the cat.

   Love,
   Mother
6. Pélé, the soccer star, brought renewed interest to an old sport.
7. After reading the newspaper, Terence Morgan decided to write to his congressman.
8. Will stood up when Mrs. Sullivan, the mayor's wife, entered the room.
9. "Please bring your camera to the game," said Juan.
10. "I would like to," Mitchell replied, "but I can't afford the film."

Practice II *Page 129.*

1. (3) Tom's brother jogs before eating breakfast.
   When a sentence begins with a complete thought followed by an incomplete thought, a comma is not used.
2. (1) Because he was late, John missed most of the lecture.
   An introductory word or group of words is separated from the complete thought by a comma.
3. (1) Hubert Humphrey, as well as Adlai Stevenson, accepted the Democratic nomination but lost the election.
   As well as Adlai Stevenson interrupts the flow of the sentence. Hubert Humphrey accepted the Democratic nomination but lost the election is the main idea of the sentence; therefore, *as well as Adlai Stevenson* must be set off by commas.

136

4. (2) The local Memorial Day Committee plans many exciting events for this summer, and the Committee will continue to function each summer.

    When two complete thoughts are connected by *and, and* must be preceded by a comma.

5. (3) The recipe calls for baking soda, eggs, flour, sugar, and milk.

    A comma precedes the *and* in a list of three or more items.

Practice III *Page 130.*

(3) For example, another story that appeared in the *Herald* on April 20, 1967, states, "Many
$$\overline{3}$$
home economists report that mothers overfeed their children and allow improper foods."

(7) The story says serious future effects can result from such habits. Many children are fed more than necessary, and they have many unnecessary sweets on their menus. These children may de-
$$\overline{7}$$
velop future, incurable diseases.

(9) These same parents donate generous sums of money for research for cures for these diseases.
$$\overline{9}$$
But on the other hand, they don't realize that their over indulgence, spoiling, and doting, are not in their children's best interests.

Commas and Semicolons

Practice IV *Page 132.*

1. (2) Use a semicolon to connect two complete, related thoughts when there is no connecting word such as *and, but, or.*

2. (1) Use a comma when connecting two complete thoughts joined by *and, but, or.*

3. (1) See answer 2 above.
4. (2) See answer 1 above.

5. (1) See answer 2 above.
6. (2) See answer 1 above.
7. (1) See answer 2 above.
8. (2) See answer 1 above.
9. (1) See answer 2 above.
10. (2) See answer 1 above.

Practice V *Page 133.*

1. (2) *guilds and* No comma; *and arose gradually and with great difficulty* is not a complete thought.

2. (1) *attend; nevertheless,* When connecting two complete thoughts by *nevertheless, however,* etc., precede the connecting word with a semicolon and follow it with a comma.

3. (2) *buildings and* See answer 1 above.
4. (5) No error
5. (3) *soldier; nevertheless,* See answer 2 above.

14.
Cumulative Review

This review covers the following concepts which have been included in the preceding chapters.

- Balanced Sentences
- Correct Sentence Structure
- Punctuation Which Affects Sentence Structure

After completing the Cumulative Review exercises, evaluate your ability using the SUMMARY OF RESULTS chart on page 149. Acceptable scores for each practice are given.

To learn your weaknesses, find the question numbers you answered incorrectly on the SKILLS ANALYSIS table. The table will show which of your skills need improvement and the necessary chapters to review.

PRACTICE

I   **Directions:** Blacken the space beneath the number which corresponds to the correct rewriting of the underlined portion of the sentence. Choice 1 is always the same as the underlined portion and is sometimes the right answer.

1 2 3 4 5

1. In the autumn of 2001 we prepared for the colonization of Venus. We encountered *difficulties although* our technology was advanced.

    1) difficulties although

    2) difficulties, although

    3) difficulties! Although

    4) difficulties. Although

    5) difficulties; although

1 2 3 4 5

2. My Aunt Bell, the woman in the *green dress speaks five languages*.

    1) green dress speaks five languages.

    2) green dress, speaks five languages.

    3) green dress; speaks five languages.

    4) green dress. speaks five languages.

    5) green dress? She speaks five languages.

1 2 3 4 5

3. *After the baseball game we* bought lettuce, tomatoes, onions, luncheon meats, and Italian bread and made hero sandwiches.

    1) After the baseball game we

    2) After the baseball game. We

    3) After the baseball game, we

    4) After the baseball game ended we

    5) After the baseball game; we

1 2 3 4 5

4. She was an attractive woman, an excellent *speaker and a charming hostess; but* she dressed outlandishly.

    1) speaker and a charming hostess; but

    2) speaker and a charming hostess, but

    3) speaker, and a charming hostess; but

    4) speaker, and a charming hostess, but

    5) speaker, and a charming hostess but

PRACTICE
II *

Directions: Blacken the space beneath the number which corresponds to the correct rewriting of the underlined portion of the sentence. Choice 1 is always the same as the underlined portion and is sometimes the right answer.

1 2 3 4 5
|| || || || ||

1. The bicycle is a fairly pleasant machine for limited use by a few *people, but claims* that it can substitute for the automobile as a device for moving people around town are grossly overstated.

    1) people, but claims

    2) people, But claims

    3) people but claims

    4) people; but claims

    5) people, but, claims

1 2 3 4 5
|| || || || ||

2. Most old people will not be happy aboard *it, and mothers who must take along small children during a shopping trip to the supermarket won't be either.*

    1) it, and mothers who must take along small children during a shopping trip to the supermarket won't be either.

    2) it, and mothers who must take along small children during a shopping trip to the supermarket won't be.

    3) it, nor will mothers who must take along small children during a shopping trip to the supermarket.

    4) it, or will mothers who must take along small children during a shopping trip to the supermarket.

    5) it, for mothers who take along small children during a shopping trip to the supermarket.

* Practice II is adapted from Russell Baker's "Backwards Wheels the Mind," *The New York Times*, July 1, 1973. © 1973 by The New York Times Company. Reprinted by permission.

1 2 3 4 5
‖ ‖ ‖ ‖ ‖

3. It is an exhausting and brutal machine in cities built on *hills, and being* the most unattractive way to travel wherever and whenever the temperature is over 90° and under 30°.

    1) hills, and being

    2) hills, and is said to be

    3) hills, and it is

    4) hills, and has been

    5) hills, but being

1 2 3 4 5
‖ ‖ ‖ ‖ ‖

4. If parked, even chained, out of eyesight for more than 10 *minutes; it is* a cinch to be stolen.

    1) minutes; it is

    2) minutes it, is

    3) minutes it is

    4) minutes, it is

    5) minutes. It is

1 2 3 4 5
‖ ‖ ‖ ‖ ‖

5. And *then, of course,* there is the awkward question of courage.

    1) then, of course,

    2) then, of course

    3) then of course,

    4) then; of course

    5) then; of course;

PRACTICE III

Directions: Blacken the space beneath the number which corresponds to the correct rewriting of the underlined portion of the sentence. Choice 1 is always the same as the underlined portion and is sometimes the right answer.

1. Because he did not enjoy last week's *lecture*,   1 2 3 4 5
    Tom decided to skip this week's.
    1) lecture, Tom
    2) lecture! Tom
    3) lecture Tom
    4) lecture; Tom
    5) lecture. Tom

2. The carnival was exciting, the games were   1 2 3 4 5
    fun but the children became very tired.
    1) fun but
    2) fun; but
    3) fun, but
    4) fun. But
    5) fun, the

3. We decided to play tennis, have lunch, *and*   1 2 3 4 5
    then we played bridge.
    1) , and then we played bridge.
    2) , and played bridge.
    3) ; and then we played bridge.
    4) , and play bridge.
    5) ; we played bridge

4. Their living room lights were *shining we* de-   1 2 3 4 5
    cided to stop to say hello.
    1) shining we
    2) shining, we
    3) shining. And we
    4) shining; and we
    5) shining; we

5.   We should first measure the room, then order the carpeting, and, finally, *we will paint the walls*.

      1) we will paint the walls.

      2) we would paint the walls.

      3) paint the walls.

      4) we will be painting the walls.

      5) to paint the walls.

6.   Among all the causes of sedition and basic changes of *the state; none* is more important than excessive wealth of the few and extreme poverty of the many.

      1) the state; none

      2) the state none

      3) the state? None

      4) the state, none

      5) the state, so none

7.   From a thousand feet, flapping his wings as hard as he could, he pushed over into a blazing steep dive toward the *waves, and* learned why seagulls don't make blazing steep power-dives.*

      1) waves, and

      2) waves and

      3) waves; and

      4) waves. And

      5) waves and,

* Quote from Richard Bach's *Jonathan Livingston Seagull.* © 1975, Macmillan Publishing Co., Inc. Reprinted by permission.

	1	2	3	4	5
	‖	‖	‖	‖	‖

8. The beach was extremely *crowded, neverthe-less,* we found Joan.
   1) crowded, nevertheless,
   2) crowded; nevertheless,
   3) crowded; nevertheless
   4) crowded nevertheless
   5) crowded, nevertheless

	1	2	3	4	5
	‖	‖	‖	‖	‖

9. Because the landlord has refused *to testify our attorney* will have to subpoena him.
   1) to testify our attorney
   2) to testify. Our attorney
   3) to testify; our attorney
   4) to testify our attorney,
   5) to testify, our attorney

	1	2	3	4	5
	‖	‖	‖	‖	‖

10. Della Mason is a competent accountant *and she cooks well.*
    1) and she cooks well.
    2) , and she cooks well.
    3) and a good cook.
    4) and she cooks competently.
    5) ; and she cooks well.

PRACTICE

IV **Directions:** Blacken the space beneath the number which corresponds to the number of the incorrect sentence in each group. If there is no error, blacken space number 5.

	1	2	3	4	5
	‖	‖	‖	‖	‖

1
1) Increasing unemployment, in my opinion, is a major problem of the decade.
2) Our babysitter never cleans the kitchen and leaves the den in a mess.
3) I, however, spoke to John and alerted him to expect the shipment.
4) I like the painting, but not enough to buy it.
5) No error

2

1 2 3 4 5
|| || || || ||

1) The aphids have eaten the roses, the mealworms have destroyed the cucumbers, and the cinchbugs have ruined the lawn.

2) After we had paid the painter, we called the mason for an estimate on rebuilding the front stairs.

3) When the carpenter ants invade your kitchen, and the termites swarm under your porch, you know that spring is here.

4) Owning a home is a pleasurable experience; however, there is a great deal of work involved.

5) No error

3

1 2 3 4 5
|| || || || ||

1) Having considered the backgrounds of the prospective candidates, the members of the Republican National Committee began to consider its options.

2) Although history records the names of many famous women, many women remain anonymous.

3) According to Tom Seaver, confidence, self-discipline, and experience are prerequisites for a successful pitcher.

4) After a massive stroke, President Woodrow Wilson was partially paralyzed; nevertheless, the White House functioned under the leadership of Edith Bolling Wilson, the president's wife.

5) No error

4

1 2 3 4 5
|| || || || ||

1) Television should instruct, inform, and entertain.

2) Arthur rushed out of the barber shop, his face buried in lather; however, the meter maid already had written out his parking ticket.

3) Although the city council's meeting was lengthy, it proved beneficial.

4) Coughing, sneezing, and wheezing, the speaker descended from the stage.

5) No error

1 2 3 4 5

5 1) I enjoy sad movies, but I dislike books which depress   ‖ ‖ ‖ ‖ ‖
me.

2) The young author had a compulsion to do the research, assemble his notes, and write the paper in
one evening.

3) If you believe that I am correct, then why won't you
support me publicly?

4) The community pool is not only crowded, but also
shadeless.

5) No error

1 2 3 4 5

6 1) If you don't like the heat, get out of the kitchen.   ‖ ‖ ‖ ‖ ‖

2) Don't jump!

3) During our trip to London, we visited Westminster
Abbey, we also viewed the Crown Jewels in the
Tower of London and saw the Changing of the
Guard.

4) Because they were planning a picnic lunch, the children asked for pretzels, potato chips, cookies, and
marshmallows for dessert.

5) No error

1 2 3 4 5

7 1) Although, in recent years, many efforts have been   ‖ ‖ ‖ ‖ ‖
made; we can never compensate for the injustice
inflicted upon the American Indian.

2) I could wait no longer because I had promised to
begin the meeting promptly at eight o'clock.

3) Once one attains freedom of purpose, any task is
possible.

4) The current hearings are interesting, but last year's
scandal bored me.

5) No error

PRACTICE
V

Directions: Blacken the space beneath the number which corresponds to the number of the incorrect word in each group. If there is no error, blacken space number 5.

1. Men are bent intently over *chessboards. They*
  <u> </u>
  1

  are men of all *ages, but* most are closer to life's
  <u> </u>
  2

  twilight than its *dawn. They* are in battle with
  <u> </u>
  3

  one *another, the* chessboard is their battle-
  <u> </u>
  4
  field. *No error*
  <u> </u>
  5

1 2 3 4 5
|| || || || ||

2. The sun is *hot. Never* mind. Sometimes a driz-
  <u> </u>
  1

  zle *begins. Never* mind. This is not some silly
  <u> </u>
  2

  pastime to idle time *away, this* is *chess! This*
  <u> </u> <u> </u>
  3   4

  outdoor chess congregation is the only one of

  its kind in the borough. *No error*
  <u> </u>
  5

1 2 3 4 5
|| || || || ||

3. *Yet, it* boasts not a single authentic chess mas-
  <u> </u>
  1

  ter. Is this *sad? No*, it's irrelevant. *For, if* a
  <u> </u>   <u> </u>
  2   3

  man is seeking out excellence in *chess he*
  <u> </u>
  4

  would do well to stay away from St. James

  Park. *No error*
  <u> </u>
  5

1 2 3 4 5
|| || || || ||

1	2	3	4	5
‖	‖	‖	‖	‖

4.   What he would find here is *grimness, determi-*
                                   1

nation, anguish, wisdom after the fact, bitter-
           2   3

ness under the breath, and *there are a number*
                                  4

of accidental brilliances. *No error*
                            5

1	2	3	4	5
‖	‖	‖	‖	‖

5.   Good chess is not being played in St. James

Park, but life is being played. Here sits
    1

Liebowitz, he has escaped again from his
    2

wife. She will be along about 7 o'clock to re-

mind him loudly that he is a married man with

children. "Your supper is cold again, Liebo-

witz!" She has never called him Liebowitz

anywhere in the *world but* in St. James Park.
                           3

It is the circumstances, the men there, the

lateness of the hour. *No error*
    4   5

SUMMARY OF RESULTS

After reviewing the Answer Key on page 151, chart your scores below for each practice exercise.

Practice Number	Your Number Right	Your Number Wrong (Including Omissions)	Acceptable Score
I			3 Correct
II			4 Correct
III			7 Correct
IV			5 Correct
V			4 Correct

SKILLS ANALYSIS

To discover your weak areas, locate the question numbers you got wrong and circle them on this Skills Analysis chart. Refer back to those chapters where you got questions wrong.

Skill	Question Number	Chapter Reference
Practice I Balanced Sentences	3, 4	*See Chapter* 12
Punctuation Which Affects Sentence Structure	2	13
Practice II Punctuation Which Affects Sentence Structure	1, 4, 5	13
Balanced Sentences	2, 3	12

Skill	Question Number	Chapter References
Practice III Punctuation Which Affects Sentence Structure	1, 4, 6, 7, 8, 9	*See Chapter*
Balanced Sentences	2, 3, 5, 10	13
Practice IV Balanced Sentences	1, 5, 7	12
Punctuation Which Affects Sentence Structure	6	13
Practice V Balanced Sentences	4	12
Punctuation Which Affects Sentence Structure	1, 2, 3, 5	13

ANSWER KEY

Chapter 14

Cumulative Review

Practice I *Page 138.*

1. (1) No error
2. (2) My Aunt Bell, the woman in the green dress, speaks five languages.
3. (3) After the baseball game, we bought lettuce, tomatoes, onions, luncheon meats, and Italian bread and made hero sandwiches.
4. (3) She was an attractive woman, an excellent speaker, and a charming hostess; but she dressed outlandishly.

Practice II *Page 140.*

1. (1) The bicycle is a fairly pleasant machine for limited uses by a few *people, but claims* that it can substitute for the automobile as a device for moving people around town are grossly overstated. Use a comma between two complete thoughts connected by *and, but, or.*
2. (3) Most old people will not be very happy aboard *it, nor will mothers who must take along small children during a shopping trip to the supermarket.* This choice states the idea most clearly.
3. (3) It is an exhausting and brutal machine in cities built on *hills, and it is* a most unattractive way to travel wherever and whenever the temperature is over 90° or under 30°. *And it is* agrees with *It is* at the beginning of the sentence.
4. (4) If parked, even chained, out of eyesight for more than 10 *minutes, it is* a cinch to be stolen. When a sentence begins with an incomplete thought followed by a complete thought, the two are separated by a comma.
5. (1) And *then, of course,* there is the awkward question of courage. Set off an interrupting group of words with commas.

Practice III *Page 141.*

1. (1) Because he did not enjoy last week's *lecture, Tom* decided to skip this week's.
2. (3) The carnival was exciting, the games were *fun, but* the children became very tired.
3. (4) We decided to play tennis, have lunch, *and play bridge.*
4. (5) Their living room lights were *shining; we* decided to stop to say hello.
5. (3) We should first measure the room, then order the carpeting, and, finally, *paint the walls.*
6. (4) Among all the causes of sedition and basic changes of *the state, none* is more important than excessive wealth of the few and extreme poverty of the many.
7. (2) From a thousand feet, flapping wings as hard as he could, he pushed over into a blazing steep dive toward the *waves and* learned why seagulls don't make blazing steep power-dives.
8. (2) The beach was extremely *crowded; nevertheless,* we found Joan.
9. (5) Because the landlord has refused *to testify, our attorney* will have to subpoena him.
10. (3) Della Mason is a competent accountant *and a good cook.*

Practice IV *Page 144.*

1. (2) Our babysitter never cleans the kitchen or the den.
2. (5) No error
3. (5) No error
4. (5) No error
5. (1) I enjoy sad movies, but I dislike depressing books.

6. (3) During our trip to London, we visited Westminster Abbey; we also viewed the Crown Jewels in the Tower of London, and saw the Changing of the Guard.
7. (4) The current hearings are interesting, but last year's scandal was boring.

Practice V *Page 147.*

1. (4) another*;* the   *or*   another*, and* the   *or*   another. *T*he
2. (3) away*; this*   *or*   away. *T*his
3. (4) chess*,* he
4. (4) *a number of accidental brilliances*
5. (2) Liebowitz*;* he   *or*   Liebowitz. *He*

15.

Effective Expression

I never say, "The trip it was a lovely cruise,"
Nor make a boorish error of that type.
  "The reason is because" I hesitate to use
  And regard "he hardly never" as sheer tripe.
When it comes to proper style, I've paid my dues.
            —Lorraine Lockwood
        from "Paying One's Dues" in
         A Housewife and Her Poems

A Word With You . . .

The common errors pointed out by the poet are all treated in Chapter 15. She "paid her dues" by learning how to avoid such repetitive expressions and how to write in a clear, concise, uncluttered fashion.

Care to pay your dues?

Style and Clarity

Many sentences which seem correctly written are, in fact, incorrect because of:

the misuse of words or phrases.

the addition of unnecessary words or phrases.

See if you can locate the errors in style and clarity in the following paragraphs. Mark your corrections directly in the paragraph.

Paragraph A:

My reason for sending the children to Happy Days Camp was that I thought they might learn to swim. Much of the time, the weather was cloudy, but they didn't go swimming. At the end of the season, the campers gave a party for their parents, but they didn't enjoy it. Since our expectations were not fulfilled, we signed the children up for the next year.

Did you find these errors?

1 INCORRECT: My reason for sending the children to Happy Days Camp was that I thought they might learn to swim.

PROBLEM: The incorrect sentence uses too many words to make the point. "My reason . . . was that" can be condensed simply to "I sent the children to Happy Days Camp because . . ."

CORRECT: I sent the children to Happy Days Camp *because* I thought they might learn to swim.

2 INCORRECT: Much of the time, the weather was cloudy, but they didn't go swimming.

PROBLEM: The sentence states that they didn't go swimming *in spite of* the cloudy weather. In fact, they didn't go swimming *because of* the cloudy weather.

CORRECT: a. Much of the time, the weather was cloudy, so they didn't go swimming.

b. Much of the time, the weather was cloudy; therefore, they didn't go swimming.

c. Much of the time, they didn't go swimming because the weather was cloudy.

3 INCORRECT: At the end of the season, the campers gave a party for their parents, but they didn't enjoy it.

PROBLEM: It is unclear whether *they* refers to the campers or their parents. The sentence must be changed in order to convey the true meaning.

CORRECT: a. At the end of the season, the campers gave a party for their parents, but the campers didn't enjoy it.

b. At the end of the season, the campers gave a party for their parents, but their parents didn't enjoy it.

c. Although they didn't enjoy it, at the end of the season, the campers gave a party for their parents.

d. At the end of the season, the campers gave a party for their parents who didn't enjoy it.

4 INCORRECT: Since our expectations were not fulfilled, we signed the children up for next year.

PROBLEM: The sentence states that we enrolled the children for next year *since* our expectations were not fulfilled. In fact, we enrolled the children for next year *although* our expectations were not fulfilled.

CORRECT: Although our expectations were not fulfilled, we enrolled the children for next year.

The corrected paragraph would look like this:

I sent the children to Happy Days Camp *because* I thought they might learn to swim. Much of the time, the weather was cloudy, *so* they didn't go swimming. At the end of the season, the campers gave a party for their parents, but *the campers* didn't enjoy it. *Although* our expectations were not fulfilled, we enrolled the children for next year.

> ### Paragraph B:

The bus tour of Philadelphia on the bus was interesting. I don't never remember a livelier group. The highlight of the trip was when we saw the Liberty Bell. The reason I enjoyed that sight was because I love history. The bus driver, he gave an informative speech.

Did you find these errors?

1 INCORRECT: The bus tour on the bus of Philadelphia was interesting.
  PROBLEM: The phrase *on the bus* is a repetition. Bus *tour* means that the tour was on the bus.
  CORRECT: The bus tour of Philadelphia was interesting.

2 INCORRECT: I don't never remember a livelier group.
  PROBLEM: The incorrect sentence uses a double negative, *don't never*. These two negative words, in effect, cancel each other. Other negative words which should not be used in combination are: hardly, scarcely, neither, only, never, no one, nobody, no, none, nothing, not.
  CORRECT: I don't ever remember a livelier group.

3 INCORRECT: The highlight of the trip was when we saw the Liberty Bell.
  PROBLEM: The use of *was when* is poor style. A more concise form of expression should be chosen.
  CORRECT: The highlight of the trip was seeing the Liberty Bell.

4 INCORRECT: The reason I enjoyed that sight was because I love history.
   PROBLEM: *The reason . . . was because* creates an awkward sentence. Simplify the sentence by stating *A* because *B* without the unnecessary words.
   CORRECT: I enjoyed that sight because I love history.

5 INCORRECT: The bus driver, he gave an informative speech.
   PROBLEM: Wordiness results from the repetition in the phrase *the bus driver, he.* Use one or the other, but not both terms. In this sentence you need to use *bus driver,* since there has been no prior reference to him.
   CORRECT: The bus driver planned an informative speech.

The corrected paragraph would look like this:

The bus tour of Philadelphia was interesting. I don't *ever* remember a livelier group. The highlight of the trip was *seeing* the Liberty Bell. I enjoyed that sight *because* I love history. The *bus driver* gave an informative speech.

PRACTICE

I **Directions:** Blacken the space beneath the number which corresponds to the number of the incorrect sentence in each group. If there is no error, blacken space number 5.

	1	2	3	4	5

1 1) He hardly never writes home.
   2) Charlie accepted the job because the pay was good.
   3) I hardly ever visit my childhood friend, Eddie.
   4) Manuel doesn't like fishing.
   5) No error

	1	2	3	4	5

2 1) My reasons for leaving the firm are personal.
   2) Leonardo Da Vinci, he painted the *Last Supper.*
   3) I had scarcely opened the book when I fell asleep.
   4) Albert Einstein was one man whom many people admired.
   5) No error

	1	2	3	4	5

3 1) Money was very tight during the early 1980's, so major automobile manufacturers offered customer rebates.

2) Britons and Americans have never spoken the same language.

3) Since I enjoy music, I never attend concerts.

4) Although the hour was late, Congress voted to remain in session.

5) No error

1 2 3 4 5

4 1) Since the weather has been unusually dry, forests are in danger of burning.

2) Dolores visited her former employer, Martha Cummins, and she gave her a lovely gift.

3) Although I like to play chess, I cannot play now.

4) I have never known anyone else who has so consistently disregarded the rules.

5) No error

1 2 3 4 5

5 1) There isn't no easy way of solving the problem.

2) Since Martin Luther King had been an advocate of non-violence, his violent death was particularly shocking.

3) An impasse occurs when either party refuses to listen.

4) If you regulate your sleeping habits, you will feel better.

5) No error

1 2 3 4 5

6 1) Good sense told the ambassador not to continue in that area of conversation.

2) When my young neighbor asked for permission to use my car, I denied it.

3) My brother, he refused to admit that he'd broken the stereo.

4) After he had signed the bill, the President gave the Boy Scout leader the pen.

5) No error

	1	2	3	4	5

7
1) The librarian had given no one permission to use the reference books.
2) Susan B. Anthony was a pioneer for women's suffrage during a period in history when it was hardly popular for a woman to be an activist.
3) The babysitter gave the child her lunch and she continued to play.
4) Since the crew had heard the twelve o'clock whistle, they knew it was lunch time.
5) No error

	1	2	3	4	5

8
1) If the play is not a success, the reason is because the actors never learned their lines well.
2) A green-eyed, black cat darted in front of us.
3) A high school graduate is neither too young nor too inexperienced for that job.
4) As the bus rounded the corner, the tourists could see the traffic jam.
5) No error

	1	2	3	4	5

9
1) Rupert cannot understand your unclear notes.
2) Maria washed her car this morning, so she is tired.
3) Don't say that you haven't been warned.
4) The reason I called this meeting is because there have been some misunderstandings.
5) No error

	1	2	3	4	5

10
1) Didn't Mattie say that she would complete the job?
2) Why don't you ask her if she would?
3) The ancient, old castle stood on the hill.
4) We visited an old, well-kept inn.
5) No error

PRACTICE

II   Directions: Blacken the space beneath the number which corresponds to the correct rewriting of the underlined portion of the sentence. Choice 1 is always the same as the underlined portion and is sometimes the right answer. These sentences are presenting a story.

1 2 3 4 5
|| || || || ||

1.   Our *family, we* went to the craft show.

   1) family, we
   2) we
   3) whole family, we
   4) family
   5) family, when we

1 2 3 4 5
|| || || || ||

2.   The *craft show* included displays of pottery, needlepoint, jewelry, leaded-glass, and other crafts.

   1) craft show
   2) crafts show
   3) show of crafts
   4) show
   5) craft's show

1 2 3 4 5
|| || || || ||

3.   My favorite part of the afternoon *was when I tried* the potter's wheel.

   1) was when I tried
   2) was trying
   3) was the time I tried
   4) was when trying
   5) is when I tried

1 2 3 4 5
|| || || || ||

4.   I *didn't never do anything* that creative before.

   1) didn't never do anything
   2) never did nothing
   3) didn't ever do nothing
   4) never did anything
   5) did not never do anything

1 2 3 4 5

5.   I had difficulty trying the spinning wheel, ‖ ‖ ‖ ‖ ‖
     and I had never done it before.
     1) and
     2) therefore
     3) but
     4) however
     5) since

1 2 3 4 5

6.   The artists permitted the children to try their ‖ ‖ ‖ ‖ ‖
     media, _**and they enjoyed**_ sharing this creative
     experience.
     1) and they enjoyed
     2) and the artists enjoyed
     3) and then they enjoyed
     4) and they also enjoyed
     5) and, despite this, they enjoyed

1 2 3 4 5

7.   When I was a child, _nobody never_ took me ‖ ‖ ‖ ‖ ‖
     to such an exciting event.
     1) nobody never
     2) anybody never
     3) anybody ever
     4) no one never
     5) nobody ever

**PRACTICE
  III**

Directions: Blacken the space beneath the number which corresponds
to the correct rewriting of the underlined portion of the sentence. Choice
1 is always the same as the underlined portion and is sometimes the
correct answer.

1 2 3 4 5

1.   The graduates and their teachers gathered in ‖ ‖ ‖ ‖ ‖
     the auditorium _where they received di-
     plomas_.
     1) where they received diplomas.
     2) in which they received diplomas.

     3) where the graduates received their diplomas.

     4) to receive diplomas.

     5) where diplomas were received.

                                            1 2 3 4 5

2.   The mailman *he comes promptly* at 12 noon. ‖ ‖ ‖ ‖ ‖

     1) he comes promptly

     2) who comes promptly

     3) comes promptly

     4) coming promptly

     5) he come promptly

                                            1 2 3 4 5

3.   *The reason I bought the outfit was because it* ‖ ‖ ‖ ‖ ‖
was on sale.

     1) The reason I bought the outfit was because it was on sale.

     2) The reason I bought the outfit was it was on sale.

     3) I bought the outfit for the reason that it was on sale.

     4) I bought the outfit because it was on sale.

     5) The reason it was on sale was because I bought the outfit.

                                            1 2 3 4 5

4.   The polite time to comment *was when he* ‖ ‖ ‖ ‖ ‖
finished his entire speech.

     1) was when he finished his entire speech.

     2) was when he had finished his entire speech.

     3) was when he was finishing his speech.

     4) was while he was finishing his speech.

     5) came after he had finished his speech.

                                            1 2 3 4 5

5.   *Don't you never* have to work on weekends? ‖ ‖ ‖ ‖ ‖

     1) Don't you never

     2) Don't you ever

3) Didn't you never

4) Haven't you never

5) Do you not never

6. All of the graduates *who graduated in the class of '74* met at the school for a party.

   1 2 3 4 5

   1) who graduated in the class of '74

   2) whom graduated in the class of '74

   3) graduated in the class of '74

   4) who graduate in the class of '74

   5) of the class of '74

7. *Since I had cooked dinner, we did not go out to eat.*

   1 2 3 4 5

   1) Since I had cooked dinner, we did not go out to eat.

   2) Since I had cooked dinner, we went out to eat.

   3) We went out to eat since I had cooked dinner.

   4) We went out to eat because I cooked dinner.

   5) Since I cooked dinner, we did not go out to eat.

PRACTICE IV

Directions: Blacken the space beneath the number which corresponds to the number of the proper completion for each sentence below.

1. Paula entered the room laughing,

   1 2 3 4

   1) because she tripped at the doorway.

   2) when she saw that her father was angry.

   3) but stopped when she saw that her father was angry.

   4) but stopped when she saw her father who was not laughing because he was angry.

1 2 3 4
|| || || ||

2. Lyndon Johnson chose not to run for reelection in 1968
   1) since the growing antiwar sentiment did not influence him.
   2) because the growing antiwar sentiment did not influence him.
   3) because the growing antiwar sentiment influenced him.
   4) because his reason was that the growing antiwar sentiment influenced him.

1 2 3 4
|| || || ||

3. The roads were flooded
   1) , so we went for a drive.
   2) since we went for a drive.
   3) although we turned back.
   4) , so we turned back.

1 2 3 4
|| || || ||

4. Because the building was old and irreparable,
   1) the city planners decided to use it for student housing.
   2) the city planners decided that the thing to do was that they should tear it down.
   3) the city planners decided to tear it down.
   4) the city planners asked the students if they would tear it down.

1 2 3 4
|| || || ||

5. After climbing thirty flights of stairs,
   1) the package was still in the delivery boy's hands.
   2) the feet of the delivery boy were sore he said.
   3) the delivery boy he refused to walk home.
   4) the delivery boy's feet were sore.

6. The combined meeting of the bus drivers and taxi drivers

    1 2 3 4

1) resulted from the passenger boycott.
2) was for the men who drove buses and taxis.
3) was because of the passenger boycott.
4) met for the bus drivers and taxi drivers.

7. I'm very sorry for leaving early,

    1 2 3 4

1) but I couldn't never understand the speaker.
2) so I couldn't understand the speaker.
3) but I couldn't hardly understand the speaker.
4) but I couldn't understand the speaker.

8. Although we celebrated the occasion,

    1 2 3 4

1) we were very happy about it.
2) was because we were happy about it.
3) we were not very happy about it.
4) was that we were happy about it.

9. Thomas Jefferson, the President of the United States,

    1 2 3 4

1) he was a creative thinker.
2) who was a creative thinker.
3) who thought creatively.
4) was a creative thinker.

10. If you did not enjoy that movie,

    1 2 3 4

1) the reason is because you have no sense of humor.

EFFECTIVE EXPRESSION | 165

2) the reason is because that you have no
   sense of humor.

3) you have no sense of humor.

4) it could also be the reason is because you
   have no sense of humor.

ANSWER KEY

Chapter 15

Effective Expression

Practice I *Page 156.*

1. (1) Do not use a negative word such as never with *hardly* or *scarcely*. The sentence should read: He hardly *ever* writes home.
2. (2) *He* is repetitious. The sentence should read: *Leonardo Da Vinci painted* the *Last Supper*.
3. (3) The second part of the sentence is contradictory to the first. The sentence should read: Since I enjoy music, *I frequently attend* concerts.
4. (2) The use of *she* and *her* makes the sentence unclear. Who gave the gift to whom? The sentence should read: Dolores *visited* her former employer, Martha Cummins, and *gave her* a lovely gift.
5. (1) Don't use *not* and *no* together. The sentence should read: There *is no* easy way of solving the problem. or There *isn't any* easy way of solving the problem.
6. (3) *He* is repetitious. The sentence should read: My *brother refused* to admit that he'd broken the stereo.
7. (3) The use of *her* and *she* make the sentence unclear. The sentence should read: The babysitter gave the child lunch, *and the child* continued to play.
8. (1) *The reason is because* makes the sentence unwieldly. The sentence should read: If the play is not a success, *it is because* the actors never learned their lines well.
9. (4) See #8. The sentence should read: *I called this meeting because* there have been some misunderstandings.
10. (3) *Old* is repetitious. The sentence should read: The *ancient castle* stood on a hill.

Practice II *Page 159.*

1. (4) *We* is repetitious. The sentence should read: Our *family* went to the craft show.
2. (4) *Craft* is repetitious. The sentence should read: The *show* included displays of pottery, needlepoint, jewelry, beaded glass objects, and other crafts.
3. (2) *Was when* is an awkward construction. The sentence should read: My favorite part of the afternoon *was trying* the potter's wheel.
4. (4) Don't use *didn't* and *never* together. The sentence should read: I *never did anything* that creative before.
5. (5) *Since* coordinates the two thoughts; *and* does not. The sentence should read: I had difficulty trying the spinning wheel, *since* I had never done it before.
6. (2) The word to which *they* refers is unclear. The sentence should read: The artists permitted the children to try their media, *and the artists* enjoyed sharing this creative experience.
7. (5) Don't use *nobody* and *never* together. The sentence should read: When I was a child, *nobody ever* took me to such an exciting event.

Practice III *Page 160.*

1. (3) The graduates and their teachers gathered in the auditorium *where the graduates received their diplomas.*
2. (3) The mailman *comes promptly* at 12 noon.
3. (4) *I bought the outfit because it was on sale.*
4. (5) The polite time to comment *came after he had finished his speech.*
5. (2) *Don't you ever* have to work on weekends?
6. (5) All of the graduates *of the class of '74* met at the school for a party.
7. (1) *Since I had cooked dinner, we did not go out to eat.*

Practice IV *Page 162.*

1. (3) Paula entered the room laughing, but stopped when she saw that her father was angry.
2. (3) Lyndon Johnson chose not to run for reelection in 1968 because the growing antiwar sentiment influenced him.
3. (4) The roads were flooded, so we turned back.
4. (3) Because the building was old and irreparable, the city planners decided to tear it down.
5. (4) After climbing thirty flights of stairs, the delivery boy's feet were sore.
6. (1) The combined meeting of the bus drivers and taxi drivers resulted from the passenger boycott.
7. (4) I'm very sorry for leaving early, but I couldn't understand the speaker.
8. (3) Although we celebrated the occasion, we were not very happy about it.
9. (4) Thomas Jefferson, the President of the United States, was a creative thinker.
10. (3) If you did not enjoy that movie, you have no sense of humor.

16.

More Punctuation

"That secretary you sent me . . . ."
"What about her?"
"She's beautiful, all right, but where did she go to school?" asked Davis.
"Anything wrong?" Osborn wanted to know, but not too desperately.
"It seems," Davis went on, "that she must have been absent when they taught about commas. In fact, she's in a coma when it comes to commas."
"Tough luck," grunted Osborn. "Imagine if she were ugly and didn't know anything about commas."

—Sloan Robinson
Drowning in the Steno Pool

A Word With You . . .

One of the mistakes made by Mr. Davis' gorgeous secretary came in the following sentence:
"Our company manager said the Mayor is an idiot."
Or should she have typed it this way?
"Our company manager," said the Mayor, "is an idiot."
Apparently, commas do make a difference. Proper use of quotation marks makes a difference, too.

Quotation Marks

Quotation marks are used to set off the *exact* words said by somebody or taken from a source.

Direct quotation: The young mother remarked, "Thank Heavens for our community's parks and recreation program!"

Indirect quotation: The young mother remarked that she was grateful for her community's parks and recreation program.

In the first sentence, the woman's exact words are quoted. In the second sentence, the word *that* signals the fact that the sentence is a report of what was said, not a direct quotation.

QUOTATION MARK
STYLE SHEET

RULES	EXAMPLES
1. Use quotation marks to set off the exact words of a speaker. Note the comma between the speaker and the words spoken in each example. Note the period *inside* the quotation marks at the end of the first sentence.	The teacher instructed, "Complete the vocabulary list at home." "Review the vocabulary list for our last class," the teacher instructed.
2. Use quotation marks to set off both parts of a broken quotation. Do not capitalize the first word of the second part of the quotation unless it is the beginning of a new sentence.	"Well," exclaimed Anita, "what did you expect?" "Stop complaining, Billy," said his brother. "It won't help."
3. Place a semicolon after the closing quotation marks.	You said, "Wait until you see me"; so I waited. Did Jane say, "Meet at our house"?
4. Never use two forms of punctuation at the end of a quotation. When the entire sentence is a question but the quoted portion is not, place a question mark *after* the closing quotation marks.	
5. Never use two forms of punctuation at the end of a quotation. When the entire sentence is an exclamation but the quoted portion is not, place the exclamation point *after* the closing quotation marks. When the quoted portion is an exclamation, place the exclamation mark *inside* the quotes.	I could scream each time you call and say, "I'll be late for dinner tonight, dear"! The guard shouted, "Stop him! Stop him!"

RULES	EXAMPLES
6. Use single quotation marks for a quotation within a quotation.	The history student asked, "Is it true that Patrick Henry said, 'Give me liberty or give me death' when America's freedom was in question?"
7. Use quotation marks to enclose titles of poems, articles, chapters, or any part of a book or magazine. If the quoted title is followed by a comma, the comma should be placed inside the quotation marks.	The third chapter of *Our World,* entitled, "Views of the Middle East," is the most interesting.

Common Errors with Quotation Marks

Quotations require marks of punctuation in addition to quotation marks. The most common errors in quotations involve the omission or misuse of commas, periods, and capital letters. Following are common examples.

1. Place a comma between what is quoted and the person quoted.

INCORRECT: "When you finish packing the last box, start loading all of them onto the truck" the shipping manager instructed.

CORRECT: "When you finish packing the last box, start loading all of them onto the truck," the shipping manager instructed.

2. In a broken quotation, do not capitalize the first word of the second part of the quotation unless it is the beginning of a new sentence.

INCORRECT: "When you finish packing the last box," the shipping manager instructed. "Start loading all of them onto the truck."

CORRECT: "When you finish packing the last box," the shipping manager instructed, "start loading all of them onto the truck."

CORRECT: "You have finished packing the last box," the foreman said. "Start loading all of them onto the truck."

3. Place the period inside the quotation marks at the end of a sentence.

INCORRECT: Dr. D'Amato said, "Before you leave the office, please give your Medicare number to the nurse".

CORRECT: Dr. D'Amato said, "Before you leave the office, please give your Medicare number to the nurse."

4. Place a question mark *after* the closing quotation marks when the entire sentence is a question, but the quoted portion is not.

INCORRECT: Did Dr. D'Amato say, "Please leave your Medicare number with the nurse?"

CORRECT: Did Dr. D'Amato say, "Please leave your Medicare number with the nurse"?

5. Place a question mark *inside* the closing quotation marks when the quoted portion is a question, but the entire sentence is not.

INCORRECT: Dr. D'Amato asked, "Is this your correct Medicare number"?
CORRECT: Dr. D'Amato asked, "Is this your correct Medicare number?"

PRACTICE
I   Directions: Punctuate the following sentences.

1.   The manager said three men must work overtime
2.   The manager said that three men must work overtime
3.   Three men said the manager must work overtime
4.   The manager asked who will work overtime
5.   Why didn't the manager say everyone must work
6.   Imagine if the manager had said everyone must work overtime
7.   Imagine if the manager had said that everyone must work overtime
8.   The manager shouted everyone must work overtime

PRACTICE
II   Directions: Blacken the space beneath the number which corresponds to the number of the error in each sentence. If there is no error, blacken space number 5.

1 2 3 4 5

1.   Mrs. Romano exclaimed, Frankie, the para-   ‖ ‖ ‖ ‖ ‖
                        1   2   3

keet has disappeared!" No error
                4   5

1 2 3 4 5

2.   Frankie answered, "Mom, I don't know   ‖ ‖ ‖ ‖ ‖
                    1   2

why; it was there when I tried to clean
$\overline{3}$

it with the vacuum cleaner. No error
$\overline{4}$ $\overline{5}$

3. "You will never catch me!" shouted Bat-
$\overline{1}$ $\overline{2}$

man. The pursuers vowed to catch him.
$\overline{3}$ $\overline{4}$

No error
$\overline{5}$

1	2	3	4	5
‖	‖	‖	‖	‖

4. The student said that he now understands the
$\overline{1}$

theory behind these problems. He said, "Sud-
$\overline{2}$ $\overline{3}$

denly, everything falls into place." No error
$\overline{4}$ $\overline{5}$

1	2	3	4	5
‖	‖	‖	‖	‖

5. The author said, "You can learn to write only
$\overline{1}$

through writing." He said that one can never
$\overline{2}$

learn to write by reading how-to books.
$\overline{3}$ $\overline{4}$

No error
$\overline{5}$

1	2	3	4	5
‖	‖	‖	‖	‖

6. Alice told Marion she was to stay at home and
$\overline{1}$

be a babysitter. Marion exclaimed, "what a
$\overline{2}$ $\overline{3}$

shame!" No error
$\overline{4}$ $\overline{5}$

1	2	3	4	5
‖	‖	‖	‖	‖

7. "Clean your room; take the laundry to the
$\overline{1}$ $\overline{2}$

1	2	3	4	5
‖	‖	‖	‖	‖

basement; and wash the car," instructed
    3   4

Mother. *No error*
        5

8. After you turn over the eart*h, a*dd some plant
   1   2

food and water. Then you'll be ready to

plant the flower," *c*oncluded the gardene*r*.
        3   4

No error
  5

1 2 3 4 5
‖ ‖ ‖ ‖ ‖

9. *W*as it Elsa who said, "*O*ur sales meeting be-
  1   2 3

gins at 9:30 A.M. sharp*?*" *No error*
                4   5

1 2 3 4 5
‖ ‖ ‖ ‖ ‖

10. "*W*hen will you ever," asked the foreman,
   1   2

"*A*rrive at work on time*?*" *No error*
  3   4   5

1 2 3 4 5
‖ ‖ ‖ ‖ ‖

11. "*I* know when I will arrive on tim*e*," an-
  1   2

swered Marie. "*i*t will be when my alarm
            3

clock is finished being repaired." *No error*
                    4   5

1 2 3 4 5
‖ ‖ ‖ ‖ ‖

12. The show is called "Day After Day;" it starts
                 1   2

at 2:30 P.M. *No error*
  3   4   5

1 2 3 4 5
‖ ‖ ‖ ‖ ‖

13. He replied encouragingly, *"R*emember that
$$\overline{1}$$
Ted said, *"L*et Irene wait. I'll interview her
$$\overline{2}\ \overline{3}$$
as soon as I return.*'"* *No error*
$$\overline{4}\quad\overline{5}$$

    1 2 3 4 5
    ‖ ‖ ‖ ‖ ‖

14. After having read the third chapter, *enti-*
$$\overline{1}$$
tled *"S*pring-time Planting*",* I felt that I was
$$\overline{2}\qquad\qquad\overline{3}$$
ready to tackle the gardening jo*b.* *No error*
$$\overline{4}\quad\overline{5}$$

    1 2 3 4 5
    ‖ ‖ ‖ ‖ ‖

15. After the vicious dog had attacked the
trespasser, the dog's owner sai*d, "D*idn't you
$$\overline{1}$$
see the sign which reads *'B*eware of Do*g'* be-
$$\overline{2}\qquad\qquad\overline{3}$$
fore you entered my property*?".* *No error*
$$\overline{4}\quad\overline{5}$$

    1 2 3 4 5
    ‖ ‖ ‖ ‖ ‖

Other Marks of Punctuation

You have already studied the major punctuation marks. There are several marks of punctuation which we encounter less frequently. These are the colon, the hyphen, the apostrophe, the dash, parentheses, and brackets.

OTHER MARKS OF PUNCTUATION STYLE SHEET

RULES	EXAMPLES
1. **<u>Colon</u>** Use a colon to introduce a list. Don't use a colon when the list is preceded by an action or linking word.	Bring the following equipment: a tent, a cot or sleeping bag, basic cooking utensils, and matches. Necessary equipment for such a trip includes a tent, a cot or sleeping bag, basic cooking utensils, and matches.

RULES	EXAMPLES
2. Use a colon after the salutation in a business letter.	Dear Mr. Williams: Dear Sir:
3. Use a colon between numbers to show time.	4:15 P.M.
4. **Hyphen** Use a hyphen to divide a word at the end of a line. Divide between syllables with a hyphen.	The new, downtown building is enormous, yet unornamented.
5. Use a hyphen to divide compound numbers from twenty-one to ninety-nine.	twenty-two, eighty-seven
6. Hyphenate descriptive words which are brought together to form a new word.	well-to-do, fly-by-night, half-yearly, self-supporting
7. Hyphenate certain prefixes and the words to which they are added. For example, ex-husband.	My favorite art form is pre-Columbian sculpture.
8. **Apostrophe** Use an apostrophe to show the omission of a letter from a word.	We aren't (are not) responsible for breakage.
9. Use an apostrophe to show possession. Note that apostrophes are placed differently according to whether the word is singular or plural and according to the way the word forms its plural. Exceptions: *Its* is the possessive form of *it. It's* means *it is. His* and *hers* are the possessive forms of *he* and *she*.	the lamb's wool, the dogs' kennels, the men's department, the ladies' club
10. Use an apostrophe to show the plural of letters and numbers.	8's, B's
11. **Dash** Use dashes to emphasize an interruption within a sentence.	Be home on time—no later than midnight—or I shall be very worried.
12. **Parentheses** Use parentheses for words not strictly related to the main thought of the sentence. Do not use a capital letter or final punc-	I managed (somehow or other) to drag three heavy suitcases to the terminal. I called you last night (or was

RULES	EXAMPLES
tuation (except the question mark) within the parentheses.	it Friday?) to give you the message.
13. **Brackets** Use brackets within parentheses and within a quotation.	They tried some French wines (Bordeaux [Medoc], Burgundy, and Chablis).
	We were asked to read a poem and Tom said, "The one I've chosen [by Wilde] is called 'The Ballad of Reading Gaol.'"

PRACTICE

III Directions: Blacken the space beneath the number which corresponds to the number of the error in each sentence. If there is no error, blacken space number 5.

1 2 3 4 5

1. The presiden*t's* desk was covered with all   ‖ ‖ ‖ ‖ ‖
$\overline{1}$

sorts of business paper*s;* invoices, receipts,
$\overline{2}$

minutes of his last meetin*g,* and projected
$\overline{3}$

plans for the new buildin*g.* *No error*
$\overline{4}$ $\quad$ $\overline{5}$

1 2 3 4 5

2. We expect to arrive at Kennedy Airport   ‖ ‖ ‖ ‖ ‖

at *8 15 P.M.* on Thursda*y, J*une *8, 1983.*
$\overline{1}$ $\qquad$ $\overline{2}$ $\quad$ $\overline{3}$ $\overline{4}$

No error
$\overline{5}$

1 2 3 4 5

3. Although we had met only once, he *rec-*   ‖ ‖ ‖ ‖ ‖
$\overline{1}$

ognized me immediately and began to regale

me with the followin*g:* he had just arrived in
$\overline{2}$

MORE PUNCTUATION | 177

tow*n;* he had bought a hous*e;* and he had
  3   4

just been promoted within his company.

No error
5

                                  1 2 3 4 5

4. Do you really *believe* that you were a differ- || || || || ||
  1

ent person at *twenty nine* from the one you
  2

are at *thirty?* *No error*
  3 4   5

                                  1 2 3 4 5

5. If you are planning to send a present to || || || || ||

Lauri*e,* go to the *half-yearly* sale in the chil-
  1   2

dren*s'* departmen*t.* *No error*
  3   4   5

                                  1 2 3 4 5

6. *Dont* forget to write two *r's* in *"d*eferr*ed."* || || || || ||
  1   2   3   4
No error
5

                                  1 2 3 4 5

7. When I arrived (*after a four hour drive*), I || || || || ||
  1

found that my *cousin's* *weren't* at hom*e.*
  2   3   4
No error
5

                                  1 2 3 4 5

8. The *ex Senator* hoped that his *protege's* bill || || || || ||
  1   2

would pass the *two-thirds* mar*k.* *No error*
  3   4   5

9. Although Septembe*r*, Jun*e*, and April have $\underset{1}{}$ $\underset{2}{}$

    thirty day*s*, December and January have
    $\underset{3}{}$

    thirty-one days. *No error*
    $\underset{4}{}$ $\quad$ $\underset{5}{}$

    1 2 3 4 5
    ‖ ‖ ‖ ‖ ‖

10. At *11:45* A.M. the *commuter's train* pulled
    $\underset{1}{}$ $\qquad$ $\underset{2}{}$ $\underset{3}{}$

    them into the *jam-packed* station. *No error*
    $\underset{4}{}$ $\qquad$ $\underset{5}{}$

    1 2 3 4 5
    ‖ ‖ ‖ ‖ ‖

PRACTICE

IV **Directions:** Blacken the space beneath the number which corresponds to the number of the incorrect sentence in each group. If there is no error, blacken space number 5.

1
1) Let's talk about Mozart's music first.

1 2 3 4 5
‖ ‖ ‖ ‖ ‖

2) If you leave after I do, do this: put the cat out, close the windows, and lock the front door.
3) Henrys new car seems to be a poor sample of this year's cars.
4) Mr. Jones is a good example of a self-satisfied person.
5) No error

2
1) In November, 1975, unusually high temperatures reached the 60's and even the 70's.

1 2 3 4 5
‖ ‖ ‖ ‖ ‖

2) Dot your i's and cross your t's.
3) Who's going to Ellen's party?
4) It's wheel is no longer round.
5) No error

3
1) Many experts skills have been brought to bear upon our energy needs.

1 2 3 4 5
‖ ‖ ‖ ‖ ‖

2) Mr. Evans hadn't stepped out of the room before the whispering began.

3) After her work's finished, she'll be home.

4) My mother-in-law's house was the scene of our recent reunion.

5) No error

1 2 3 4 5
|| || || || ||

4 1) The United Nations' subcommittees meet regularly.

2) Have you ever bought tickets to the Firemens' Ball?

3) My friends' letters demand that I be a good correspondent.

4) The children's club meets at 3:45 P.M. on Tuesdays.

5) No error

1 2 3 4 5
|| || || || ||

5 1) Yesterday I had lunch with Mr. Templeton.

2) Learn the meanings of the following words—"petition," "council," and "electorate."

3) The children—in the midst of our frantic activity—asked for chocolate ice cream sundaes.

4) Take the bicycle (John's), and don't forget my fishing rod.

5) No error

1 2 3 4 5
|| || || || ||

6 1) If you consult James Beard's newest cookbook, you will find some excellent shellfish recipes.

2) I'd rather you didn't do that.

3) When I heard (last night) that you were ill, I drove all night to get here.

4) Is that pen his or her's?

5) No error

1 2 3 4 5
|| || || || ||

7 1) Take my shirts to the laundry tomorrow!

2) We listed the stolen items a ring, a bracelet, and a TV set.

3) All of this pre-Christmas rush has ruined Terry's disposition.

4) Jan's sister-in-law agreed to join us for bridge.

5) No error

1 2 3 4 5

8 1) When it is 10:30 A.M. in New York, what time is it in Chicago?

2) A famous critic (Lionel Trilling) said that a nation's literature reflects its deepest philosophies.

3) Listening to everyone's ideas sometimes confuses me.

4) I've decided to take a year's subscription to *Your Health.*

5) No error

1 2 3 4 5

9 1) We've discovered that students' absences have decreased this month.

2) The seashore is only an hour's ride from here.

3) Have you read *The Record's* lead article?

4) This book's most important theme is the development of the Puritan ethic.

5) No error

1 2 3 4 5

10 1) A person's health depends somewhat upon his mental attitude.

2) Don't call him un American because he disagrees with your opinions.

3) While you're at the store, buy wire, nails, and a hammer.

4) Almost three-fourths of our organization voted against the admission of new members.

5) No error

ANSWER KEY

Chapter 16

More Punctuation

Quotation Marks

Practice I *Page 171.*

1. The manager said, "Three men must work overtime."
2. The manager said that three men must work overtime.
3. "Three men," said the manager, "must work overtime."
4. The manager asked, "Who will work overtime?"
5. Why didn't the manager say, "Everyone must work"?
6. Imagine if the manager had said, "Everyone must work overtime"!
7. Imagine if the manager had said that everyone must work overtime!
8. The manager shouted, "Everyone must work overtime!"

Practice II *Page 171.*

For explanations of answers, refer to the punctuation rules on pages 174–176.

1. (2) Mrs. Romano exclaimed, *"F*rankie, the parakeet has disappeared!"
   See Rule 1
2. (4) Frankie answered, "Mom, I don't know why, since it was there when I tried to clean it with the vacuum cleaner*."*
   See Rule 1
3. (5) No error
4. (5) No error
5. (5) No error
6. (3) Alice told Marion she was to stay at home and be a babysitter. Marion exclaimed, *"W*hat a shame!"
   See Rule 1
7. (5) No error
8. (1) *"After* you turn over the earth, add some plant food and water. Then you'll be ready to plant the flower," concluded the gardener.
   See Rule 1
9. (4) Was it Elsa who said, "Our sales meeting begins at 9:30 A.M. shar*p"?*
   See Rule 4
10. (3) "When will you ever," asked the foreman, *"arrive* at work on time?"
    See Rule 2
11. (3) "I know when I will arrive on time," answered Marie. *"It* will be when my alarm clock is finished being repaired."
    See Rule 2
12. (2) The show is called "Day After Da*y"*; it starts at 2:30 P.M.
    See Rule 3
13. (3) He replied encouragingly, "Remember that Ted said, *'L*et Irene wait. I'll interview her as soon as I return.' "
    See Rule 6
14. (3) After having read the third chapter, entitled "Spring-time Planting*," I* felt that I was ready to tackle the gardening job.
    See Rule 7
15. (4) After the vicious dog had attacked the trespasser, the dog's owner said, "Didn't you see the sign which reads 'Beware of Dog' before you entered my propert*y?"*
    See Rule 4

Other Marks of Punctuation

Practice III *Page 176.*

For explanations of answers, refer to the punctuation rules on pages 174–176.

1. (2) The president's desk was covered with all sorts of business paper*s:* *i*nvoices, receipts, minutes of his last meeting, and projected plans for the new building.
See Rule 1

2. (1) We expect to arrive at Kennedy Airport at <u>8:15</u> on Thursday, June 8, 1983.
See Rule 3

3. (1) Although we had met only once, he <u>re-</u>cognized me immediately.
See Rule 4

4. (2) Do you really believe that you were a different person at <u>*twenty-nine*</u> from the one you are at thirty?
See Rule 5

5. (3) If you are planning to send a present to Laurie, go to the half-yearly sale in the <u>*children's*</u> department.
See Rule 8

6. (1) <u>*Don't*</u> forget to write two r's in "deferred".
See Rule 8

7. (2) When I arrived (after a four hour drive), I found that my <u>*cousins*</u> weren't at home.
See Rule 8

8. (1) The <u>*ex-Senator*</u> hoped that his protege's bill would pass the two-thirds mark.
See Rule 7

9. (5) No error

10. (2) At 11:45 A.M., the <u>*commuters'*</u> train pulled them into the jam-packed station.
See Rule 9

Practice IV *Page 178.*

For explanations of answers, refer to the punctuation rules on pages 174–176.

1. (3) <u>*Henry's*</u> new car seems to be a poor sample of this year's cars.
See Rule 9

2. (4) <u>*Its*</u> wheel is no longer round.
See Rule 9

3. (1) Many <u>*experts'*</u> skills have been brought to bear upon our energy needs.
See Rule 8

4. (2) Have you ever bought tickets to the <u>*Firemen's Ball?*</u>
See Rule 9

5. (2) Learn the meanings of the following <u>*words:*</u> petition, council, and electorate.
See Rule 1

6. (4) Is that pin his or <u>*hers?*</u>
See Rule 9

7. (2) We listed the stolen <u>*items:*</u> a ring, a bracelet, and a TV set.
See Rule 1

8. (5) No error

9. (4) This book's theme is the <u>*develop-*</u>ment of the Puritan ethic.
See Rule 4

10. (2) Don't call him <u>*un-American*</u> because he disagrees with your opinions.
See Rule 7

17.
Capitalization

When I was a young writer, submitting poems and thought pieces to arty little magazines, I refused to capitalize anything—not my own name, not kentucky, not broadway, not belgium, not even e. e. cummings or don marquis' cockroach, archy.

It was a period I was going through when I explained to my courtiers that only God was deserving of capitalization. You can't imagine how that nonsensical pose won approbation with my admirers, but, come to think of it, it never made much of an impression on the editors of *Partisan Review*. When they sent me my usual rejection slip, they always used CAPITAL LETTERS.

—Tim Wolfe
The Child That's Got His Own

A Word With You . . .

Some writers, for purposes best known to themselves, use lowercase letters at all times, refusing to capitalize anything. Instead of "Dear Sir" in the salutation of a letter, they prefer "dear sir," that is, when they take the trouble to write a formal letter.

When one is a professional writer with a philosophical point of view about capitalization, one can afford to use lowercase letters. The rest of us had better learn where and when to capitalize. Chapter 17 will help.

CAPITALIZATION STYLE SHEET

Capitalization, like punctuation, is applied according to rules. Study the style sheet and then take the survey test which follows.

RULES	EXAMPLES
1. Capitalize the first letter of the first word in a sentence, unless it is a sentence within parentheses.	Language changes continually (note all the once-slang words in your current dictionary) but slowly.

RULES	EXAMPLES
2. Capitalize the first word of a direct quotation.	He cautioned, "If you buy a ticket beforehand, you will secure a seat for the performance."
3. Capitalize the word *I*.	In case you are late, *I* will cover for you.
4. Capitalize the diety, place names, street names, persons' names, organization names, languages, and specific course names.	God and His universe, Blue Ridge Mountains, Delaware River, Forty-second Street, John Masters, Knights of Columbus, Spanish, History II (not sociology, math, etc.)
5. Capitalize names of important historical events, documents, and ages.	World War I, Magna Carta, Declaration of Independence, Victorian Era
6. Capitalize days of the week, months, and special holidays.	Monday, January, Memorial Day
7. Capitalize east, west, north, and south only when they are used as sections of the country, not as directions.	Rod Lewis lived in the East for three years, then moved to the Midwest. Turn east at the next corner.
8. In a title (of a play, book, poem, magazine, etc.) capitalize the first word and each important word.	*Death of a Salesman, The Odyssey, The Wasteland, The Last of the Mohicans*
9. Capitalize the initials of a person's name.	T.J. Phillips
10. Capitalize a title when it precedes the name.	Captain T.J. Phillips
Do not capitalize a title when it does not precede the name.	T.J. Phillips, captain of *Star Lady*,... The captain of *Star Lady*, T.J. Phillips....
11. Capitalize the first word in each line of poetry.	"A thing of beauty is a joy forever: Its loveliness increases . . ."

Survey Test

Directions: Place capital letters where they are needed in the following sentences.

1. after considering all the facts, i have chosen an appropriate action.

2. don't you think that fred might enjoy owning a french-english dictionary?

3. he said, "leave new jersey at noon, and you will reach new york city by 1 p.m. at the latest."

4. john is planning to take german, geography, history, and economics this year at city college.

5. we're expecting king farouk for dinner on friday night. i hope you can join us.

6. mary stark bought a chevrolet last tuesday, although she hadn't planned on buying a car this year.

7. in history II we will study the industrial revolution, world war I, world war II, and the atomic age.

8. this course will be offered to adults on mondays, wednesdays, and fridays in the spring only.

9. his original home, in california, was his favorite; and he plans on returning to the west in november.

10. captain and mrs. ryan made reservations at island beach motel on the cape's north shore for labor day.

Before beginning *Practice 1,* check your answers on the Survey Test and review the rules pertaining to the errors you made.

PRACTICE
I   **Directions:** Blacken the space beneath the number which corresponds to the number of the capitalization error in each sentence. If there is no error, blacken space number 5.

1.   *Our History* course this semester highlights   1 2 3 4 5
     1   2
    civilizations of the *East.* *No error*
        3   4   5

2.   *My* family plans to move to *Cypress street* in   1 2 3 4 5
   1   2
    Millville, *Ohio.* *No error*
      3   4   5

3.   *"If* you plan to see the entire *art* exhibit,"   1 2 3 4 5
   1   2

Joan said, "*Be* sure to arrive at 10 A.M."
   3   4

No error
 5

                            1 2 3 4 5

4.   The *Thompkins'* plans for *Labor day* include ‖ ‖ ‖ ‖ ‖
             1   2

a *visit* to the *beach.* *No error*
  3   4   5

                            1 2 3 4 5

5.   *Proceed* two blocks *north* to the traffic light, ‖ ‖ ‖ ‖ ‖
      1   2

and turn right onto *Rumson Lane.* *No error*
             3   4   5

                            1 2 3 4 5

6.   I asked *father* to lend me the *Chevrolet* so that ‖ ‖ ‖ ‖ ‖
            1   2

we can drive to the *Rosemont Club* which is
                3

on the *east* side of town. *No error*
      4   5

                            1 2 3 4 5

7.   Speaking to the *town's Community Action* ‖ ‖ ‖ ‖ ‖
                  1   2

Council, Dr. j. l. Raio suggested revamping
  2   3

mental health *services.* *No error*
             4   5

                            1 2 3 4 5

8.   This *September,* both of my children, Bob and ‖ ‖ ‖ ‖ ‖
           1

Ronny, will be attending *Cedar High school.*
                     2   3   4

No error
 5

9. Waiting for the _Twenty-second Street_ bus, we
   <u>   1   </u>

   had time to admire the **arrow shirts** displayed
                           <u>   2   </u>

   in _Stone's_ _Haberdashery_. _No error_
      <u> 3 </u> <u>   4   </u> <u> 5 </u>

1 2 3 4 5
|| || || || ||

10. _"Why_ don't you read the _Winston Item,"_ said
    <u>1</u>   <u>   2   </u>

    Mother, _"and_ check for sales on air condition-
    <u> 3   </u> <u> 4 </u>

    ers?" _No error_
         <u> 5 </u>

1 2 3 4 5
|| || || || ||

11. _Uncle_ John and my _father_ are going to
    <u> 1 </u>   <u> 2   </u>

    Crystal Lake on _saturday_ to try out their new
    <u>   3   </u>   <u>   4   </u>

    fishing gear. _No error_
                  <u> 5 </u>

1 2 3 4 5
|| || || || ||

12. I've already crossed the _Atlantic ocean_ by air;
                            <u> 1 </u> <u> 2 </u>

    but this summer, in _July,_ I hope to make the
                        <u> 3 </u>

    crossing on an _Italian_ freighter. _No error_
                   <u>   4   </u>   <u> 5 </u>

1 2 3 4 5
|| || || || ||

13. _More_ and more elementary _schools_ are
    <u> 1 </u>   <u>   2   </u>

    teaching in _spanish_ in order to meet the needs
                <u> 3   </u>

    of the _community_. No error.
           <u>   4   </u> <u>   5   </u>

1 2 3 4 5
|| || || || ||

14. You recall *Reverend* *Hempstead* saying that
                1   2

    he will study *religious* philosophies of the *east*.
              3   4

    No error
      5

    1 2 3 4 5

15. The Ridgedale *Garden* *club* developed a hy-
               1   2

    brid *rose* and named it *Everlasting Beauty*.
         3   2

    No error
      5

    1 2 3 4 5

16. Including *caucasians*, *Blacks*, and *Orientals*,
             1   2   3

    the population of *Winfield*, Pennsylvania has
                 4

    grown to one and a half million. *No error*
                                5

    1 2 3 4 5

PRACTICE

II   Directions: Blacken the space beneath the number which corresponds to the number of the incorrect sentence in each group. If there is no error, blacken space number 5.

1 2 3 4 5

1 1) Each year our community celebrates the Fourth Of July with races, entertainment, and fireworks.

2) Because of its beauty and natural resources, the state of Colorado now boasts many new residents.

3) John works for the Ford Motor Company in Cleveland.

4) I asked Gerry, "Do you think we'll get to the game in time for the first quarter?"

5) No error

2 1) Last year we celebrated that Holiday on a Monday.

   2) This year the holiday falls in the third week of September.

   3) Shall we cross the bridge or take the tunnel?

   4) Archaeologists found evidence that the pagan gods were worshipped on that spot.

   5) No error

1 2 3 4 5

3 1) Dean Jones just became an administrator this September.

   2) Andy joined the travel-American Club and enjoyed a six week tour with the group.

   3) We have a subscription to the *Reader's Digest*.

   4) The *Odessa File* was a very popular book.

   5) No error

1 2 3 4 5

4 1) "Don't forget your umbrella," Aunt Jean said, "for you know the forecast indicates rain for today."

   2) At Ohio State university, students take courses year round.

   3) Our curriculum needs to stress reading skills in the areas of science, social studies, and American literature.

   4) Evan Greene, who lives in Syracuse, New York, joined the Professional Photographers Club.

   5) No error

1 2 3 4 5

5 1) The train trip was most scenic since the route wound through the White Mountains and ended at Pleasant Lake.

   2) when did you say that Bud had called me?

   3) Last summer, in July, we camped in Colorado.

   4) That company, Ferro Metals, has increased its volume of business through advanced advertising and promotion techniques.

   5) No error

			1	2	3	4	5

6 1) In the West, we plan to visit the Grand Canyon as well as the southern half of California.

2) The course, interestingly enough, was entitled, "God and His Relationship to Man."

3) Let's make a date to meet on Sunday, June 2nd.

4) The poem reads: Up the airy mountain,
   down the rushy glen . . .

5) No error

7 1) We're leaving Kennedy International Airport at 8 P.M., and we arrive in Lisbon seven hours later.

2) My friend, Fred, was elected President of the Rescue Squad.

3) "This new wing contains our intensive care unit," explained the director.

4) France and Belgium are both French-speaking countries.

5) No error

8 1) The group turned its attention to a tall, drawling Texan in its midst.

2) A well-known senator was accused of un-American activities.

3) "Don't do that!" said Jack. "you'll ruin the machine!"

4) Each time I see the Tappan Zee Bridge, I am impressed by its size and beauty.

5) No error

9 1) A river in Wisconsin is called the Fox River.

2) The Indian language is composed of many dialects.

3) The Empire State Building is still an impressive sight although it is no longer the tallest building in the world.

4) While you are in London, be sure to shop at Simpson's, Ltd.

5) No error

1 2 3 4 5
‖ ‖ ‖ ‖ ‖

10 1) It was two years ago that judge Billings was appointed to the bench.

2) I remember seeing Uncle John at the family gathering; but, as I recall, my aunt was not there.

3) Our study group discussed a few books of the Bible.

4) An essay question regarding the French Revolution might involve the major causes leading up to the disquiet of the times.

5) No error

ANSWER KEY

Chapter 17

Capitalization

Survey Test *Page 184.*

1. After considering all the facts, I have chosen an appropriate action.
2. Don't you think that Fred might enjoy owning a French-English dictionary?
3. He said, "Leave New Jersey at noon, and you will reach New York City by 1 P.M. at the latest."
4. John is planning to take German, geography, history and economics this year at City College.
5. We're expecting King Farouk for dinner on Friday night. I hope you can join us.
6. Mary Stark bought a Chevrolet last Tuesday, although she hadn't planned on buying a car this year.
7. In History II we will study the Industrial Revolution, World War I, World War II, and the Atomic Age.
8. This course will be offered to adults on Mondays, Wednesdays, and Fridays in the spring only.
9. His original home, in California, was his favorite; and he plans on returning to the West in November.
10. Captain and Mrs. Ryan made reservations at Island Beach Motel on the Cape's north shore for Labor Day.

Practice I *Page 185.*

1. (2) Our *history* course this semester highlights civilization of the East.
   Capitalize only *specific* course names, ie., History IA.
2. (2) My family plans to move to *Cypress Street* in Millville, Ohio.
   Capitalize entire street names.
3. (4) "If you plan to see the entire art exhibit," Joan said, *"be* sure to arrive at 10 A.M."
   Do not capitalize the first word in a broken quotation unless it is the beginning of a complete thought.
4. (2) The Thompkins' plans for *Labor Day* include a visit to the beach.
   Capitalize the name of a holiday.
5. (5) No error.
6. (1) I asked *Father* to lend me the Chevrolet so that we can drive to the Rosemont Club which is in the east side of town.
   Capitalize Father or Mother when they are used as names.
7. (3) Speaking to the town's Community Action Council, Dr. *J. L.* Raio suggested revamping mental health services.
   Capitalize initials in a name.
8. (4) This September both of my children, Bob and Ronny, will be attending Cedar High *School.*
   Capitalize the entire name of a school.
9. (2) Waiting for the Twenty-second Street Bus, we had time to admire the *Arrow* shirts displayed in Stone's Haberdashery.
   Capitalize the name of a company.
10. (5) No error.
11. (4) Uncle John and my father are going to Chrystal Lake on *Saturday* to try out their new fishing gear.
    Capitalize the names of the days of the week.
12. (2) I've already crossed the Atlantic *Ocean* by air; but this summer, in July, I hope to make the crossing on an Italian freighter.
    Capitalize the entire name of an ocean.
13. (3) More and more elementary schools are teaching in *Spanish* in order to meet the needs of the community.
    Capitalize the name of a language.

14. (4) You recall Reverend Hempstead saying that he will study religious philosophies of the *East.*
    Capitalize North, South, East, and West when they designate an area.
15. (2) The Ridgedale Garden *Club* developed a hybrid rose and named it Everlasting Beauty.
    Capitalize the entire name of a club.
16. (1) Including *Caucasians,* Blacks and Orientals, the population of Winfield, Pennsylvania has
    grown to one and a half million.
    Capitalize the name of a race.

Practice II *Page 188.*

1. (1) Each year our community celebrates the Fourth *of* July with races, entertainment, and fire-
    works.
2. (1) Last year we celebrated that *holiday* on a Monday.
3. (2) Andy joined the *Travel-American Club* and enjoyed a six-week tour with the group.
4. (2) At Ohio State *University,* students take courses year round.
5. (2) *When* did you say that Bud had called me?
6. (4) The poem reads:
    Up the airy mountain
    Down the rushy glen . . .
7. (2) My friend, Fred, was elected *president* of the Rescue Squad.
8. (3) "Don't do that!" said Jack. *"You'll* ruin the machine!"
9. (5) No error.
10. (1) It was two years ago that *Judge* Billings was appointed to the bench.

18.

Spelling

"The other people that was involved in the Lincoln assination later exequded or killed themselves. Mary Tood Lincoln locked herself up in a closet and went crazy. She was declared mentally insane and put in a insane silome.

One day a long time later a man walked into Lincoln's office and found his son, Robert Tood, burning some of his daddy's old pappers. The man asked him why he was burning the pappers and Robert Tood said, 'Maybe they will criminate one of the members of the goverment,' which his daddy was in."

—Bill Lawrence, Editor
Then Some Other Stuff Happened

A Word With You . . .

It isn't easy to become a good speller; in fact, many people never master the art. The high school student whose work is quoted above proves our point.

One famous English writer, George Bernard Shaw, was critical of our many spelling rules and the strange appearance of many of our words. He invested a goodly sum of money in a campaign to reform certain spelling practices. Shaw, however, was an excellent speller, regardless of his complaints.

There is no magic formula for learning how to spell. The ability to spell correctly results from persistent study. Here are some useful suggestions for studying spelling:

1. Use a small notebook exclusively for recording your personal spelling problem words.
2. Each time that you discover a problem word, enter it in

your notebook. Check a dictionary for the correct syl-labification and pronunciation.

3. Look at the word and say it in syllables.
4. Try to apply a rule which will help you to understand *why* the word is spelled as it is.
5. Close your eyes and picture the way the word looks.
6. Write the word. Check it. Rewrite it if necessary.
7. Review words you have already studied until you are absolutely sure that you know how to spell them.

There are many commonly misspelled words. Careful study of the list beginning on page 212 of this chapter will improve your spelling. There are also a number of hints and rules which are helpful in learning to spell.

Building Blocks of Words: Consonants, Vowels, Syllables

Of the twenty-six letters in the alphabet, twenty-one letters are consonants: b, c, d, f, g, h, j, k, l, m, n, p, q, r, s, t, v, w, x, y, z. The other five letters of the alphabet are vowels: a, e, i, o, u. Sometimes the consonant y is used as a vowel. When a consonant or consonants are combined with at least one vowel, a word or syllable results.

Example: let

A syllable is a word or part of a word pronounced with a single uninterrupted sound.

Nonsense syllable: ki

Meaningful syllable: sat

Learning to spell a long word is a much easier task if you divide the word into syllables.

Example: complacency = com • pla • cen • cy

You can learn to spell each syllable and, finally, put the word together.

Adding to Words

Many words are formed by adding to the root (basic part) of the word. Prefixes are added to the beginning of a word, while suffixes are added to the end of a word. *For example:*

prefix	root	suffix
*dis*quiet	quiet	quiet*ly*

Rule 1: In most cases, a prefix can be added to a word without changing the spelling of that word. *For example:*

PREFIX	(MEANING)	WORD	COMBINATION
il	(not)	literate =	illiterate
ir	(not)	regular =	irregular

PRACTICE

I **Directions:** Add the correct prefix from the list below to each of the following words.

ac-	il-	in-	mis-	over-	mal-
dis-	ir-	un-	re-	im-	co-

1. _____ instate
2. _____ illusion
3. _____ necessary
4. _____ operate
5. _____ mortal
6. _____ spell
7. _____ reverent
8. _____ legal
9. _____ climate
10. _____ rate
11. _____ content
12. _____ accurate

Rule 2: When adding a suffix which begins with a consonant, the spelling of most words does not change. For example:

WORD	SUFFIX		
careless	ness	=	carelessness
active	ly	=	actively

Exceptions:	true	ly	=	truly
	due	ly	=	duly

Rule 3: Suffixes do change the spelling of words which end in *y. For example:*

WORD	SUFFIX		
happy	ness	=	happiness
hearty	ly	=	heartily

Rule 4: When adding a suffix which begins with a vowel to a word which ends in *e*, drop the final *e. For example:*

WORD	SUFFIX		
fame	ous	=	famous
continue	ous	=	continuous

Exceptions: Words which end in *-ge* or *-ce* must retain the final *e* to maintain the soft sound of the *g* or *c*. *For example:*

WORD	SUFFIX		
courage	ous	=	courageous
notice	able	=	noticeable

Another exception is the word *dye.*

dye	ing	=	dyeing

PRACTICE II

Directions: Opposite each word below is a suffix which, when combined with the word, forms a new word. In the space provided, write the new word making sure to spell it correctly.

	WORD	SUFFIX	
1.	announce	ment	= _____
2.	dye	ing	= _____
3.	snappy	ness	= _____
4.	associate	ion	= _____
5.	dispense	able	= _____
6.	definite	ly	= _____
7.	economic	al	= _____
8.	courage	ous	= _____
9.	move	able	= _____
10.	necessary	ly	= _____
11.	practical	ly	= _____
12.	port	able	= _____
13.	rude	ness	= _____
14.	guide	ance	= _____
15.	true	ly	= _____

PRACTICE III

Directions: Blacken the space beneath the number which corresponds to the number of the incorrectly spelled word in each group. If there is no error, blacken space number 5.

1 2 3 4 5
‖ ‖ ‖ ‖ ‖

1. 1) unimportant 2) revelation
    3) cumulative 4) irational 5) no error

		1	2	3	4	5
2.	1) brighter 2) happyness 3) unaccustomed 4) berate 5) no error	‖	‖	‖	‖	‖
3.	1) impossible 2) cooperation 3) inactive 4) mispell 5) no error	‖	‖	‖	‖	‖
4.	1) commencment 2) coverage 3) practically 4) extraction 5) no error	‖	‖	‖	‖	‖
5.	1) safty 2) forgiveness 3) shining 4) amusement 5) no error	‖	‖	‖	‖	‖
6.	1) becoming 2) truly 3) plainness 4) actually 5) no error	‖	‖	‖	‖	‖
7.	1) adorable 2) contagious 3) acumulate 4) supervise 5) no error	‖	‖	‖	‖	‖
8.	1) loneliness 2) personal 3) barely 4) noticable 5) no error	‖	‖	‖	‖	‖
9.	1) continuation 2) arguement 3) ridiculous 4) usage 5) no error	‖	‖	‖	‖	‖
10.	1) surprised 2) acquisitiveness 3) carefully 4) virtuous 5) no error	‖	‖	‖	‖	‖

The Role of Accent Marks

A word that contains more than one syllable has an accent on one of those syllables. Say this word in syllables: punc • tu • ate. Which syllable is stressed? Yes, the first syllable is stressed or accented, and its accent is marked in this way:

punc′ • tu • ate

PRACTICE

IV Directions: The following words have been divided into syllables. In each word, place an accent mark to show which syllable is stressed. The first word is done for you.

1. paint′ • er
2. pri • vate
3. of • fice
4. e • con • o • my
5. ad • vise
6. bal • ance
7. dis • sat • is • fy
8. de • vel • op • ment
9. in • di • vid • u • al
10. pre • fer
11. pref • er • ence
12. psy • chol • o • gy
13. vac • il • late
14. u • nan • i • mous
15. wretch • ed

Rule 5: When changing the form of a one-syllable action word which ends in a consonant preceded by a vowel, double the final consonant. *For example:*

plan	planned
sun	sunning
run	runner

Rule 6: Double the final consonant when changing the form of a two-syllable word which ends in a consonant preceded by a vowel *and* which is accented on the second syllable. *For example:*

re<u>fer</u>	re<u>fer</u>red
oc<u>cur</u>	oc<u>cur</u>red
oc<u>cur</u>	oc<u>cur</u>rence

Rule 7: In a two or three syllable word, if the accent changes from the final syllable to a preceding one when a suffix is added (prefer, preference), do not double the final consonant. *For example:*

re<u>fer</u>	reference
con<u>fer</u>	conference

PRACTICE V

Directions: Blacken the space beneath the number which corresponds to the number of the incorrectly spelled word in each group. If there is no error, blacken space number 5.

```
                                          1  2  3  4  5
```

1. 1) referred 2) preferrence 3) stunning   ‖ ‖ ‖ ‖ ‖
    4) winding 5) no error

2. 1) thinner 2) conferred 3) reference   ‖ ‖ ‖ ‖ ‖
    4) detered 5) no error

3. 1) binder 2) funnier 3) pictured   ‖ ‖ ‖ ‖ ‖
    4) reared 5) no error
                                              ‖ ‖ ‖ ‖ ‖
4. 1) cunning 2) preferable 3) deterent
    4) banning 5) no error

5. 1) preferred 2) canning 3) fanned   ‖ ‖ ‖ ‖ ‖
    4) occurence 5) no error

Rule 8: Use *i* before *e* except after *c,* e.g., relief, receipt. Exception: Use *e* before *i* in words which sound like ā, e.g., neighbor, weigh.

Other exceptions: weird, seize, either, leisure, neither.

PRACTICE VI

Directions: Complete the following words with *ei* or *ie.*

1. n____ce
2. dec____ve
3. th____f
4. rel____ve
5. n____gh

6. rec____ve
7. conc____ve
8. bel____f
9. n____ther
10. s____ze

Rule 9: There are rules for forming the plurals of words. Following are the rules and a few examples of each.

A Most words form plurals by adding *s.*

radio	radios
towel	towels
chair	chairs
tray	trays

B Words ending in *y* preceded by a consonant form plurals by changing *y* to *i* and adding *es.*

sky	skies
story	stories

C Words ending in *o* preceded by a consonant form plurals by adding *es.*

tomato	tomatoes
hero	heroes

Exception: words ending in o, preceded by a consonant, but referring to music, form their plurals by adding only *s.*

alto	altos
piano	pianos

D Words ending in *s, sh, ch,* and *x* form plurals by adding *es.*

bunch	bunches
sex	sexes
boss	bosses
crush	crushes

E A compound word forms its plural by adding *s* to the principal word.

fathers-in-law

baby*sitters*

F Words ending in *-ful* form their plurals by adding *s.*

mouthfuls

cupfuls

G Some words have one spelling for singular and plural.

deer

trout

Chinese

sheep

H Numbers and letters form plurals by adding *'s.*

5's   h's

I Some words form their plurals by irregular changes.

thief	thieves
knife	knives
leaf	leaves
woman	women
child	children
tooth	teeth
louse	lice
crisis	crises
alumnus	alumni
datum	data
appendix	appendices

PRACTICE VII

Directions: Blacken the space beneath the number which corresponds to the number of the incorrectly spelled word in each group. If there is no error, blacken space number 5.

1 2 3 4 5

1. 1) geese 2) mouthsful
3) commanders-in-chief 4) firemen
5) no error
‖ ‖ ‖ ‖ ‖

2. 1) Chinese's 2) bases 3) workmen
4) P's 5) no error
‖ ‖ ‖ ‖ ‖

3. 1) bacilli 2) son-in-laws 3) series
4) handkerchiefs 5) no error
‖ ‖ ‖ ‖ ‖

4. 1) women 2) alumni 3) passersby
4) mice 5) no error
‖ ‖ ‖ ‖ ‖

5. 1) 8s 2) Frenchmen 3) alumni
4) men-of-war 5) no error
‖ ‖ ‖ ‖ ‖

Rule 10:

Following are rules regarding *sede, ceed,* and *cede.*

A Only one word is spelled with an *sede* ending:

supersede

B Only three words are spelled with a *ceed* ending:

succeed   exceed   proceed

C All other words of this type are spelled with a *cede* ending. *For example:*

precede   recede   concede

Spelling Review

PRACTICE VIII

Directions: Blacken the space beneath the number which corresponds to the number of the incorrectly spelled word in each group. If there is no error, blacken space number 5.

1 2 3 4 5

1. 1) acknowledge 2) fireman
3) conclusivly 4) commodity 5) no error
‖ ‖ ‖ ‖ ‖

2.   1) incurred   2) coranation   3) voluntary
      4) herald   5) no error

3.   1) simular   2) bulletin   3) bored
      4) quizzes   5) no error

4.   1) duchess   2) achevement   3) monarchial
      4) fertile   5) no error

5.   1) distribute   2) sieze   3) premises
      4) tonnage   5) no error

6.   1) monthly   2) primarily   3) condemned
      4) dupped   5) no error

7.   1) cancellation   2) derrick   3) pertinant
      4) utilize   5) no error

8.   1) nowadays   2) courtesies   3) negotiate
      4) guardian   5) no error

9.   1) loot   2) faculties   3) loveable   4) axle
      5) no error

10.   1) fragrance   2) accompanied
      3) preference   4) athletic   5) no error

PRACTICE
IX

Directions: Blacken the space beneath the number which corresponds to the number of the incorrectly spelled word in each group. If there is no error, blacken space number 5.

	1	2	3	4	5

1.   1) liquify   2) disappear   3) swirling
      4) dissolve   5) no error

2.   1) inexorable   2) mercyful   3) potable
      4) arboreal   5) no error

3.   1) disolution   2) agreeable   3) planned
      4) diseases   5) no error

4.   1) minimize   2) sophomore   3) attorneys
      4) candidacy   5) no error

5.   1) unnecessary   2) carnage   3) wierd
      4) judgment   5) no error

		1	2	3	4	5
6.	1) roses 2) goverment 3) absence 4) churches 5) no error	‖	‖	‖	‖	‖
7.	1) emergency 2) eager 3) cordialy 4) citizen 5) no error	‖	‖	‖	‖	‖
8.	1) benefit 2) boxes 3) consequence 4) peice 5) no error	‖	‖	‖	‖	‖
9.	1) journey 2) majority 3) necessarily 4) relief 5) no error	‖	‖	‖	‖	‖
10.	1) yacht 2) traveler 3) profession 4) principle 5) no error	‖	‖	‖	‖	‖

**PRACTICE
X**

Directions: Blacken the space beneath the number which corresponds to the number of the incorrectly spelled word in each group. If there is no error, blacken space number 5.

		1	2	3	4	5
1.	1) overrate 2) misapprehend 3) habitualy 4) greenness 5) no error	‖	‖	‖	‖	‖
2.	1) deferred 2) hoping 3) approval 4) defference 5) no error	‖	‖	‖	‖	‖
3.	1) candys 2) valleys 3) torches 4) files 5) no error	‖	‖	‖	‖	‖
4.	1) immaterial 2) dissapoint 3) practically 4) unabated 5) no error	‖	‖	‖	‖	‖
5.	1) potatos 2) teeth 3) radios 4) sopranos 5) no error	‖	‖	‖	‖	‖
6.	1) preparing 2) writing 3) propeling 4) controlled 5) no error	‖	‖	‖	‖	‖
7.	1) crises 2) geese 3) concertos 4) trucksful 5) no error	‖	‖	‖	‖	‖
8.	1) truely 2) moving 3) running 4) famous 5) no error	‖	‖	‖	‖	‖
9.	1) shelves 2) benches 3) knives 4) churches 5) no error	‖	‖	‖	‖	‖
10.	1) salarys 2) basketfuls 3) reddest 4) nameless 5) no error	‖	‖	‖	‖	‖

		1	2	3	4	5
11.	1) disagree 2) benefited 3) gases 4) casually 5) no error	‖	‖	‖	‖	‖
12.	1) oxen 2) desirable 3) data 4) solves 5) no error	‖	‖	‖	‖	‖

PRACTICE XI

Directions: Blacken the space beneath the number which corresponds to the number of the incorrectly spelled word in each group. If there is no error, blacken space number 5.

		1	2	3	4	5
1.	1) belief 2) achieve 3) neice 4) weigh 5) no error	‖	‖	‖	‖	‖
2.	1) yield 2) neighbor 3) deceive 4) releif 5) no error	‖	‖	‖	‖	‖
3.	1) benefited 2) appealed 3) refered 4) equipped 5) no error	‖	‖	‖	‖	‖
4.	1) preference 2) reference 3) asessment 4) colonel 5) no error	‖	‖	‖	‖	‖
5.	1) stationery 2) stationary 3) sophomore 4) similar 5) no error	‖	‖	‖	‖	‖
6.	1) primarily 2) principal 3) principle 4) receit 5) no error	‖	‖	‖	‖	‖
7.	1) aquired 2) brief 3) contemptible 4) height 5) no error	‖	‖	‖	‖	‖
8.	1) erred 2) millionaire 3) misanthrope 4) lieutenent 5) no error	‖	‖	‖	‖	‖
9.	1) adjournament 2) caucus 3) contagious 4) digestible 5) no error	‖	‖	‖	‖	‖
10.	1) cheff 2) calendar 3) macaroni 4) preceding 5) no error	‖	‖	‖	‖	‖

PRACTICE XII

Directions: Blacken the space beneath the number which corresponds to the number of the incorrectly spelled word in each group. If there is no error, blacken space number 5.

		1	2	3	4	5
1.	1) changeable 2) atheletic 3) grammar 4) fortissimo 5) no error	‖	‖	‖	‖	‖

		1	2	3	4	5
2.	1) filial 2) leisure 3) temperture 4) treachery 5) no error	‖	‖	‖	⧧	‖
3.	1) bulletin 2) amendment 3) incessent 4) kindergarten 5) no error	‖	‖	‖	‖	‖
4.	1) legitiment 2) vivisection 3) pervade 4) courtesies 5) no error	‖	‖	‖	‖	‖
5.	1) prefer 2) preferred 3) preference 4) patrolled 5) no error	‖	‖	‖	‖	‖
6.	1) ninth 2) correspondent 3) canon 4) hideous 5) no error	‖	‖	‖	‖	‖
7.	1) apparently 2) foreign 3) carriage 4) forfeit 5) no error	‖	‖	‖	‖	‖
8.	1) aggregate 2) massacre 3) omissions 4) tetnus 5) no error	‖	‖	‖	‖	‖
9.	1) exceed 2) intercede 3) proceed 4) procedure 5) no error	‖	‖	‖	‖	‖
10.	1) fundimental 2) misspell 3) odyssey 4) penitentiary 5) no error	‖	‖	‖	‖	‖

PRACTICE XIII

Directions: Blacken the space beneath the number which corresponds to the number of the incorrectly spelled word in each group. If there is no error, blacken space number 5.

		1	2	3	4	5
1.	1) torches 2) salaries 3) valleys 4) shelves 5) no error	‖	‖	‖	‖	‖
2.	1) absense 2) gases 3) accident 4) citizen 5) no error	‖	‖	‖	‖	‖
3.	1) executive 2) divide 3) discusion 4) eager 5) no error	‖	‖	‖	‖	‖
4.	1) contrary 2) atheletic 3) critical 4) banquet 5) no error	‖	‖	‖	‖	‖
5.	1) association 2) character 3) earliest 4) decide 5) no error	‖	‖	‖	‖	‖
6.	1) Wenesday 2) knives 3) concerning 4) executive 5) no error	‖	‖	‖	‖	‖

		1	2	3	4	5
7.	1) appreciate 2) except 3) scene 4) numerous 5) no error	‖	‖	‖	‖	‖
8.	1) national 2) posession 3) industrious 4) volume 5) no error	‖	‖	‖	‖	‖
9.	1) patient 2) quantity 3) boundary 4) probably 5) no error	‖	‖	‖	‖	‖
10.	1) warrant 2) laboratory 3) interesting 4) libary 5) no error	‖	‖	‖	‖	‖

PRACTICE XIV

Directions: Blacken the space beneath the number which corresponds to the number of the incorrectly spelled word in each group. If there is no error, blacken space number 5.

		1	2	3	4	5
1.	1) biased 2) aberation 3) wholly 4) vacuum 5) no error	‖	‖	‖	‖	‖
2.	1) capitol 2) ecstasy 3) embarrass 4) essential 5) no error	‖	‖	‖	‖	‖
3.	1) asertain 2) correlation 3) abeyance 4) diocese 5) no error	‖	‖	‖	‖	‖
4.	1) ninth 2) resileince 3) nickel 4) official 5) no error	‖	‖	‖	‖	‖
5.	1) salable 2) ordinance 3) illegitimate 4) policy 5) no error	‖	‖	‖	‖	‖
6.	1) subversive 2) predatory 3) lucritive 4) prairie 5) no error	‖	‖	‖	‖	‖
7.	1) pacifist 2) senior 3) source 4) surfiet 5) no error	‖	‖	‖	‖	‖
8.	1) weild 2) vacillate 3) vengeance 4) transaction 5) no error	‖	‖	‖	‖	‖
9.	1) queue 2) masquerade 3) loose 4) marital 5) no error	‖	‖	‖	‖	‖
10.	1) psicology 2) possession 3) imminent 4) impeccable 5) no error	‖	‖	‖	‖	‖

PRACTICE

XV   Directions: Blacken the space beneath the number which corresponds to the number of the incorrectly spelled word in each group. If there is no error, blacken space number 5.

		1	2	3	4	5
1.	1) derogatory 2) neglagible 3) rehearsal 4) yacht 5) no error	‖	‖	‖	‖	‖
2.	1) queue 2) jeopardy 3) forfiet 4) gelatin 5) no error	‖	‖	‖	‖	‖
3.	1) bureau 2) blamable 3) desecration 4) harass 5) no error	‖	‖	‖	‖	‖
4.	1) falibility 2) heinous 3) myriad 4) remnant 5) no error	‖	‖	‖	‖	‖
5.	1) hygienic 2) medallion 3) midget 4) prommisory 5) no error	‖	‖	‖	‖	‖
6.	1) complacency 2) efemeral 3) exaggerate 4) realize 5) no error	‖	‖	‖	‖	‖
7.	1) lacquer 2) currency 3) exortation 4) emolument 5) no error	‖	‖	‖	‖	‖
8.	1) apologetic 2) coroner 3) clique 4) exzema 5) no error	‖	‖	‖	‖	‖
9.	1) disatisfied 2) moribund 3) warrant 4) surgeon 5) no error	‖	‖	‖	‖	‖
10.	1) defered 2) extraordinary 3) journal 4) intercede 5) no error	‖	‖	‖	‖	‖

PRACTICE

XVI   Directions: Blacken the space beneath the number which corresponds to the number of the incorrectly spelled word in each group. If there is no error, blacken space number 5.

		1	2	3	4	5
1.	1) responsibility 2) resonence 3) rheostat 4) rhetoric 5) no error	‖	‖	‖	‖	‖
2.	1) salient 2) patronize 3) pateint 4) parliament 5) no error	‖	‖	‖	‖	‖
3.	1) secretery 2) piquancy 3) integrity 4) innocuous 5) no error	‖	‖	‖	‖	‖

		1	2	3	4	5
4.	1) diphtheria 2) distinguised 3) category 4) cemetery 5) no error	‖	‖	‖	‖	‖
5.	1) abscess 2) chamois 3) effects 4) ingenuous 5) no error	‖	‖	‖	‖	‖
6.	1) accessible 2) chauffur 3) elaborate 4) inimitable 5) no error	‖	‖	‖	‖	‖
7.	1) impromptu 2) incongruity 3) permissable 4) precede 5) no error	‖	‖	‖	‖	‖
8.	1) tremendous 2) punctilious 3) recognizible 4) tariff 5) no error	‖	‖	‖	‖	‖
9.	1) reasonable 2) mischivous 3) picnicking 4) repetitious 5) no error	‖	‖	‖	‖	‖
10.	1) sobriquet 2) soveriegn 3) staunch 4) stretch 5) no error	‖	‖	‖	‖	‖

PRACTICE XVII

Directions: Blacken the space beneath the number which corresponds to the number of the incorrectly spelled word in each group. If there is no error, blacken space number 5.

		1	2	3	4	5
1.	1) addressee 2) carburator 3) intercede 4) murmuring 5) no error	‖	‖	‖	‖	‖
2.	1) biscut 2) financier 3) previous 4) preceding 5) no error	‖	‖	‖	‖	‖
3.	1) hearth 2) bounteous 3) judgment 4) heritage 5) no error	‖	‖	‖	‖	‖
4.	1) aversion 2) aquatic 3) facilitation 4) bookkeeping 5) no error	‖	‖	‖	‖	‖
5.	1) dilapidated 2) function 3) relevent 4) regrettable 5) no error	‖	‖	‖	‖	‖
6.	1) dearth 2) deceive 3) proceed 4) wethar 5) no error	‖	‖	‖	‖	‖
7.	1) excede 2) feudal 3) grandeur 4) vacuum 5) no error	‖	‖	‖	‖	‖
8.	1) realize 2) foriegn 3) nevertheless 4) matinee 5) no error	‖	‖	‖	‖	‖

		1	2	3	4	5
9.	1) criticism 2) plagiarism 3) equiped 4) preferably 5) no error	‖	‖	‖	‖	‖
10.	1) beatitude 2) corruggated 3) existence 4) succeed 5) no error	‖	‖	‖	‖	‖

PRACTICE XVIII

Directions: Blacken the space beneath the number which corresponds to the number of the incorrectly spelled word in each group. If there is no error, blacken space number 5.

		1	2	3	4	5
1.	1) angle 2) conciliatory 3) exersise 4) compel 5) no error	‖	‖	‖	‖	‖
2.	1) description 2) hindrence 3) memoir 4) publicity 5) no error	‖	‖	‖	‖	‖
3.	1) belligerent 2) dearth 3) equator 4) decieve 5) no error	‖	‖	‖	‖	‖
4.	1) bankruptcy 2) deliberate 3) histrionic 4) demurrer 5) no error	‖	‖	‖	‖	‖
5.	1) crystallized 2) mackeral 3) maintenance 4) masquerade 5) no error	‖	‖	‖	‖	‖
6.	1) sandwich 2) peculiar 3) neumonia 4) scissors 5) no error	‖	‖	‖	‖	‖
7.	1) temperment 2) summarize 3) scripture 4) occur 5) no error	‖	‖	‖	‖	‖
8.	1) abundence 2) citation 3) clamorous 4) colossal 5) no error	‖	‖	‖	‖	‖
9.	1) acumulation 2) circumstantial 3) adoption 4) adage 5) no error	‖	‖	‖	‖	‖
10.	1) apparatus 2) anceint 3) amplify 4) allege 5) no error	‖	‖	‖	‖	‖

PRACTICE XIX

Directions: Blacken the space beneath the number which corresponds to the number of the incorrectly spelled word in each group. If there is no error, blacken space number 5.

		1	2	3	4	5
1.	1) consumation 2) anemia 3) corporal 4) emphasis 5) no error	‖	‖	‖	‖	‖

		1	2	3	4	5
2.	1) crucial 2) disappearance 3) eminently 4) asessment 5) no error	‖	‖	‖	‖	‖
3.	1) impartiality 2) impecable 3) indictment 4) scissors 5) no error	‖	‖	‖	‖	‖
4.	1) maneuver 2) preparation 3) fasinated 4) presumptuous 5) no error	‖	‖	‖	‖	‖
5.	1) rythm 2) pamphlet 3) panicky 4) interruption 5) no error	‖	‖	‖	‖	‖
6.	1) controler 2) labyrinth 3) judiciary 4) scripture 5) no error	‖	‖	‖	‖	‖
7.	1) similar 2) mediocrity 3) emphatically 4) column 5) no error	‖	‖	‖	‖	‖
8.	1) commandant 2) aquaint 3) across 4) commemorate 5) no error	‖	‖	‖	‖	‖
9.	1) demurring 2) detrimental 3) conversent 4) laboratory 5) no error	‖	‖	‖	‖	‖
10.	1) liquidate 2) matinee 3) mecanical 4) medieval 5) no error	‖	‖	‖	‖	‖

PRACTICE
XX   **Directions:** Blacken the space beneath the number which corresponds to the number of the incorrectly spelled word in each group. If there is no error, blacken space number 5.

		1	2	3	4	5
1.	1) wholly 2) thorough 3) symetrical 4) adjunct 5) no error	‖	‖	‖	‖	‖
2.	1) arouse 2) superceed 3) actually 4) proceed 5) no error	‖	‖	‖	‖	‖
3.	1) accede 2) succeed 3) appellate 4) arraignment 5) no error	‖	‖	‖	‖	‖
4.	1) adjunct 2) advise 3) preceed 4) amendment 5) no error	‖	‖	‖	‖	‖
5.	1) anoyance 2) antipathy 3) biased 4) actually 5) no error	‖	‖	‖	‖	‖

Commonly Misspelled Words

Give special review to all those words which have given you trouble. Do not try to learn more than 10 new words at one time.

abandoned	allege	attendants	candle
aberration	allies	attorneys	cannon
abeyance	all right	authentic	canon
abscess	ambassador	aversion	capital
absence	amendment	awkward	capitol
absurd	amplify	axle	(a building)
abundance	ancient		carburetor
abutting	anecdote	baccalaureate	carnage
academy	anemia	bachelor	carriage
accent	angle	bacteria	category
accede	annoyance	balance	caucus
accessible	annum	banana	cauldron
acclimate	anticipate	bankruptcy	cavalier
accommodate	antipathy	barely	cavalry
accumulation	antique	beaker	cease
accusation	apologetic	beatitude	ceiling
achievement	apparatus	beleaguered	cemetery
acknowledge	apparently	belligerent	certain
acquaint	appellate	benefit	certified
acquired	appetite	biased	chagrined
acquisition	appreciation	bigamy	chamois
across	appropriation	bimonthly	chancellor
actually	apricot	biscuit	changeable
acutely	aquatic	blamable	character
adage	architecture	blight	charitable
addressee	arduous	bookkeeping	chauffeur
adequate	arguing	border	chef
adieu	arouse	bored	chisel
adjournment	arraignment	bounteous	Christian
adjunct	arrest	breeding	circumstantial
adopted	article	brief	citation
adoption	artificial	bulletin	clamorous
advise	ascertain	bungalow	classified
advisable	aspirations	bureau	clique
advising	assassination	burglaries	clothe
affirmative	assessment	business	colonel
aggravate	assigned		colossal
aggregate	association	cafeteria	column
agitation	assurance	calendar	comedian
agreeable	athletic	cameos	commandant
agreement	attach	campaign	commemorate
aisle	attempt	cancel	commenced
alcohol	attendance	candidacy	

committal
committing
community
comparative
compel
competition
competitors
complacency
conciliatory
conclusively
condemned
confectionery
congenial
congestion
conjunction
connoisseur
conquer
conscript
consequently
conservatory
consistent
consummation
contagious
contemptible
continually
control
controller
convenient
conversant
cooperate
coronation
coroner
corporal
corral
 (an enclosure)
correlation
correspondence
correspondent
corrugated
corset
countenance
courtesies
criticism
crochet
cronies
crowded
crucial
crystallized
currency

death
deceive
decision
declaration
deferred
definite
delegate
deliberate
delicious
delinquent
democrat
demurrage
denunciatory
deodorize
derogatory
description
desecration
desert
desirable
despair
dessert (food)
destruction
detrimental
development
digestible
dilapidated
dining room
diocese
diphtheria
dirigible
disappear
disappearance
disapprove
discipline
discretion
diseases
disgust
dispatch
dispensable
dissatisfied
dissatisfy
dissolution
distillery
distinguished
distributor
dizzy
doctor
dormitory
drastically

dual
duchess
duly
dungarees
duped
dyeing

economical
economy
ecstasy
eczema
effects
efficient
elaborate
electrolysis
embarrass
embassies
emergency
eminently
emolument
emphasis
emphasize
emphatically
endurance
enlargement
enormous
enthusiastic
ephemeral
equilibrium
equinoctial
equipped
error
essential
everlasting
exaggerate
exceed
excel
exercise
exhibition
exhortation
existence
extradite
extraordinary
extravagant

facilitation
faculties
fallibility

falsify
falsity
fascinated
fatal
feudal
filial
finally
financial
financier
finely
fireman
flexible
foggy
foliage
forcible
foreign
foretell
forfeit
fortissimo
forty
fragrance
fraternally
freshman
frightfully
frostbitten
function
fundamental
furl

gallery
galvanized
gelatin
glimpse
guaranteed
guardian
gout
government
grammar
grandeur
grapevines
grease
grieve
guidance
guild
guitar

handicapped
harass
hearth

height
heinous
hence
herald
heritage
hideous
hindrance
histrionic
holly
hosiery
humorists
hybrid
hygienic
hysterics

idiomatic
ignoramus
ignorant
illegitimate
illuminate
illustrative
imminent
impartiality
impeccable
impromptu
incongruity
indecent
indictment
individual
ingenuity
ingenuous
inimitable
innocent
innocuous
insulation
insurance
integrity
intelligence
intercede
interruption
irreparably
itemized

jealous
jeopardy
journal
jovial
judgment

judiciary
jurisdiction

kindergarten
kinsman

label
laboratory
labyrinth
laceration
lacquer
ladies
larceny
latter
leased
legend
leggings
legitimate
leisure
libel
lieutenant
ligament
lightning
likeness
likewise
liquidate
literally
logical
loose
loot
lose
losing
lovable
loveliness
loyalty
lucrative
luxury
lynch

macaroni
mackerel
magnificent
maintain
maintenance
malice
maneuver
mania
manual
marital

marmalade
masquerade
massacre
matinee
matrimony
mattress
maturity
mayonnaise
mechanical
medal
medallion
medicine
medieval
mediocrity
melancholy
memoir
mercantile
mercury
merely
midget
midriff
military
millinery
millionaire
misanthrope
mischievous
misdemeanor
mislaid
misspell
misstep
monarchical
monkeys
morale
moribund
mortgage
movable
murmuring
muscle
museum
myriad

necessity
negligible
negotiate
nervous
nevertheless
nickel
niece
ninety

ninth
notary
notoriety
nowadays
nuisance

obedient
obliged
obstacles
occasionally
occur
occurrence
odyssey
official
omissions
omitted
operated
opportunity
option
ordinance
overwhelming

pacifist
pageant
pamphlet
panel
panicky
papal
parachute
paradoxical
parasite
parliament
parole
partisan
partner
patient
patronize
pattern
peculiar
penitentiary
people's
perilous
perjury
permanent
permissible
persevere
pervade
phrenologist
physical

physician
picnicking
piquancy
pitiful
plagiarism
plague
planned
playwright
pneumonia
policy
politician
portable
portend
portiere
possession
possibilities
post office
postpone
potato
poultry
prairie
preceding
precious
predatory
predilection
preferably
preference
premises
preparation
prestige
presume
presumptuous
previous
primarily
primitive
principal
principalship
prisoner
privilege
probably
proffer
profit
proletarian
promissory
promptness
propaganda
proprietor
psychology
publicity

publicly
punctilious

quantities
quartet
questionnaire
queue
quinine

rabid
raisin
realize
reasonable
receipted
receipts
receptacle
recognizable
recommend
recompense
reconcile
recruit
refrigerator
regrettable
regretted
rehearsal
relevant
relieve
religious
remodel
renaissance
renascence
repetitious
requisition
reservoir
resilience
resonance
resources
response
responsibility
responsible
restaurant
rheostat
rhetorical
rheumatism
rhubarb
rhythm
rickety
ridiculous
righteous

roommate
routine

Sabbath
sacrilegious
salable
salaries
salient
sandwiches
Saturn
saucy
scenes
scissors
screech
scripture
scrutiny
secretary
seize
senior
serenity
series
session
sieges
significant
silhouette
similar
sincerely
sitting
sobriquet
society
solemn
soliciting
sophomore
soporific
source
sovereign
specialized
specific
specifically
speech
spiritualist
squalor
squirrels
staid
staunch
standard
stationary (fixed)
statistics
statutes

steak
strengthen
strenuous
stretch
studying
subsidy
suburb
subversive
succeed
successor
suffrage
summarize
superb
surfeit
surgeon
symmetrical
sympathy
systematic

tableaux
  (or tableaus)
taciturn
talcum
tantalizing
tariff
taunt
technical
temperament
temperature
temporarily
tenet
tennis
terse
tetanus
thermometer
thesis
thorough
thought
together
tournament
tragedy
traitor
transaction
transient
transparent
treachery
tremendous
triumph
troupe (theatrical)

truce
tuition
turkeys
twelfth
twins
typewriting
typhoid
tyranny

unanimous
unauthorized
unbearable
unconscious
undecided
undoubtedly
undulate

unfortunately
uniform
unify
universe
unnecessary
utilize

vacancy
vacillate
vacuum
vague
valuing
vegetable
velvet
vengeance

verbal
villain
visible
vivisection
voluntary
voucher

warrant
warranted
weather
Wednesday
weird
welfare
we're
whether

wholly
width
wield
wiring
witnesses
woman's
women's
worlds
wrapped
wretched

yacht
yoke

zephyr

ANSWER KEY

Chapter 18

Spelling

Practice I *Page 196.*

1. reinstate
2. disillusion
3. unnecessary
4. cooperate
5. immortal
6. misspell
7. irreverent
8. illegal
9. acclimate
10. overrate
11. malcontent
12. inaccurate

Practice II *Page 197.*

1. announcement
2. dyeing
3. snappiness
4. association
5. dispensable
6. definitely
7. economical
8. courageous
9. movable
10. necessarily
11. practically
12. portable
13. rudeness
14. guidance
15. truly

Practice III *Page 197.*

1. (4) irrational
2. (2) happiness
3. (4) misspell
4. (1) commencement
5. (1) safety
6. (5) No error
7. (3) accumulate
8. (4) noticeable
9. (2) argument
10. (5) No error

Practice IV *Page 198.*

1. paint´. er
2. pri´. vate
3. of´. fice
4. e . con´. o . my
5. ad . vise´
6. bal´. ance
7. dis . sat´. is . fy
8. de . vel´. op . ment
9. in . di . vid´. u . al
10. pre . fer´
11. pref´. er . ence
12. psy . chol´. o . gy
13. vac´. il . late
14. u . nan´. i . mous
15. wretch´. ed

Practice V *Page 199.*

1. (2) preference
2. (4) deterred
3. (5) No error
4. (3) deterrent
5. (4) occurrence

Practice VI *Page 200.*

1. niece
2. deceive
3. thief
4. relieve
5. neigh
6. receive
7. conceive

8. belief
9. neither
10. seize

Practice VII *Page 202.*

1. (2) mouthfuls
2. (1) Chinese
3. (2) sons-in-law
4. (5) No error
5. (1) 8's

Practice VIII *Page 202.*

1. (3) conclusively
2. (2) coronation
3. (1) similar
4. (2) achievement
5. (2) seize
6. (4) duped
7. (3) pertinent
8. (5) No error
9. (3) lovable
10. (5) No error

Practice IX *Page 203.*

1. (5) No error
2. (2) merciful
3. (1) dissolution
4. (5) No error
5. (3) weird
6. (2) government
7. (3) cordially
8. (4) piece
9. (5) No error
10. (5) No error

Practice X *Page 204.*

1. (3) habitually
2. (4) deference
3. (1) candies
4. (2) disappoint
5. (1) potatoes
6. (3) propelling
7. (4) truckfuls
8. (1) truly
9. (5) No error
10. (1) salaries
11. (5) No error
12. (5) No error

Practice XI *Page 205.*

1. (3) niece
2. (4) relief
3. (3) referred
4. (3) assessment
5. (5) No error
6. (4) receipt
7. (1) acquired
8. (4) lieutenant
9. (1) adjournment
10. (1) chef

Practice XII *Page 205.*

1. (2) athletic
2. (3) temperature
3. (3) incessant
4. (1) legitimate
5. (5) No error
6. (5) No error
7. (5) No error
8. (4) tetanus
9. (5) No error
10. (1) fundamental

Practice XIII *Page 206.*

1. (5) No error
2. (1) absence
3. (3) discussion
4. (2) athletic
5. (5) No error
6. (1) Wednesday
7. (5) No error
8. (2) possession
9. (5) No error
10. (4) library

Practice XIV *Page 207.*

1. (2) aberration
2. (5) No error
3. (1) ascertain
4. (2) resilience
5. (5) No error
6. (3) lucrative
7. (4) surfeit
8. (1) wield
9. (5) No error
10. (1) psychology

Practice XV *Page 208.*

1. (2) negligible
2. (3) forfeit
3. (5) No error
4. (1) fallibility
5. (4) promissory
6. (2) ephemeral
7. (3) exhortation
8. (4) eczema
9. (1) dissatisfied
10. (1) deferred

Practice XVI *Page 208.*

1. (2) resonance
2. (3) patient
3. (1) secretary
4. (2) distinguished
5. (5) No error
6. (2) chauffeur
7. (3) permissible
8. (3) recognizable
9. (2) mischievous
10. (2) sovereign

Practice XVII *Page 209.*

1. (2) carburetor
2. (1) biscuit
3. (5) No error
4. (5) No error
5. (3) relevant
6. (4) weather
7. (1) exceed
8. (2) foreign
9. (3) equipped
10. (2) corrugated

Practice XVIII *Page 210.*

1. (3) exercise
2. (2) hindrance
3. (4) deceive
4. (5) No error
5. (2) mackerel
6. (3) pneumonia
7. (1) temperament
8. (1) abundance
9. (1) accumulation
10. (2) ancient

Practice XIX *Page 210.*

1. (1) consummation
2. (4) assessment
3. (2) impeccable
4. (3) fascinated
5. (1) rhythm
6. (1) controller
7. (5) No error
8. (2) acquaint
9. (3) conversant
10. (3) mechanical

Practice XX *Page 211.*

1. (3) symmetrical
2. (2) supersede
3. (5) No error
4. (3) precede
5. (1) annoyance

19.

Building Vocabulary

Costard: "O, they have liv'd long on the
                almsbasket of words. I marvel thy
                master hath not eaten thee for a word;
                for thou art not so long by the head
                as honorificabilitudinitatibus;
                thou art easier swallowed than a
                flapdragon."
                                    —William Shakespeare
                    from *Love's Labour's Lost, Act V, Scene 1*

A Word With You . . .

Costard, a clown in Shakespeare's comedy, uses one of the longest words in the English language (almost as long as *antidisestablishmentarianism*) in his conversation with Holofernes, the schoolmaster. Not only did Shakespeare know that 27-letter word, but he knew thousands upon thousands of other choice vocabulary words. Youngsters in his time were exposed to Latin and Greek in the schools and were able to develop a mastery of English words through their knowledge of prefixes, suffixes, and roots in those languages.

You may not catch up to Shakespeare, but you can get started in a modest way with the hints offered in this chapter.

Some Facts about Vocabulary:

We use words to think. A large and precise vocabulary leads to clear thinking.

The words we use "talk" about us. They create an impression of intelligence or dullness, success or failure.

The average person stops collecting new words early in life—probably during the twenties. Only by a conscious effort do we continue to add words to our vocabulary. This chapter will show you how to expand your vocabulary.

There are many ways to increase your vocabulary. If you are an avid reader, you've found the most natural way. But what if you're not? You can choose one or more of the following methods to help you. You may find that certain ways appeal to you more than others.

To increase your vocabulary, take advantage of what you like to do. When we like what we're doing, we learn faster. Building vocabulary may not be your idea of fun, but if you start with a topic you like, you might develop an interest.

Are you interested in history? Learn new words by studying their histories. Many English words include Latin, Greek, and other languages in their histories. One of our most frequently used words is an example of this. The word *television* came to English from the French: *télévision*. But television was not originally a French word. In fact, its journey through history includes both Latin and Greek.

tele from the Greek *tēle*, meaning at a distance, or far off

vision from the Latin *vīsiō*, meaning see

Put the two parts together and you have a good definition of what television is: pictures which were taken at a distance and which you can see. Let's see how this works with other common words.

PRACTICE

I **Directions:** Draw a line from the Latin and Greek word parts in the left-hand column to the English words in the right-hand column.

Note: In the dictionary, histories of words follow definitions and are placed in brackets.

LATIN AND GREEK WORD PARTS	ENGLISH WORDS
1. [Greek *teknē*, skill, art + *logos*, word speech]	video
2. [Latin *alere*, to nourish]	computer
3. [Latin *com*, together, jointly + Latin *dominium*, property]	alimony
4. [Latin *com*, together + Latin *putare*, to think, reckon]	technology
5. [Latin *videre*, to see]	condominium

PRACTICE

II **Directions:** Use your dictionary to discover the histories of the following words. Notice that a word may have gone through more than one language before it reached English. A word's most recent history is found at the beginning of the bracketed information. Its earliest history is at the end. Copy the earliest history.

1. compress _____

2. vindictive _____

3. pedicure _____

4. manicure _____

5. unique _____

Latin roots are found over and over again in English words. Once you know the meanings of these roots, you can unlock the meanings of many English words. The following are just a few examples:

COMMON LATIN ROOTS

bene	well
dicere	to say
facere	to do, to make
volens	wishing
unus	one, single
signum	sign
portare	to carry
manu	by hand

PRACTICE

III   **Directions:** Can you guess from which Latin root each of the following words was formed? Use the above list to make your decision.

1. united _____

2. factory _____

3. benefit _____

4. insignia _____

5. portable _____

6. dictation _____

7. volunteer _____

Sometimes two roots combine to make another word. *For example:*
bene + dicere = benediction = a blessing, or "saying well"
bene + facere = benefactor =   one who does something good for another
bene + volens = benevolent = wishing others well, kindly

Perhaps you're interested in building things. You can build words by learning how prefixes add to the meanings of roots.

PRACTICE

IV   **Directions:** Think about the meaning each prefix adds to these words. The prefixes are underlined. Answer the questions. If you are in doubt about the meanings, check your dictionary. Prefixes appear in this way: pre-

PREFIXES	MEANINGS.
<u>pre</u>date	1. Which prefixes make root words negative? _____
<u>im</u>possible	_____
<u>dis</u>organize	_____
<u>re</u>turn	2. Which prefix means "evil"?
<u>ex</u>tract	_____
<u>un</u>tie	3. Which prefix means "self"? _____
<u>mal</u>odorous	4. Which prefix means "back" or "again"? _____
<u>post</u>natal	_____
<u>a</u>moral	5. Which prefix means "after"? _____
<u>auto</u>mobile	6. Which prefix means "out"? _____
	7. Which prefix means "before"? _____

PRACTICE

V   **Directions:** Make new words by adding one of the above prefixes to each word below.

1. _____view
2. _____agree
3. _____biography
4. _____live
5. _____dress
6. _____theist

How would you like to enlarge your vocabulary and improve your writing skills—*at the same time?* You can accomplish both by increasing the number of action and descriptive words you know. Begin by using the word *get* less frequently and by using precise words more.

LESS INTERESTING	PRECISE
1. We should *get* a new typewriter for the office.	1. We should (*buy, rent, lease*) a new typewriter for the office.
2. Milton tried to *get* me to take his side in the dabate.	2. Milton tried to *persuade* me to take his side in the debate.
3. The first baseman *got* hit by the pitcher's fast ball.	3. The pitcher's fast ball *struck* the first baseman.
4. When he spoke of his war buddies, he *got* sad.	4. When he spoke of his war buddies, he *grew* sad.

Try to avoid overused words. Learn new words to replace them. Start with the word *very*. *Very*, plus an overused word hides a precise word.

OVERUSED WORDS	PRECISE WORDS
very pretty	captivating
very new	novel
very lazy	indolent
very funny	amusing
very slow	languid

PRACTICE

VI   **Directions:** Replace the italicized words in each sentence with a descriptive one chosen from the list below.

ancient   swift   overjoyed   terrified   craves

1. I am *very afraid* of night noises. _____

2. We toured a *very old* ruin in Rome. _____

3. A *very fast* runner won the marathon. _____

4. My friend, Sheila, *really wants* fame. _____

5. I was *very glad* to hear of your good fortune. _____

This chapter offers only a few techniques for increasing your vocabulary. There are many more. In fact, entire books have been written on the subject. Now that you have completed a sample improvement program, don't stop building your vocabulary. Be aware of new words. Keep a list of them, define them, and write them in sentences. Try to use them in your everyday conversations, letters, or memos. Your personal gains will make it well worth the effort.

ANSWER KEY

Chapter 19

Building Vocabulary

Practice I *Page 221*

1. technology
2. alimony
3. condominium
4. computer
5. video

Practice II *Page 221*

1. [Latin: com-, together + premere, to press]
2. [Latin vindicare, to revenge]
3. [French pédicure: pedi + Latin cūrāre, to take care of]
4. [Latin manus, hand + cūra, care]
5. [Latin ūnicus, only]

Practice III *Page 222*

1. unus—one, single
2. facere—to do
3. benefit—well
4. signum—sign
5. portare—to carry
6. dicere—to say
7. volens—wishing

Practice IV *Page 223*

1. im-, dis-, un-, a-
2. mal-
3. auto-
4. re-
5. post-
6. ex-
7. pre-

Practice V *Page 223*

1. preview
2. disagree
3. autobiography
4. relive
5. undress
6. atheist

Practice VI *Page 224*

1. terrified
2. ancient
3. swift
4. craves
5. overjoyed

20.

Word Usage

I was a pretty good student back in Wilberforce in the 1930's but there were a few things that always gave me trouble. I never felt comfortable with *affect* and *effect, capital* and *capitol, beside* and *besides*—and hundreds of others like that with which Miss Conway used to torture us every Friday.

"Now we come to words frequently confused," she would drool, adjusting wig and lorgnette, her eyes brightening with anticipation.

I think what really turned me off on that subject was when old Mr. Wentworth tried to show me the difference between *principal* and *principle*, pontificating that "Your princi*pal* is your *pal*," and spraying me with tobacco juice in the process.

I didn't believe him then, and I still have trouble with those words, forty years later. Traumatic, I guess.

—Oliver L. Kenworthy
Bluegrass Lawyer

A Word With You . . .

English seems to have so many more words that sound alike and words that are frequently confused than any other language. The same problems which young Oliver Kenworthy found in Wilberforce, Kentucky may have plagued you, too.

In the following pages, you will find some of the more troublesome sets of words. See how well you can handle them.

Many words are easily confused. Some words sound the same but are spelled differently and have different meanings. These are *homonyms*. *For example:*

1. A full moon *shone* brightly last night.

The film was *shown* on TV.

2. Once we nail up this *board*, the tool shed will be finished.

I was very *bored* during that long, rainy week.

3. The *pain* in my lower back increases during rainy weather.

Could you please replace the cracked *pane* of glass?

Other words are confusing because they sound almost the same.
For example:

1. The legislators had an angry debate before *adopting* a policy on school funding.

Since we moved from the West Coast to the Midwest, we've had to *adapt* to colder weather.

2. The politician's *allusions* to his opponent's past errors in judgment were unnecessary.

In the story *The Christmas Carol,* Scrooge's visitors were *illusions.*

3. How do you think the current job action will *affect* management?

I think the *effect* will be that management will meet labor's demands.

In order to improve your understanding of easily confused words, study the following list. An example of correct usage is given for each commonly confused word.

Commonly Misused Words

accept - except

I *accept* your apology.

Everyone *except* John may leave.

adapt--adopt

When visiting a foreign country, you must *adapt* yourself to the customs practiced there.

The Grays plan to *adopt* several hard-to-place children.

advice - advise

Because of Michael's excellent *advice,* Bob completed a successful business deal.

Michael will *advise* Bob to be daring.

affect - effect

The accident did not *affect* Thomas.

The *effect* on his brother, however, was great.

aggravate - annoy

If you continue to scratch that rash, you will *aggravate* your condition.

Your constant scratching *annoys* me.

all ready - already

Call me when you are *all ready* to go.

By the time Sue arrived, we had *already* finished dinner.

all right   (*Alright* is not an acceptable word.)

Is it *all right* to leave this window open?

all together - altogether

The four of us were *all together* at the coffee shop.

This book is *altogether* too long.

allude - refer

In passing, the speaker *alluded* to the new technology in business.

The speaker *referred* to statistics that demonstrated the rise of technology in

allusion - illusion

I resent your *allusion* to my cooking as comparable with Mac-Donald's.

You have the *illusion* that I enjoy classical music; I don't.

altar--alter

Many a would-be-bride has been left at the *altar*.

Would it be inconvenient for you to *alter* your plans for this weekend?

among--between

The campaign director divided the state *among* his *three* most competent assistants.

In many of today's homes, the care of the children is divided *between* the *two* parents.

amount - number

You would not believe the *amount* of time I have spent on this project.

I wish I could reuse the *number* of hours I have spent on this project.

angry at - angry with

Ira was *angry at* the thought of working overtime.

Ira was *angry with* his boss for insisting that Ira work overtime.

anxious - eager

I am *anxious* about the diagnosis.

I am *eager* to see your new car.

anywhere (There is no such word as *anywheres*.)

Marlene cannot find her glasses *anywhere*.

as - like

Paula looks very much *like* her sister.

Rosemary swims *as* well as Pam does.

Carl looks *as* if he needs a nap.

ascent - assent

The *ascent* to the tower was frighteningly steep.

Because I value his opinion, I will not go ahead with the project without his *assent*.

awful - very - real

This fish tastes *awful*.

This fish tastes *very* bad.

Are these pearls *real* or imitation?

because of - due to

Because of our tight budget, we're vacationing at home.

We're vacationing at home *due to* our tight budget.

beside - besides

Linda likes to sit *beside* Ellen at the table.

Who, *besides* Pam, is taking swimming lessons?

born - borne

Our youngest child was *born* last month.

John has *borne* the burden by himself for long enough.

borrow from (*borrow off* is unacceptable.)

Mickey borrowed the soldering iron from Allen.

borrow - lend - loan

May I *borrow* your pocket calculator?

I can *lend* you my mechanical pencil.

I need a $500 *loan*.

brake - break

I prefer a bicycle with a foot *brake*.

Because he did not *brake* in time, Herman crashed into the tree.

If you are not careful, you will *break* that dish.

can - may

Some fortunate people *can* arrange their time to include work and pleasure.

You *may* hunt deer only during certain seasons.

capital - capitol - Capitol

Ricardo has 90% of the necessary *capital* for his new business venture.

Trenton is the *capital* of New Jersey.

New Jersey's *capitol* building is in Trenton.

Did you visit the *Capitol* when you were in Washington, D.C.?

cite - sight - site

An attorney often *cites* previous cases which support his argument.

One of the most beautiful *sights* in the country is the Grand Canyon.

The alternative school will be built on this *site*.

coarse - course

I find this *coarse* fabric to be abrasive.

That is an acceptable *course* of action.

complement - compliment

Rice nicely *complements* a chicken dinner.

I'd like to *compliment* you for doing such a thorough job.

communicate with - contact

I will *communicate with* (call, write, speak) you in May.

Contact (call, write, speak) me when you return.

continually - continuously

Tom is *continually* late.

The river runs *continuously* through several towns.

council - counsel

Our neighbor has just been elected to the town *council.*

The troubled man sought his friend's *counsel.*

credible - creditable - credulous

Because the defendant had a good alibi, his story seemed *credible.*

As a result of many hours of hard work, Joe presented a *creditable* report.

Sally is so *credulous* that one could sell her the Brooklyn Bridge.

currant - current

His unusual recipe called for *currant* jelly.

Because the *current* was swift, the canoe was difficult to maneuver.

desert - dessert

The *desert* is very hot and dry.

More and more young soldiers have been *deserting* the army.

Apple pie is America's favorite *dessert.*

die - dye

Eventually, every living thing *dies.*

I'll never *dye* my hair.

discover - invent

The builders *discovered* oil on our land.

Whitney *invented* the cotton gin.

disinterested - uninterested

The *disinterested* observer of the accident was certain that the driver of the blue car was at fault.

Because Sheila was *uninterested* in the lecture, she paid no attention.

draw - drawer

Marlene *draws* very well.

She keeps her pads and pencils in the top *drawer* of her desk.

emigration - immigration

The Harlows *emigrated* from England.

After *immigrating* to the United States, the Harlows settled in Kansas.

famous - infamous

John Simpson is a *famous* pianist.

Arthur Jones is an *infamous* car thief.

farther - further

My car can run *farther* on this other brand of gasoline.

I cannot continue this discussion any *further*.

fewer - less

Gerry invited *fewer* people to her office party this year.

Since she moved from a house to an apartment, she has *less* space.

formally - formerly

Please dress *formally* for the wedding.

I was *formerly* employed by a jewelry company, but I am now working in a bank.

good - well

Maria performed a *good* job.

Maria performed the job *well*.

Maria doesn't feel *good*.

Maria doesn't feel *well*.

grate - great

The continuous harsh and rasping sound *grated* on my nerves.

A *grate* in the sidewalk covered the opening to the sewer.

Ernest Hemingway was considered a *great* writer in his own lifetime.

healthful - healthy

Orange juice is *healthful*.

If you eat properly and exercise sufficiently, you will be *healthy*.

imply - infer

Although he did not state it directly, the candidate *implied* that his opponent was dishonest.

From the mayor's constructive suggestions, the townsfolk *inferred* that he was trying his best to do a good job.

in - into

Marlene stood *in* the living room.

Wayne came rushing *into* the room.

it's - its

I think *it's* a fine idea!

The dog wagged *its* tail.

kind of - sort of - type of

(These expressions can be used interchangeably. They should never be followed by "a.")

Mrs. Peterson always buys that *kind of* meat.

I like that *sort of* book.

This is my favorite *type of* record.

later - latter

Sue can finish the report *later* this week.

I can meet you Tuesday or Thursday. The *latter* would be more convenient.

lead - led

I'll need one more *lead* pipe to complete this plumbing job.

I only enjoy a race when I am in the *lead*.

John was unfamiliar with that route, so Jules *led* the way.

learn - teach

Harriet is having great difficulty with her efforts to *learn* flowcharting.

Leslie is patiently trying to *teach* Harriet how to flowchart.

leave - let

If the customs officer finds nothing wrong with a traveler's baggage, the officer *lets* the traveler *leave* the area.

loose - lose

Eric was excited about his first *loose* tooth.

If you step out of line, you will *lose* your place.

manor - manner

The *manor*, or landed estate, dates back to feudal times in England.

They don't like the *manner* in which you responded to my sincere question.

miner - minor

The coal *miners* were trapped during the cave-in.

The young man was not allowed to enter the bar because he was a *minor*.

moral - morale

Because of Ed's high *moral* standards, he returned the wallet to its owner.

The story of *The Boy Who Cried Wolf* has a *moral* which applies to everyone.

Because the war was *immoral*, the *morale* of the troops was low.

nauseated - nauseous

When we drove past the skunk, the car was filled with a *nauseous* odor.

The odor of the skunk *nauseated* Sara.

pail - pale

The amount of paint needed to finish the job would fill a one-gallon *pail*.

Because of her long illness, Maria's complexion was very *pale*.

passed - past

We *passed* the Model T on the parkway.

You cannot always try to recapture the *past*.

peace - piece

If we work together, perhaps we can end the war and achieve a truly lasting *peace*.

In time, we will be paying an extremely high price for a *piece* of paper.

persecute - prosecute

Older children frequently *persecute* their younger siblings.

If you do not return the stolen money, you will be *prosecuted*.

personal - personnel

The items written in a young girl's diary are very *personal.*
When applying for a job at a large company, you must go to
the *personnel* office.

plain - plane

The meaning is quite *plain* and requires no further explanation.

We rode for miles across the open *plains* of Kansas.

The *plane* landed smoothly.

Please *plane* that wood so that I can build a birdhouse with
it.

precede - proceed

A preface always *precedes* the body of a book.

Don't let me interrupt you; *proceed* with your work.

practicable - practical

Studying computer programming is a *practicable* plan for
the future.

Computerizing payroll is a *practical* business decision.

principal - principle

A school is as good as the teachers and *principal.*

The *principal* actors in the play remained for a final rehearsal
of the second act.

The *principle* upon which many simple machines are based
is frequently the lever.

quiet - quite

As the campers lay down for the night, *quiet* settled over the
campsite.

That is *quite* a strong accusation.

raise - rise

When we *raise* the flag, we'd like everyone in the audience to *rise*.

sit - set

The chairman requested committee members to *sit* down.

The artist *set* his clay on the workbench and began to create a sculpture.

stationary - stationery

Theater seats are most often *stationary*.

When I write letters, I always use my engraved *stationery*.

sure - surely

I am *sure* Alice will be at the meeting.

Surely, you don't expect me to take notes.

teach - learn

Miss Smith *teaches* math every Thursday.

Ron Jonas, a student, *learns* math from Miss Smith.

than - then

New York is smaller *than* Wyoming, but Wyoming has a much smaller population *than* New York.

First the eastern seaboard was colonized, *then* settlers moved westward.

their - there - they're

When leaving *their* war-torn country, most of the refugees left all *their* possessions behind.

There are no easy answers to the problem of world-wide hunger.

As for the members of Congress, *they're* not always responsible for the wisest decisions.

through - threw

The special crew worked *through* the night to repair the damaged wires.

When the Little League pitcher *threw* the ball, her teammates cheered.

to - too - two

United States presidents often travel *to* foreign countries.

Many foreign heads of state visit the United States, *too*.

Two visitors were the late Anwar Sadat and Margaret Thatcher.

vain - vane - vein

The *vain* man peered at his reflection in every window as he strolled down the street.

A rooster is the traditional weather *vane* symbol.

Veins are passageways which carry deoxygenated blood to the heart.

vale - veil

Vale is an uncommonly used synonym for valley.

The mourning woman hid her grief behind her *veil*.

wade - weighed

The smaller children were told to *wade* near the shore.

The clerk *weighed* and priced the fresh vegetables.

waist - waste

If you measure your *waist* before you go to buy a pattern, you will avoid much confusion.

Don't *waste* precious time gossiping on the phone.

weather - whether

Tomorrow morning the general *weather* conditions will determine the distance of our first day's hike.

Whether or not you wish to pay taxes, you must.

who's - whose

The teacher asked, "*Who's* responsible for clean-up today?"

We must determine *whose* turn it is.

writes - rights - rites

Kurt Vonnegut *writes* excellent fiction.

Their attorney explained the family's *rights* in the lawsuit.

The religious *rites* of many Indian tribes are an impressive part of their culture.

your - you're

Where is *your* car parked?

You're attempting something that's too difficult for you.

PRACTICE

I   **Directions:** Blacken the space beneath the number which corresponds to the number of the correct word to complete each sentence.

                                               1   2

1.   *Your* *You're* on the right track. || ||
             1   2

                                                 1   2

2.   I enjoy a cold *bier* *beer* on a warm day. || ||
                                 1   2

                                                 1   2

3.   Please use the main *aisle* *isle* in the theater. || ||
                                      1   2

                                                 1   2

4.   We left early because we were *bored* *board*. || ||
                                         1   2

                                                 1   2

5.   The ship travelled through the *straight* *strait*. || ||
                                           1   2

                                                 1   2

6.   The *sum* *some* collected was not significant. || ||
            1   2

7. Please, don't *waist* *waste* my time.

                            1   2

8. The queen sat gracefully on her *thrown*

                                              1

    throne.

      2

9. Buddy would never *steal* *steel* from anyone.

                                 1   2

10. The wise old Indian knew many interesting

    tales *tails*.
      1   2

PRACTICE

II   **Directions:** Blacken the space beneath the number which corresponds to the number of the sentence in each group which contains an incorrectly used word. If there is no error, blacken space number 5.

            1 2 3 4 5

1 1) The jewel was shown to the prospective buyer.

    2) Her hair shown in the bright sunlight.

    3) The sun shone brightly this morning.

    4) I have never been shown how to use this machine.

    5) No error

            1 2 3 4 5

2 1) I would like you to cite at least three examples.

    2) Her husband was cited for contempt.

    3) For that sight, we're planning a municipal parking lot.

    4) When the bridge is within your sight, start looking for our street.

    5) No error

            1 2 3 4 5

3 1) The some total of these facts spells disaster.

    2) Take some cake with you to the picnic.

    3) I have some clothes that are no longer useful to me.

4) That sum of money is to be labeled petty cash.

5) No error

         1 2 3 4 5

4 1) Since the development of the tape recorder, Braille   ‖ ‖ ‖ ‖ ‖
is no longer the sole method of communicating fine
literature to sightless people.

2) Lemon sole is one of the many varieties of fish that
can enhance a meatless diet.

3) Sole music is very popular among people of all ages.

4) The concept of the soul does not have the same
meaning in all religions.

5) No error

         1 2 3 4 5

5 1) Napoleon had a great deal at steak when he decided   ‖ ‖ ‖ ‖ ‖
to invade Russia.

2) Finally, William hammered the last stake into the
ground.

3) I would enjoy a steak dinner tonight.

4) Sue was upset because her job was at stake.

5) No error

         1 2 3 4 5

6 1) Please, remain stationary while I draw your picture.   ‖ ‖ ‖ ‖ ‖

2) Irene wrote the letter on her finest stationary.

3) I believe you can buy staples at the stationery store.

4) This appliance cannot be moved; it is stationary.

5) No error

         1 2 3 4 5

7 1) Ilene attended a conference there.   ‖ ‖ ‖ ‖ ‖

2) There is the book I've been wanting to read.

3) There's is a truly open relationship.

4) I have never been to their summer home.

5) No error

			1	2	3	4	5

8 1) Those two stairs make this house bi-level.
   2) Hers was hardly a friendly stair.
   3) We've already swept the stairs today.
   4) Don't stare at me!
   5) No error

			1	2	3	4	5

9 1) I think it's time that he buys a new suite of furniture.
   2) We've already eaten our portion of sweets for this day.
   3) The visiting lecturer's hotel suite was paid for by the university.
   4) Don't make the chocolate pudding overly sweet.
   5) No error

			1	2	3	4	5

10 1) The boat was taken in toe after its motor failed.
   2) We were towed all the way to shore.
   3) At the football game we had a bad case of frozen toes.
   4) When you go beyond your own authority, you must step on somebody's toes.
   5) No error

PRACTICE

III   **Directions:** Blacken the space beneath the number which corresponds to the number of the incorrect word in each sentence. If there is no error, blacken space number 5.

1. The guide *led* us to a *straight* path *through*
        1   2   3
   the woods and to a lovely *veil. No error*
                            4   5

2. My neighbor *dies* her *hair* *two* times every
               1   2   3
   week. No error
    4   5

3. We had *already* planned our vacation to an
      1
 unknown *isle* when our friends said that they
        2
 were *all ready* to come along *to.* *No error*
       3   4   5

  1 2 3 4 5
  ‖ ‖ ‖ ‖ ‖

4. You are *all together* mistaken about *their*
         1   2
 decision *to* *write* to the newspaper.
       3   4
 No error
   5

  1 2 3 4 5
  ‖ ‖ ‖ ‖ ‖

5. Ira Swanson *writes* about the religious *rights*
           1   2
 of the Indians who inhabit the island *right* off
                              3
 the coast *of* Japan. *No error*
         4   5

  1 2 3 4 5
  ‖ ‖ ‖ ‖ ‖

6. The *capital* of each state is the *cite* of the
      1   2
 capitol building of that state and main
        3
 attraction for *sightseers.* *No error*
           4   5

  1 2 3 4 5
  ‖ ‖ ‖ ‖ ‖

7. Because the *currant* was *strong,* we had *great*
         1   2   3
 difficulty reaching *shore.* *No error*
          4   5

  1 2 3 4 5
  ‖ ‖ ‖ ‖ ‖

8. I, for one, *didn't appreciate* the *manor* in
           1   2   3
 which she answered. *No error*
   4   5

  1 2 3 4 5
  ‖ ‖ ‖ ‖ ‖

	1	2	3	4	5

9. We *truly* felt that the *exorbitant* *expenditure*
      1   2   3

was a *waist*. *No error*
     4   5

	1	2	3	4	5

10. We *wade* both *arguments,* and we decided in
       1   2

favor of the *contract*. *No error*
   3   4   5

	1	2	3	4	5

11. The *nutritious* food, the fine *weather,* and the
        1   2

exercise made us feel *grate*. *No error*
   3   4   5

	1	2	3	4	5

12. The *members* of the *panel* were asked to
       1   2

leave *their* jackets in the *outer* office.
      3   4

No error
 5

	1	2	3	4	5

13. We *heard* Pete *moan,* and we saw that he
    1   2

had become deadly *pail*. *No error*
   3   4   5

PRACTICE
IV   **Directions:** Blacken the space beneath the number which corresponds to the number of the incorrect word in each passage. If there is no error, blacken space number 5.

	1	2	3	4	5

1. Because I was *anxious* to avoid another argu-
             1

ment, I *accepted* Roy's apology. His story
        2

seemed <u>*credible*</u> so there was no point in
      3

carrying the argument any <u>*further.*</u> <u>*No error*</u>
                 4   5

                  1 2 3 4 5

2.   Sue left the elevator and <u>*proceeded*</u> to the ‖ ‖ ‖ ‖ ‖
                                   1

<u>*personal*</u> office. The cold, efficient inter-
  2

viewer lowered Sue's <u>*morale,*</u> but she was
                      3

<u>*eager*</u> to obtain the job. <u>*No error*</u>
4   5

                  1 2 3 4 5

3.   The <u>*effect*</u> of the unusual visitor on the family ‖ ‖ ‖ ‖ ‖
           1

was startling. Mother <u>*adopted*</u> Mrs. Chug-
                  2

gley's speech habits; father <u>*altered*</u> his smok-
                         3

ing habits to suit Mrs. Chuggley's allergy; and

I found myself <u>*continuously*</u> saying, "Yes,
                  4

Ma'am." <u>*No error*</u>
        5

                  1 2 3 4 5

4.   The <u>*course*</u> of action determined by the city ‖ ‖ ‖ ‖ ‖
           1

<u>*counsel*</u> at its last meeting has <u>*already*</u> begun
2   3

to <u>*affect*</u> us. <u>*No error*</u>
   4   5

                  1 2 3 4 5

5.   Family gatherings are <u>*always*</u> interesting. ‖ ‖ ‖ ‖ ‖
                      1

Grandpa is usually <u>*angry with*</u> Aunt Jean.
                  2

Rhoda insists upon sitting *besides* Grandma.
3

Mother tries to divide her attention equally

among all of the guests. *No error*
4   5

		1	2	3	4	5

6.   I was *altogether* shocked when Sam returned
1

the ice bucket which he had *borrowed from*
2

us last spring. When I *complemented* him for
3

returning it so promptly, Sam's red face told

me that he understood my *implied* sarcasm.
4

No error
5

7.   Please put the change *into* your pocket be-
1

fore you lose it. It's hard enough to keep pace

with today's prices without carelessly *losing*
2

money. That *kind of* carelessness makes me
3

loose my temper. *No error*
4   5

8.   The *minor led* his *team* into the shaft. After
1   2   3

several hours of dangerous work, they

ascended jubilantly. *No error*
4   5

9. I am *formally* engaged in a program of good
    1

    nutrition. I always eat a *healthy* breakfast. I
    2

    consume *fewer* sweets and I spend *less* time
    3   4

    stalking the refrigerator for snacks. *No error*
    5

    1 2 3 4 5
    ‖ ‖ ‖ ‖ ‖

10. Sue asked if she *might* go swimming at the
    1

    pool. Although Sue *can* swim *quite* well, her
    2   3

    mother refused permission. Sue was angry

    and said she was being *prosecuted*. *No error*
    4   5

    1 2 3 4 5
    ‖ ‖ ‖ ‖ ‖

PRACTICE
V   **Directions:** Blacken the space beneath the number which corresponds to the number of the sentence in each group which contains an incorrectly used word. If there is no error, blacken space number 5.

1 1) The damage has all ready been done.
   2) Father was altogether too surprised to speak.
   3) Events have borne out my prediction.
   4) Perry is an altar boy at Queen of Peace Church.
   5) No error

   1 2 3 4 5
   ‖ ‖ ‖ ‖ ‖

2 1) The family was all together for the annual picnic.
   2) Terry's mother cautioned, "If you break a window, you will have to pay for it."
   3) Paris is the capital of France.
   4) My mother was borne in Canada.
   5) No error

   1 2 3 4 5
   ‖ ‖ ‖ ‖ ‖

1 2 3 4 5

3 1) Was his work all right?

2) I use old shirts for cleaning cloths.

3) The dome on the capital is lighted each night.

4) Everyone was wearing his best clothes.

5) No error

1 2 3 4 5

4 1) I applied the brakes immediately.

2) Cars are borne across the river on a ferry.

3) Are you feeling all right?

4) When you are all ready, I will pick you up.

5) No error

1 2 3 4 5

5 1) John is considered an imminent member of congress.

2) The duke was received formally at the ambassador's home.

3) Out of deference to her loss, we did not resume the music.

4) We could hear a vigorous discussion of current problems.

5) No error

1 2 3 4 5

6 1) When you give your report, be sure to cite as many concrete examples as possible.

2) "I am surely not guilty of excessive spending!" he shouted.

3) We are not likely to meet again in the near future.

4) Because of several miner disagreements, the discussion came to a halt

5) No error

1 2 3 4 5

7 1) The politician was asked to accede to the council's wishes.

2) I am opposed to the construction of the bridge for two good reasons.

3) Do not hire anyone whose personality doesn't complement the rest of the staff.

4) Prospective homeowners are eager for reduction of the mortgage interest rate.

5) No error

	1	2	3	4	5

8 1) The attorney set fourth his ideas and told us all of the angles of his case.

2) Will you sign this senior citizen petition?

3) The beauty of the mountains exceeded all our expectations.

4) Mike is quite an athlete.

5) No error

	1	2	3	4	5

9 1) Wayne is likely to be defeated.

2) There was nothing to do but accept his plan.

3) I am opposed too airing family matters in public.

4) The crowd was quiet until the rocket ascended.

5) No error

	1	2	3	4	5

10 1) After listening with great patience, the diplomat listed his objectives.

2) No one knew him as well as I.

3) Choose your coarse of action and stick to it.

4) I think the skirt is too loose on you.

5) No error

PRACTICE
VI

Directions: Blacken the space beneath the number which corresponds to the number of the incorrect word in each passage. If there is no error, blacken space number 5.

	1	2	3	4	5

1. The *principal* members of the committee de-
      1

   cided to *lead* a discussion about the *peace*
      2   3

movement and the *type of a* person attracted
$$\underline{\qquad}$$
4

to it. *No error*
      5

1 2 3 4 5

2. Many of the *minors* in the audience began to ‖ ‖ ‖ ‖ ‖
                     1

lose *there* tempers because the discussion
 2   3

seemed partisan. *No error*
  4   5

1 2 3 4 5

3. The chairman *tryed* *to* explain that the ‖ ‖ ‖ ‖ ‖
                 1   2

principle of freedom to pursue one's beliefs
   3

was not the *main* issue. *No error*
            4   5

1 2 3 4 5

4. It was not the committee's intention to ‖ ‖ ‖ ‖ ‖

persecute anyone but rather to make *plain*
  1   2

the *already* divergent viewpoints and to
       3

precede to bring them together. *No error*
  4   5

1 2 3 4 5

5. The *main* effect of the chairman's speech was ‖ ‖ ‖ ‖ ‖
       1

to quiet the audience so that the discussion
 2 3

could continue *farther.* *No error*
               4   5

1 2 3 4 5

6. The next speaker *waisted* more time by ‖ ‖ ‖ ‖ ‖
                     1

expressing anger with the young people

present rather than *formally* addressing the
2   3

issues at hand. *No error*
4   5

                                   1 2 3 4 5

7.   I am certain that the committee *learned* a les- ‖ ‖ ‖ ‖ ‖
                                          1

son about discussing *volatile* issues. Next time
                          2

it will *altar* *its* presentation so that speakers
         3   4

will be more to the point. *No error*
                        5

                                   1 2 3 4 5

8.   That way, *less* misunderstandings will occur. ‖ ‖ ‖ ‖ ‖
                   1

The Lakeview Town *Council* had planned a
                         2

similar discussion, but changed *its* program.
   3   4

No error
5

                                   1 2 3 4 5

9.   It will have a speaker on the new *adoption* ‖ ‖ ‖ ‖ ‖
                                      1

laws. Many people need *advise* on this topic.
                             2

It *plainly* will be less controversial than the
       3

peace movement was. *No error*
4   5

                                   1 2 3 4 5

10.   The council has *all ready* advertised in local ‖ ‖ ‖ ‖ ‖
                         1

papers and *expects* a large *number* of people
              2   3

to be *eager* to attend. *No error*
      4   5

PRACTICE
VII   **Directions:** Circle the error in each incorrect sentence. If there is no error, put a "C" next to the sentence. Write the correct word to replace each error.

1. Sam wants to lend your calculator for a few days.   _____
2. Please contact me by phone.   _____
3. The book alluded to the Civil War in great depth.   _____
4. Company B's continued dumping into the stream has aggravated the pollution problem.   _____
5. His foot-tapping really aggravated me.   _____
6. Please rise your hand if you know the answer.   _____
7. She gives the allusion of being much thinner than she is.   _____
8. Bill sure doesn't want to work overtime.   _____
9. John promised to learn Maria English.   _____
10. José felt awful bad about the accident.   _____

Words and Phrases to Avoid

Some incorrect words and phrases are used frequently. Because of their common use, we begin to think they are *correct*. No amount of usage will make the following words acceptable as proper English. Just as Eliza Doolittle's dialect labeled her as "lower class," our use of certain words and phrases can label us "uneducated." This may sound unfair, but most employers are looking for people who can give their businesses the best "image." "Ain't" won't do it.

> **ain't**
>
> We used to be able to say, "Ain't" ain't in the dictionary. Now it is! Most educated people do not accept this word. You would do well to avoid it. *Ain't* is used incorrectly in place of **am not, is not, isn't, are not, aren't.**

> **could of**
>
> This is incorrect grammar. You mean **could have.** The contraction for **could have** is **could've** which sounds like **could of** but is not written that way. Example: I *could have* danced all night.

> **disregardless, irregardless**

This is incorrect grammar. The word you want is **regardless**. Example: *Regardless* of the weather, I plan to wear my new suit.

> **graduate (high school or college)**

You did not *graduate high school*, you **graduated from** *high school*, or any other school.

> **nowheres**

This is incorrect grammar. Use **nowhere**. Example: This debate is going *nowhere*.

> **off of**

Incorrect grammar. The word *of* is to be omitted. Example: He climbed *off* the bleachers.

> **you all**

This is incorrect grammar. Examples: *All of you* must attend. *You must all* attend.

PRACTICE VIII

Directions: Underline the error in each of the following sentences. Rewrite each sentence correctly.

1. This project is going nowheres.

   _____

2. You all are dressed incorrectly.

   _____

3. He ain't a very good businessman.

   _____

4. Wilma could of had the promotion if she had wanted it.

   _____

5. Please take your feet off of my desk.

   _____

6. I graduated high school in 1979.

   _____

7. Irregardless of your opinion, I plan to hire the person I interviewed Tuesday.

ANSWER KEY

Chapter 20

Word Usage

Practice I *Page 240.*

1. (2) you're (you are)
2. (2) beer
3. (1) aisle
4. (1) bored
5. (2) strait
6. (1) sum
7. (2) waste
8. (2) throne
9. (1) steal
10. (1) tales

Practice II *Page 241.*

1. (2) shone
2. (3) site
3. (1) sum
4. (3) soul
5. (1) stake
6. (2) stationery
7. (3) Theirs
8. (2) stare
9. (5) No error
10. (1) tow

Practice III *Page 243.*

1. (4) vale
2. (1) dyes
3. (4) too
4. (1) altogether
5. (2) rites
6. (2) site
7. (1) current
8. (3) manner
9. (4) waste
10. (1) weighed
11. (4) great
12. (5) No error
13. (4) pale

Practice VI *Page 245.*

1. (4) type of
2. (3) their
3. (1) tried
4. (4) proceed
5. (4) further
6. (1) wasted
7. (3) alter
8. (1) fewer
9. (2) advice
10. (1) already

Practice V *Page 248.*

1. (1) already
2. (4) born
3. (3) Capitol
4. (5) No error
5. (1) eminent
6. (4) minor
7. (5) No error
8. (1) forth
9. (3) to
10. (3) course

Practice IV *Page 250.*

1. (1) eager
2. (2) personnel
3. (4) continually
4. (2) council
5. (3) beside
6. (3) complimented
7. (4) lose
8. (1) miner
9. (2) healthful
10. (4) persecuted

Practice VII *Page 253.*

1. Sam wants to *borrow* your calculator for a few days.
2. Please *communicate with* me by phone.
3. The book referred to the Civil War in great depth.
4. C (correct)
5. His foot-tapping really *annoys* me.
6. Please *raise* your hand if you know the answer.
7. She gives the *illusion* of being much thinner than she is.
8. Bill *surely* doesn't want to work overtime.
9. John promised to *teach* Maria English.
10. José felt *very* bad about the accident. Or, José felt *really* bad about the accident.

Practice VIII *Page 254.*

1. This project is going *nowhere*.
2. *You* are dressed incorrectly. *You are all* dressed incorrectly.
3. He *isn't* a very good businessman.
4. Wilma *could have* had the promotion if she had wanted it.
5. Please take your feet *off* my desk.
6. I *graduated from* high school in 1979.
7. *Regardless* of your opinion, I plan to hire the person I interviewed Tuesday.

21.

Cumulative Review

This review covers the following concepts which have been included in the preceding chapters.

- Effectiveness of Expression
- Punctuation
- Capitalization
- Spelling
- Vocabulary
- Word Usage

After completing the Cumulative Review exercises, evaluate your ability on the SUMMARY OF RESULTS chart on page 272. Acceptable scores for each practice are given.

To identify your weaknesses, find the question numbers you answered incorrectly on the SKILLS ANALYSIS table. The table will show which of your skills need improvement and the necessary chapters to review.

PRACTICE

I   **Directions:** Blacken the space beneath the number which corresponds to the number of the incorrect sentence in each group. If there is no error, blacken space number 5.

	1	2	3	4	5
	‖	‖	‖	‖	‖

1 1) Doctor Smith ordered a mahogany, octagonal-shaped table for his office.

2) I wasn't never told to take this highway to your house.

3) My aunt baked that cake for me because I'm giving a party for my friend Joan.

4) The plumber left the job almost immediately because he did not have the parts he needed.

5) No error

1 2 3 4 5

2 1) After the clerk gave the customer his change; he heard the store's closing bell ring.

2) We went to a concert at City Center and heard an especially fine pianist, Van Cliburn.

3) The best part of our day occurred when we realized we were seated behind Woody Allen.

4) The traveling lecturer hardly ever has time for lunch.

5) No error

1 2 3 4 5

3 1) The lecturer prepared slides to accompany his talk.

2) Since the hour was late, the Senate adjourned its session.

3) Our weekly discussion club, which meets each week on Thursday, invited William Buckley to comment on his latest book.

4) Although our building was painted last year, it looks as if it needs to be painted again.

5) No error

1 2 3 4 5

4 1) Our group, we visited the museum to see a display of mobiles.

2) The supplies included pencils, papers, rulers, and blackboards.

3) I have never seen a neater room!

4) The President meets with his aides at 11:55 A.M.

5) No error

1 2 3 4 5

5 1) I cancelled the meeting because I expected to be too busy to attend.

2) Do you ever feel pressured by a too-full schedule?

3) Because the plane arrived late, we missed our connecting flight.

4) The resettled Vietnamese refugees, they finally got jobs.

5) No error

			1	2	3	4	5

6 1) The best part of the book occurs when the brothers   ‖ ‖ ‖ ‖ ‖
meet after a 25-year separation.

     2) The most exciting event in the movie is the auto race.

     3) The reason for his absence is because he has the flu.

     4) Richard Robinson hasn't been seen for weeks.

     5) No error

                                                                 1   2   3   4   5

7 1) What the sergeant wanted to know was what sup-   ‖ ‖ ‖ ‖ ‖
plies the unit needed.

     2) Because it's Monday, the stores are open late.

     3) The reason for my confusion is that my notes are
incomplete.

     4) My children left for day camp at 9:00 A.M.

     5) No error

                                                                 1   2   3   4   5

8 1) Because the power steering fluid had evaporated,   ‖ ‖ ‖ ‖ ‖
the wheel would not turn.

     2) An insect, it is difficult to eliminate after it has
become established in an area.

     3) William the Conqueror and the barons of Nor-
mandy were not in agreement about the invasion
of England.

     4) His parents said that John was neither too young nor
too busy to hold a part-time job.

     5) No error

                                                                 1   2   3   4   5

9 1) If history doesn't repeat itself, why is there never   ‖ ‖ ‖ ‖ ‖
an end to war?

     2) Why is it that nothing never goes smoothly?

     3) On the subject of the dangerous effects of spray
cans, one cannot hope for scientists' accord.

     4) An automobile accident occurred when two drivers
proceeded into the intersection at the same time.

     5) No error

1 2 3 4 5
|| || || || ||

10 1) More and more people are buying small cars because the price of gas is very high.

2) There are many solutions to the energy crisis.

3) A man, carrying a fishing pole and wearing hip boots, stood knee-high in the flooded street.

4) None of Albert Schweitzer's expenses was borne by the Evangelical Mission which had sent him to Lambaréné.

5) No error

1 2 3 4 5
|| || || || ||

11 1) The football team played football well yesterday at the football game.

2) Mark's hockey team is the best in the league.

3) None of the basketball players was at the victory party.

4) Chris Evert rarely plays tennis with a player who isn't a pro.

5) No error

1 2 3 4 5
|| || || || ||

12 1) Sylvester Stallone's latest movie seems to be a variation on his famous *Rocky* movies.

2) The novel which the customer requested was out of print.

3) Herbert Hoover, a man of humble beginnings, he was the son of a blacksmith.

4) Because the restriction on misleading food labels is vague, the consumer must be vigilant.

5) No error

1 2 3 4 5
|| || || || ||

13 1) The reason the ERA was defeated was a lack of understanding of the benefits.

2) The reason the primitive people relied on witch doctors was because these people thought they had been attacked by evil spirits.

3) Our specialty is good service.

4) We feature the finest service in the field.

5) No error

	1	2	3	4	5
	‖	‖	‖	‖	‖

14 1) Although I am exhausted, I plan to rest this afternoon.

2) Please don't leave early; we are enjoying your company.

3) The world's future population is hardly ever discussed without mention of food and other resources.

4) If you continue to smoke, I'll continue to ask you to stop.

5) No error

	1	2	3	4	5
	‖	‖	‖	‖	‖

15 1) Don't you find talk shows boring?

2) Are you not Mary Smith's aunt?

3) The business manager, who was ranting uncontrollably, lost the respect of his colleagues.

4) Although it isn't none of my business, I'm concerned about your health.

5) No error

PRACTICE

II   **Directions:** Blacken the space beneath the number which corresponds to the number of the best completion for each sentence.

	1	2	3	4
	‖	‖	‖	‖

1. The mailman slipped on the steps
    1) because he was wearing boots.
    2) even though they were icy.
    3) because the steps, they were icy.
    4) because they were icy.

	1	2	3	4
	‖	‖	‖	‖

2. Jules continues to smoke
    1) because he cannot read the warning.
    2) since smoking is hazardous to his health.
    3) although smoking is hazardous to his health.
    4) when it's hazardous to his health.

1 2 3 4

3. The camping trip was uncomfortable
   1) in spite of the heat and the bugs.
   2) although it was hot and buggy.
   3) even though it was hot and buggy.
   4) because of the heat and the bugs.

1 2 3 4

4. The Giants played well
   1) because they feared the fans.
   2) because the day was unseasonably hot.
   3) even though the day was unseasonably hot.
   4) even though the weather was perfect.

1 2 3 4

5. That man, who speaks at every public meeting,
   1) he is my uncle Joe.
   2) he is a town nuisance.
   3) never offers an acceptable suggestion.
   4) hardly never offers an acceptable suggestion.

1 2 3 4

6. I'd like draperies made of a transparent fabric
   1) that sees through and is durable.
   2) that is durable.
   3) that I can see through and is durable.
   4) that is durable and I can see through.

1 2 3 4

7. My favorite scene in *Romeo and Juliet*
   1) is when Romeo kills himself.
   2) is the one where Romeo kills himself.
   3) is because Romeo kills himself.
   4) is the one in which Romeo kills himself.

8.   Bob Rice, my brother's friend,

    1) he's a male chauvinist.

    2) is a male chauvinist.

    3) he is a male chauvinist.

    4) are male chauvinists.

1	2	3	4
||	||	||	||

9.   The reason for the meeting

    1) was that the principal had resigned.

    2) was because the principal had resigned.

    3) was when the principal had resigned.

    4) was to discuss the principal's resignation.

1	2	3	4
||	||	||	||

10.   The game was dull

    1) because the teams were not evenly matched.

    2) although the teams were not evenly matched.

    3) in spite of the fact that the teams were not evenly matched.

    4) since both the teams played well.

1	2	3	4
||	||	||	||

**PRACTICE
III**

Directions: Blacken the space beneath the number which corresponds to the number of the error in each sentence. If there is no error, blacken space number 5.

1.   "Would you like to record the song you
    1

wrote?", the conductor asked the singer.
      2 3 4

No error
    5

1	2	3	4	5
||	||	||	||	||

2. If you wish, you may pick some flowers—only
   1   2
   those along the side of the house—for your
                                      3
   centerpiece." *No error*
             4   5

       1 2 3 4 5

3. "My favorite book," said Melissa "is *Animal*
   1   2   3
   Farm." *No error*
        4   5

       1 2 3 4 5

4. The show *(for which you have tickets)* begins
                1   2
   promptly at 7:45 and ends (believe it or not at
               3   4
   11:00. *No error*
            5

       1 2 3 4 5

5. Last Sunday, I met my *ex* roommate *(whom*
                1   2   3
   I haven't seen for twelve years*)* in the super-
                                  4
   market. *No error*
              5

       1 2 3 4 5

6. "After you've practiced writing r's," said Miss
   1   2
   Green, go right on to s's." *No error*
      3   4   5

       1 2 3 4 5

7. The *Brownies* annual party was at the home
          1
   of Jane *Simpson* on Friday, at *4:15* P.M.
            2   3   4
   No error
      5

8. *Two thirds* of the membership voted—de-
 $\overline{1}$ $\overline{2}$

   spite last year *'s* increase—to increase the *dues*
 $\overline{3}$ $\overline{4}$

   for the next fiscal year. *No error*
 $\overline{5}$

   1 2 3 4 5

9. The painter called this morning to say *"that*
 $\overline{1}$

   he won *'t* be able *to* begin working until next
 $\overline{2}$ $\overline{3}$

   weekend. *No error*
 $\overline{4}$ $\overline{5}$

   1 2 3 4 5

10. Please *take* that envelope *(the* one on the hall
 $\overline{1}$ $\overline{2}$

   table) across the street to Mrs. *Jones.* *No error*
 $\overline{3}$ $\overline{4}$ $\overline{5}$

   1 2 3 4 5

PRACTICE IV

Directions: Blacken the space beneath the number which corresponds to the number of the error in each sentence. If there is no error, blacken space number 5.

1. *Sue Simpson,* the lead in *The Glass menagerie,*
 $\overline{1}$ $\overline{2}$ $\overline{3}$

   is a really competent *actress.* *No error*
 $\overline{4}$ $\overline{5}$

   1 2 3 4 5

2. *When* you leave *School* today, take a *bus* and
 $\overline{1}$ $\overline{2}$ $\overline{3}$

   meet me in New York *City.* *No error*
 $\overline{4}$ $\overline{5}$

   1 2 3 4 5

3. *Our course, history IA,* will include discussion
 $\overline{1}$ $\overline{2}$ $\overline{3}$

   of the settlement of the *American* colonies.
 $\overline{4}$

   No error
 $\overline{5}$

   1 2 3 4 5

1 2 3 4 5

4. <u>*Remember*</u> that <u>*Ellie*</u> said we should meet <u>*Her*</u>
    1   2   3

for lunch on <u>*Tuesday.*</u> <u>*No error*</u>
              4   5

1 2 3 4 5

5. <u>*On*</u> <u>*Twenty-second*</u> <u>*Street*</u> there's a charming
   1   2   3

restaurant called <u>*Lou's.*</u> <u>*No error*</u>
               4   5

1 2 3 4 5

6. <u>*Mr.*</u> <u>*Goren*</u> reminded <u>*us,*</u> <u>*"all*</u> lights must be
   1   2   3   4

turned off in the laboratory at the end of the

work day." <u>*No error*</u>
           5

1 2 3 4 5

7. The <u>*lieutenant*</u> asked <u>*captain*</u> <u>*John Forbes*</u> to
        1   2   3

cut the ribbon at the ceremonies marking the

opening of <u>*Fort Titan.*</u> <u>*No error*</u>
             4   5

1 2 3 4 5

8. <u>*This*</u> <u>*October,*</u> <u>*halloween*</u> falls on a <u>*Tuesday.*</u>
   1   2   3   4

<u>*No error*</u>
  5

1 2 3 4 5

9. "We can learn much," said <u>*Edith,*</u> <u>*"from*</u> the
   1   2   3

cultures of the <u>*east.*</u>" <u>*No error*</u>
           4   5

1 2 3 4 5

10. <u>*One*</u> of the earliest and most significant <u>*British*</u>
    1   2

<u>*documents*</u> is the <u>*magna carta.*</u> <u>*No error*</u>
    3   4   5

PRACTICE

V   **Directions:** Blacken the space beneath the number which corresponds to the number of the incorrectly spelled word in each group. If there is no error, blacken space number 5.

	1	2	3	4	5

1. 1) reinstitute   2) overated   3) happily 4) foxes   5) No error   ‖ ‖ ‖ ‖ ‖

2. 1) dyeing   2) dying   3) dies   4) dice 5) No error   ‖ ‖ ‖ ‖ ‖

3. 1) truly   2) noticable   3) famous   4) duly 5) No error   ‖ ‖ ‖ ‖ ‖

4. 1) guidance   2) necessarily   3) mispell 4) edibles   5) No error   ‖ ‖ ‖ ‖ ‖

5. 1) safely   2) proceed   3) preceed 4) recede   5) No error   ‖ ‖ ‖ ‖ ‖

6. 1) merrily   2) quickly   3) niece   4) theif 5) No error   ‖ ‖ ‖ ‖ ‖

7. 1) succeed   2) willingly   3) reference 4) wierd   5) No error   ‖ ‖ ‖ ‖ ‖

8. 1) canning   2) caning   3) confering 4) radios   5) No error   ‖ ‖ ‖ ‖ ‖

9. 1) seize   2) secede   3) skys   4) axes 5) No error   ‖ ‖ ‖ ‖ ‖

10. 1) recede   2) ilegal   3) disillusion 4) hunches   5) No error   ‖ ‖ ‖ ‖ ‖

11. 1) sheep   2) data   3) datum   4) exrays 5) No error   ‖ ‖ ‖ ‖ ‖

12. 1) sevens   2) courtisans   3) 9s   4) loosens 5) No error   ‖ ‖ ‖ ‖ ‖

13. 1) atheletic   2) exceed   3) supersede 4) mice   5) No error   ‖ ‖ ‖ ‖ ‖

14. 1) vaccinate   2) mouthsful   3) oxen 4) height   5) No error   ‖ ‖ ‖ ‖ ‖

15. 1) befitting   2) allegiance   3) tonage 4) leisure   5) No error   ‖ ‖ ‖ ‖ ‖

16.   1) deceive   2) relieve   3) ferret   4) heroes || || || || ||
       5) No error

17.   1) contraltoes   2) trout   3) brothers-in-law || || || || ||
       4) duly   5) No error

18.   1) crises   2) knifes   3) disappoint || || || || ||
       4) seeing   5) No error

19.   1) colonel   2) interceed   3) release || || || || ||
       4) concurred   5) No error

20.   1) rheostat   2) tariff   3) trafic   4) vacuum || || || || ||
       5) No error

PRACTICE
VI   Directions: Blacken the space beneath the number which corresponds
              to the number of the incorrect sentence in each group. If there is no error,
              blacken space number 5.

                                                                1 2 3 4 5

1 1) Once the Equal Rights Amendment was defeated, || || || || ||
          it was too late to argue its merits.

    2) In this decade of shortages, the large scale waist of
        paper is outrageous.

    3) During the 1984 election, Ronald Reagan led the Re-
        publicans to victory.

    4) Most American first ladies have been outwardly
        plain women.

    5) No error

                                                                1 2 3 4 5

2 1) The headlights of a solitary car shone down the de- || || || || ||
          serted country road.

    2) All of the museum's newest paintings were shone
        at the recent exhibition.

    3) The weather vane is broken again.

    4) Beneath his unruffled exterior were the falsely ar-
        rested gentleman's true feelings of rage.

    5) No error

3 1) Napoleon would not settle for a small piece of   1 2 3 4 5

Europe.

     2) The judge carefully weighed both arguments.

     3) Crew is a sport in which races with row boats take place.

     4) Bart Starr was a principle player on the Green Bay Packers.

     5) No error

4 1) During the summer of 1975, many American fami-   1 2 3 4 5

lies adopted Vietnamese children.

     2) Many Vietnamese adults have had difficulty adapting to living in America.

     3) If you plan to film the entire Thanksgiving Day Parade, you'll need more than one real of film.

     4) Even an expert fisherman has, on occasion, lost a rod and reel.

     5) No error

5 1) The United States had overlooked many acts of   1 2 3 4 5

aggression towards other nations, until the Germans sank the *Lusitania*.

     2) Mark lifts weights every morning.

     3) My wait has dropped considerably since I've been on that diet.

     4) Phil refuses to wait in line for a movie, a show, or dinner.

     5) No error

6 1) Some people enjoy camping.   1 2 3 4 5

     2) The sum of my camping experience is two days.

     3) Martha is too vane to travel without a mirror.

     4) All of our efforts were in vain because the project failed.

     5) No error

7 1) A bird flew past the window.
   2) Ira is home with the flu.
   3) A squirrel was trapped in the chimney flue.
   4) Did you bring a flie-swatter?
   5) No error

	1	2	3	4	5
	‖	‖	‖	‖	‖

8 1) A female pig is called a sow.
   2) Jeannette cannot sew well at all.
   3) That gift is so nice!
   4) The ball crashed through the pain of glass.
   5) No error

	1	2	3	4	5
	‖	‖	‖	‖	‖

9 1) The old man could not walk without his cane.
   2) Sugar comes from sugar cane.
   3) Queen Elizabeth had a peaceful rein.
   4) That sprained ankle caused me great pain.
   5) No error

	1	2	3	4	5
	‖	‖	‖	‖	‖

10 1) The bough was full of blossoms.
    2) Everyone cheered when the pitcher through the third strike.
    3) I don't like to sit in the bow of the boat.
    4) Suzy enjoys wearing bows in her hair.
    5) No error

	1	2	3	4	5
	‖	‖	‖	‖	‖

11 1) Do you like to walk in the rain?
    2) Have you ever seen a ewe?
    3) The canoe floated silently down the straight.
    4) Please, straighten your tie.
    5) No error

	1	2	3	4	5
	‖	‖	‖	‖	‖

1 2 3 4 5

12 1) Some girls will not marry because they are waiting for nights in shining armor.

2) My favorite fish dinner is baked fillet of sole.

3) Many poems have been written about the journeys of the soul.

4) Because I was the sole tennis player in the group, I played a great deal of golf.

5) No error

1 2 3 4 5

13 1) Do you grate potatoes into that recipe?

2) No, but I beet the eggs thoroughly.

3) Have you tried beet soup?

4) Yes, it's delicious.

5) No error

1 2 3 4 5

14 1) I am not fond of that newscaster.

2) His manor is very offensive.

3) Did you visit the Manor House at Batsto?

4) In what manner would you like the idea presented?

5) No error

1 2 3 4 5

15 1) Since the meat shortage began, I've been freezing a great deal of meat.

2) Did you see the lovely freeze on the Smith's living room wall?

3) Please meet me at the florist.

4) Lately, loud noises wear on my nerves.

5) No error

**PRACTICE
VII**

Directions: Blacken the space beneath the number which corresponds to the number of the incorrect word in each sentence. If there is no error, blacken space number 5.

1 2 3 4 5

1. Please *leave* Marie go to the movies *with* me
      1   2

because I *may* not go to town *alone*. *No error*
       3   4   5

1 2 3 4 5

2. If you don't _want_ to _build_ shelves for me, _then_
         1   2   3

learn me how to build them myself. _No error_
  4   5

1 2 3 4 5

3. Because this is a _real_ problem in _our_ commu-
                   1   2

nity, we need a _real_ dedicated group of citi-
               3

zens _to_ study possible solutions. _No error_
      4   5

1 2 3 4 5

4. Many reports indicate that sugar-coated

serials are not _healthful; therefore,_ more
  1   2   3

nutritious breakfast foods _are_ appearing on
                        4

the market. _No error_
           5

1 2 3 4 5

5. When Stuart gives the signal, _everyone_ must
                                  1

rise to his feet, _raise_ his hands above his head,
  2   3

and _set_ down. _No error_
     4   5

1 2 3 4 5

6. Because so _many_ campers had cut down trees,
              1

there were _less_ trees this year _than_ ever
  2   3   4

before. _No error_
     5

7. Mr. Smith *taught* the science *class* the *affect*
                    1   2   3
    of radiation *upon* cells. *No error*
                4   5

1	2	3	4	5
‖	‖	‖	‖	‖

8. That *author* carries the *principle* of free will
             1   2
    farther than any *previous* author. *No error*
       3   4   5

1	2	3	4	5
‖	‖	‖	‖	‖

9. Mrs. Kelly Warren, *formally* Miss Kelly
                        1
    O'Rourke, *emigrated from* Ireland this *past*
              2   3   4
    year. *No error*
         5

1	2	3	4	5
‖	‖	‖	‖	‖

10. *Its* an *illusion* to expect that *course* of action
     1   2   3
    to have a positive *effect* on our long-range
                   4
    plan. *No error*
         5

1	2	3	4	5
‖	‖	‖	‖	‖

SUMMARY OF RESULTS

After reviewing the Answer Key on page 275, chart your scores below for each practice exercise.

Practice Number	Your Number Right	Your Number Wrong (Including Omissions)	Acceptable Score
I			11 Correct
II			7 Correct

Practice Number	Your Number Right	Your Number Wrong (Including Omissions)	Acceptable Score
III			7 Correct
IV			7 Correct
V			15 Correct
VI			11 Correct
VII			15 Correct

SKILLS ANALYSIS

To discover your weak areas, locate the question numbers you got wrong and circle them on this Skills Analysis chart. Refer back to those chapters where you got questions wrong.

Skill	Question Number	Chapter Reference
Practice I		*See Chapter*
Double Negative	1, 9, 15	15
Unclear Pronoun Reference	2	15
Repetition	3, 4, 5, 8, 11, 12	15
Wordiness	6, 7, 13	15
Coordination of Ideas	14	15
Practice II		
Coordination of Ideas	1, 2, 3, 4, 10	15
Repetition	6, 8	15
Wordiness	7, 9	15
Practice III		
Quotation Marks	1, 2, 3, 6, 9	16
Parenthesis	4	16

Skill	Question Number	Chapter References
Hyphen	5, 8	*See Chapter* 16
Apostrophe	7	16
Practice IV Capitalization	1 to 10	17
Practice V Spelling	1 to 20	18
Practice VI Word Usage	1 to 15	20
Practice VII Word Usage	1 to 20	20

ANSWER KEY

Chapter 21

Cumulative Review

Practice I *Page 256.*

1. (2) I wasn't *ever* told to take this highway to your house. Never use *not* (n't) and *never* together.
2. (1) After giving the customer change, *the clerk* heard the store's closing bell ring.
   Substitute *the clerk* for *he* in order to clarify who *heard*.
3. (3) *Our discussion club, which meets each Thursday,* invited William Buckley to comment on his latest book.
   Using *weekly* and *each week* in the same sentence is repetitious.
4. (1) *Our group visited* the museum to see a display of mobiles.
   We refers to *our group* and is, therefore, repetitious.
5. (4) The resettled Vietnamese *refugees finally* got jobs.
   They refers to the *Vietnamese* and is, therefore, repetitious.
6. (3) *He is absent* because he has the flu.
   Is because is unacceptable form. The sentence reads more smoothly as corrected.
7. (1) *The sergeant wanted* to know what supplies the unit needed.
   What . . . was is poor form. The sentence reads more smoothly as corrected.
8. (2) *An insect is difficult* to eliminate after it has become established in an area.
   The first *it* referred to *insect* and was, therefore, repetitious.
9. (2) Why is it that nothing *ever* goes smoothly?
   Never use *nothing* and *never* together.
10. (5) No error
11. (1) *The football team played well yesterday.*
    Football is repetitious.
12. (3) Herbert Hoover, a man of humble beginnings, *was* the son of a blacksmith.
    He refers to *Herbert Hoover* and is, therefore, repetitious.
13. (2) *Primitive people relied on witch doctors because* those people thought they had been attacked by evil spirits.
    Was because is unacceptable form. The sentence reads more smoothly as corrected.
14. (1) *Because* I am exhausted, I plan to rest this afternoon.
    Although contradicts the intended meaning of the sentence.
    Because clarifies the meaning.
15. (4) Although it isn't *any* of my business, I'm concerned about your health.
    Never use *not* and *none* together.

Practice II *Page 260.*

1. (4) The mailman slipped on the steps *because they were icy.*
   Because they were icy explains, simply, why the mailman slipped on the steps. The word *because* makes the connection between the mailman's slipping and the icy steps.
2. (3) Jules continues to smoke *although smoking is hazardous to his health.*
   Although smoking is hazardous to his health shows that Jules continues to smoke despite the hazards.
3. (4) The camping trip was uncomfortable *because of the heat and the bugs.*
   Because of the heat and the bugs explains, simply, why the camping trip was uncomfortable. The word *because* makes the connection between the discomfort and the heat and the bugs.
4. (3) The Giants played well *even though the day was unseasonably hot.*
   Even though the day was unseasonably hot shows that the Giants played well despite the heat.

5. (3) That man, who speaks at every meeting, *never offers an acceptable suggestion.*
   Never offers an acceptable suggestion is the only grammatically correct completion for this sentence.

6. (2) I'd like draperies made of a transparent fabric *that is durable.*
   That is durable is the only possible completion for this sentence. All other choices are grammatically incorrect and repetitive.

7. (4) My favorite scene in *Romeo and Juliet is the one in which Romeo kills himself.*
   Is the one in which Romeo kills himself is the only completion which conforms to correct style.

8. (2) Bob Rice, my brother's friend, *is a male chauvinist.*
   Is a male chauvinist is the only grammatically and stylistically correct completion for this sentence.

9. (4) The reason for the meeting *was to discuss the principal's resignation.*
   Was to discuss the principal's resignation is the simplest completion for this sentence. *Was that, was when,* and *was because* are poor style.

10. (1) The game was dull *because the teams were not evenly matched.*
    Because the teams were not evenly matched explains, simply, why the game was dull. The word *because* makes the connection between the dull game and the unevenly matched teams.

Practice III *Page 262.*

1. (4) "Would you like to record the song you wrote?" the conductor asked the singer.
   Never place a comma *outside* quotation marks. Never use two marks of punctuation at the end of a sentence.

2. (4) If you wish, you may pick some flowers—only those along the side of the house—for your centerpiece.
   This sentence is not a quotation; therefore, the quotation mark at the end of the sentence is incorrect.

3. (3) "My favorite book," said Melissa, "is *Animal Farm.*"
   Use a comma to separate *said Melissa* from the remainder of the quotation.

4. (4) The show (for which you have tickets) begins promptly at 7:45 and ends (believe it or not) at 11:00.
   The writer shows by the use of parentheses that *believe it or not* is not necessary to the meaning of the sentence. Once opened, parentheses must be closed.

5. (2) Last Sunday, I met my *ex-*roommate (whom I haven't seen for twelve years) in the supermarket.
   When the prefix *ex-* means former or previously, as in *ex-roommate,* it is followed by a hyphen.

6. (3) "After you've practiced writing r's," said Miss Green, "go right on to s's."
   When continuing an interrupted quotation, precede the quoted portion with quotation marks.

7. (1) The *Brownies'* annual party was at the home of Natalie Simpson on Friday at 4:15 P.M.
   Use an apostrophe to show possession. The apostrophe follows the *s* in *Brownies* to show that the party belonged to them.

8. (1) *Two-thirds* of the membership voted—despite last year's increase—to increase the dues for the next fiscal year.
   Two-thirds is an example of two descriptive words brought together to form a new word; therefore, it is hyphenated.

9. (1) The painter called this morning to say *that* he won't be able to begin working until next weekend.

10. (5) No error

Practice IV *Page 264.*

1. (3) Sue Simpson, the lead in *The Glass Menagerie,* is really a competent actress.
   Capitalize the complete title of a play, book, or long poem.

2. (2) When you leave *school* today, take a bus and meet me in New York City.
   School is not capitalized because it does not refer to a particular school.

3. (3) Our course, *History IA,* will include discussion of the settlement of the American colonies.
   History IA is the name of a particular course and, therefore, should be capitalized.
4. (3) Remember that Ellie said we should meet *her* for lunch on Tuesday.
   Never capitalize a pronoun unless it is the first word of a sentence or a quotation.
5. (5) No error
6. (4) Mr. Goren reminded us, "*All* lights must be turned off in the laboratory at the end of the work day."
   All is the first word of the quotation and must be capitalized.
7. (2) The lieutenant asked *Captain* John Forbes to cut the ribbon at ceremonies marking the opening of Fort Titan.
   Captain refers to a particular captain, *Captain John Forbes,* and must be capitalized.
8. (3) This October, *Halloween* falls on a Tuesday.
   Halloween is the name of a holiday and, therefore, must be capitalized.
9. (4) "We can learn much," said Edith, "from the cultures of the *East.*"
   East refers to a particular section of the world and, therefore, must be capitalized.
10. (4) One of the earliest and most significant British documents is the *Magna Carta.*
    Magna Carta is the title of a document and, therefore, must be capitalized.

Practice V *Page 266.*

For explanations of the following answers, see spelling rules in Chapter 18.

1. (2) overrated	11. (4) x-rays
2. (5) No error	12. (3) 9's
3. (2) noticeable	13. (1) athletic
4. (3) misspell	14. (2) mouthfuls
5. (3) precede	15. (3) tonnage
6. (4) thief	16. (5) No error
7. (4) weird	17. (1) contraltos
8. (3) conferring	18. (2) knives
9. (3) skies	19. (2) intercede
10. (2) illegal	20. (3) traffic

Practice VI *Page 267.*

For explanations of the following answers, see word list and examples in Chapter 19.
1. (2) In this decade of shortages, the large scale *waste* of paper is outrageous.
2. (2) All of the museum's newest paintings were *shown* at the recent exhibition.
3. (4) Bart Starr was a *principal* player on the Green Bay Packers.
4. (3) If you plan to film the entire Thanksgiving Day Parade, you'll need more than one *reel* of film.
5. (3) My *weight* has dropped considerably since I've been on that diet.
6. (3) Martha is too *vain* to travel without a mirror.
7. (4) Did you bring a *fly*-swatter?
8. (4) The ball crashed through the *pane* of glass.
9. (3) Queen Elizabeth had a peaceful *reign.*
10. (2) Everyone cheered when the pitcher *threw* the third strike.
11. (3) The canoe floated silently down the *strait.*
12. (1) Some girls will not marry because they are waiting for their *knights* in shining armor.
13. (2) No, but I *beat* the eggs thoroughly.
14. (2) His *manner* is very offensive.
15. (2) Did you see the lovely *frieze* on the Smith's living room wall?

Practice VII *Page 270.*

For explanations of the following answers, see word list and examples in Chapter XIX.

1. (1) Please *let* Marie go to the movies with me because I may not go to town alone.
2. (4) If you don't want to build shelves for me, then *teach* me how to build them myself.
3. (3) Because this is a real problem in our community, we need a *very* dedicated group of citizens to study possible solutions.
4. (1) Many reports indicate that sugar-coated *cereals* are not healthful; therefore, more nutritious breakfast foods are appearing on the market.
5. (4) When Stuart gives the signal, everyone must rise to his feet, raise his hands above his head, and *sit* down.
6. (3) Because so many campers had cut down trees, there were *fewer* trees this year than ever before.
7. (3) Mrs. Smith taught the science class the *effect* of radiation upon cells.
8. (3) The author carries the principle of free will *further* than any previous author.
9. (1) Mrs. Kelly Warren, *formerly* Miss Kelly O'Rourke, emigrated from Ireland this past year.
10. (1) *It's* an illusion to expect that course of action to have a positive effect on our long-range plan.

22.
Writing Right

May 13, 1987

Golden Oldie Records
WOR-TV
1440 Broadway
New York City, NY 10019

Dear Dumbbells:

What's the matter with you people? I sent
you my hard-earned money (I'm a construction worker) for the Lawrence Welk records
you advertised, and after waiting eight
weeks I received a Rolling Stones album.
Can't you get anything right? I hate rock'n
roll music. It gives me a splitting headache.
I have a good mind to punch you in the
nose!

Boiling mad,

Harry Flowers

Harry Flowers

National Association of Retailers
How Not to Get Results

A Word With You . . .

Harry Flowers' letter is one of the horrible examples presented in
the National Association of Retailers' booklet, *How Not to Get Results*.
Mr. Flowers has a legitimate complaint, but he should realize that he
will not win friends or influence people by abusing them. Further-
more, a letter of complaint should contain all the necessary information needed to help a merchant redress your grievance.

Homework assignment for Mr. Flowers: Study this chapter . . . and
clean up your act!

Thinking Before You Write

Whether you intend to write a letter, memo, report, or essay, one thing is certain. You should make some important decisions before you get started. You could delay making those decisions — as many people do — and end up writing your piece again and again until you hit upon what you want to say. By doing some critical thinking before you write, you could save yourself a great deal of time and frustration. Following are some questions to help you plan your writing.

Should You Write?

If you can accomplish your purpose by talking to someone, then talk! During your work day, if you see an associate three, four, perhaps five times, there may be no need to write a memo regarding a simple matter. Say what you want if the issue can be concluded with that conversation, and save time and paper. Do not, however, expect a busy co-worker to carry your request in his or her head for an hour, a day, or a week. Do yourself and the person with whom you are communicating a favor. Put the question, the information, or the request in writing, if the issue can not be concluded with a brief conversation. If you don't commit your request or message to paper, the person receiving it will have to remember it or write it down. You risk having your message ignored or forgotten.

If you have a complaint about the dangerous cracks in the sidewalk on your block, your request to the Town Administrator will get faster attention if it arrives on paper. If you are a student with an assignment to write a term paper, of course you have no choice but to put your thoughts down on paper. When you write, you must make those thoughts clear to your reader. You want your message to be understood.

What Do You Want to Say?

Recognizing what you feel and think can still be worlds apart from understanding the "purpose" of your writing. For example, you may feel angry that the dress you bought shrunk when you had it dry-cleaned, but the purpose of your writing a letter to the store will be to persuade them to refund your money. Consider your basic motivation in writing. Are you going to berate your senator for voting against the Clean Air Bill or will you congratulate him for his veto? Will your term paper support the idea that Hamlet had a tragic flaw or will it show him as a victim of circumstance? Before you write, you must know what you want to say.

Who Is Your Reader?

A first step in writing is determining who will read what you write. Your audience will determine what type of writing you will do. Think of one idea going to two different people. For example, the following two letters describe a job, first to a friend, then to a potential employer. Notice how Jane's tone changes, depending on whether she is writing to someone she knows well or a potential employer.

Dear Judy,

    I've finally decided to pack in this dead-end job. I can no longer calmly listen to Mr. B. present my ideas as his accomplishments. He is so convinced they're his, he even brags to me about them. Most recently, I developed a training program for new employees. I sent him a draft. A week later, a manual was circulated with his name on it. He didn't even correct my typing error. I've applied for a comparable position in another company and hope to have good news for you soon.

Love,
Jane

16 Sunset Road
Boise, Idaho 83701
April 3, 1988

Ms. Eunice Munson
General Manager
ABC Corporation
Boise, Idaho 83720

Dear Ms. Munson:

    I am writing in response to your ad in Sunday's *Inquirer* for an assistant manager. I believe my experience is directly related to the position offered.

    For the past five years, I have assisted the manager of XYZ Corporation. My duties have included drafting speeches, devising company manuals, and providing administrative support. Most recently, we worked together on a training manual for new employees. While I still find my present position challenging, I am seeking employment with greater growth potential.

    I enclose a copy of my résumé and look forward to hearing from you at your earliest convenience.

Sincerely,
Jane Brody

How Do You Say It Best?

Writing takes many forms: letters, memos, reports, notes, lists, and books, to name just a few. Depending on your intention, the form you choose will determine the structure of your writing. We discuss letters, memos, reports, and essays in the following pages.

Letters

In the age of audiovisual miracles, letter writing has become a forgotten art. When phones were not available to exchange news or greetings, letters were common. Because people wrote often, they wrote well.

We still need letters on occasion in our personal lives: thank you notes, concolence notes, letters to distant friends or relatives, and greetings of all kinds. Letter writing is also helpful when we want to request information, complain about a product, let our congressmen know our views, or apply for a job.

Another type of letter that has not been eliminated by the telephone is the business letter. Anyone who works for a business, large or small, should be able to write a clear business letter. While modern office technology may somewhat reduce the need for letters, it won't eliminate it. Although word processing equipment increasingly will correct human error, the machines will only be as good as their operators.

This chapter will not attempt to deal with all the skills necessary to write a perfect letter. Elements such as grammar, spelling, and punctuation, covered earlier, play an important role. This chapter provides you with models and helpful hints for form and style.

Headings

Headings consist of your address, the date, the name and address of the recipient, and the salutation or greeting. Business letters include each of these elements (see The Business Letter style sheet on page 284). However, when writing to a friend or relative, your address and the recipient's address need not be included. The sample letters later in the chapter will show you the correct formats to use for both informal letters and business letters.

Part of the heading is the salutation or greeting — the "Dear [Somebody]." Changes in language usage and business itself have made "Dear [Somebody]" increasingly complicated. Once upon a time, if you were addressing an unknown group, the term "Gentlemen:" was appropriate. Today, those gentlemen include women who would not take kindly to that greeting. Often, business people sign letters that give no clue to the signator's gender. For example: "T. Warren" or "Terry Smith." "Ladies and Gentlemen:",

"Dear T. Warren:", or "Dear XYZ Company:" could replace more conventional salutations. Some sample salutations follow.

FRIENDLY SALUTATIONS	FORMAL SALUTATIONS
Dear Aunt Sue,	Gentlemen:
Dear Rosa,	Dear Sir:
Dearest William,	Dear Sirs:
	Dear Mr. Wright:
	Dear Ms. Smith:
	Dear Dr. Schwarz:
	Dear Director of Personnel:
	Dear Salespeople:
	Ladies and Gentlemen:
	Dear T. Warren:
	Dear XYZ Company:

Introduction, Body, Conclusion

Since your opening paragraph is like a first meeting with your reader, the impression you make is a lasting one. The reader expects to have your purpose revealed. Whether it is to complain, compliment, or inform, it should be clear immediately.

Throughout the letter, say what you want to say as clearly and as briefly as possible. Your letter may be long, but it should not ramble. Every sentence should be a necessary one.

The traditional interviewer-reporter questions help keep a letter clear and concise. Note which questions apply to your letter: *who, what, when, where, why.* If you answer these questions, you will probably give all the necessary information for situations ranging from a party invitation to a complaint about a broken radio.

Just as your first impression is a lasting one, so is your final one. Make sure your reader knows what you expect. If you plan a follow-up phone call, say so and say when. If you want a written or telephone response, ask for it. If you began the letter by thanking the person, reinforce your appreciation in the final paragraph.

Closings

Closings range from "Love," to "Very truly yours," depending upon the purpose and audience of your letter. The closing should be in the same style as the salutation. A letter would not begin "Dear Sir:" and end with "Love."

FRIENDLY CLOSINGS	FORMAL CLOSINGS
Sincerely,	Very truly yours,
Warmly,	Yours very truly,
With love,	Yours truly,
Love,	Sincerely yours,
Fondly,	Yours sincerely,
Warmest regards,	Sincerely,
(Any other nice thought you may	Respectfully yours,
want to use)	Very respectfully yours,
	Yours respectfully,

BUSINESS LETTER FORMAT

Sender's Address:

This is obviously not necessary on printed stationery. If typing on plain paper, your address should be placed in the upper right-hand corner.

Date:

Spell out the month in a business letter.

Recipient's Address:

On the left-hand side of the page, include the name (and title or position if you know it) of the person to whom you are writing. Then, put the name of the company or organization and, finally, the complete address of the organization.

Salutation:

See page 283 for examples of formal salutations.

Introduction:

One short paragraph states the subject or purpose of the letter. Make your purpose clear immediately.

Body:

One, two, three or more paragraphs contain the relevant details. Each paragraph should expand on one main point.

Conclusion:

The conclusion should give direction. One short paragraph finishes the letter with a summary, a recommendation, an instruction, or a thank you.

Closing:

See page 284 for formal closings.

Name and Signature

Business form dictates typing your name and title beneath your signature. If your title is on your letterhead, do not repeat it. If you are writing a business letter as a consumer, print your name beneath your signature. You want the response addressed to you correctly.

SAMPLE PERSONAL LETTER

July 15, 1988

Dear Aunt Polly,

Thank you so much for the leather-bound dictionary. It was a perfect graduation gift. I will treasure it always.

My family and I were sorry you couldn't come to Arizona for the graduation and party. We all missed you very much. I'm enclosing some photos for you.

Love,
David

SAMPLE BUSINESS LETTER

ABC Corporation
_____

231 West 53 Street, New York, New York 10022

July 10, 1987

Ms. Cary Jeffers
66 Columbus Avenue
Tarrytown, New York 10571

Dear Ms. Jeffers:

Thank you for your letter (dated June 25, 1987), asking about employment possibilities at the ABC Corporation. We receive a number of such requests each year, and must therefore limit interviews to individuals with prior work experience. Your resume indicates that you have no such prior experience, and therefore I cannot offer you any hope at this time. However, should you still want to work for our company after having gained a few years experience in the field, we would be most happy to reconsider your application.

Thank you for considering ABC Corporation. We wish you luck in securing employment very soon.

Very truly yours,

David Green
Personnel Director

DG/sl

SAMPLE COMPLAINT LETTER

106 Goodtree Drive
Columbus, Ohio 43201
March 10, 1988

Mr. William Wellington, President
Cool-It, Inc.
738 Second Avenue
New York, New York 10017

Dear Mr. Wellington:

On February 23, 1988, while a local Cool-It, Inc., representative was servicing my air-conditioner, the tank of freon exploded in my basement. The tank was located next to my clothes dryer, so this explosion caused damage to my dryer as well as some clothing that was in the dryer at the time. This event led to an expensive dryer service call and the need to replace a complete load of laundry. I would appreciate full reimbursement for the items listed on the attached bills.

The serviceman who repaired the dryer suggested that the malfunction was mostly caused by the freon. The spilled freon permanently froze the dryer thermostat, preventing the dryer from cooling down. A full load of towels and underwear that were in the dryer at the time became excessively dried out to the point of disintegration. In fact, when I removed the laundry from the dryer, the laundry fell apart in my hands. Prior to the explosion, the load of laundry was fine and the dryer worked perfectly.

I've always had an excellent relationship with your company and look forward to your continuing service. Your representative, by the way, was courteous and thorough in his job of repairing the air-conditioning system. I look forward to your payment within a reasonable amount of time.

Thank you.

Sincerely,

Mary Edwards

Mary Edwards

Practice I

> **Directions:** Read the following facts and write a letter of complaint from Tom Williams based on those facts. You can include your opinion or attitude toward the problem in the letter.

Tom Williams bought a clock radio at Warren's Department Store on May 15, 1982. Tom could not get the alarm to work properly from the start. He brought the clock radio back to the store on May 19, 1982, and was told he would have to mail the item to the manufacturer for repair. Tom lives at 1419 Maple Street, Dayton, Ohio 82050. The clock radio was made by the Wake-Up Corporation located at 2042 Main Street, Chicago, Illinois 60791.

Practice II

> **Directions:** Rewrite Matthew Manager's letter. Remember to write simply and clearly.

February 10, 1988

Ms. Suzanne Jones
1 Willow Way
Edison, New Jersey 08817

Dear Ms. Jones:

I wish to thank you for choosing to inform me about the incident which occurred at MarketRite last Friday. It is important to us in management to know what is going on when salespeople help--or don't help--as the case may be customers.

John Rich is usually a generally friendly person. He has been under very extreme personal pressure even though that should not enter into it. I have taken the liberty of speaking with John and am assured that what happened to you won't happen again at least from him.

Please be kind enough to accept the enclosed herewith gift certificate as a small token of our regret.

Thank you for shopping at MarketRite.

Sincerely,

Matthew Manager

Matthew Manager
Vice President
Customer Relations

Memorandums

A memorandum is commonly used for interoffice communications, such as sharing information, setting procedures, or asking questions within a company or organization. Every business has its preferred style for memos, but the tips that follow can be applied in most situations. Treat a memo as you would any other kind of writing. Plan ahead and then construct clear and concise sentences that convey your intentions. Either write a brief outline or jot down phrases that will help you organize your thinking. Stick to the subject at hand. State your purpose first, then give all the necessary facts. Tell what you want done or request information. If you are informing the reader, do so simply and clearly, keeping your tone friendly and positive. A memo need not be an edict. Simply answer the question, "What do I want to accomplish?" Again, make sure that what you say is accurate because memos, when filed, become records.

Format for Memos

Although a memo is very much like a letter in purpose, its format is different. The memo style sheet that follows shows you how.

MEMO STYLE SHEET

```
                          MEMO


    TO:    The name of the recipient, including the person's
           title and/or department

    FROM:  Your name, title, and department

    DATE:  The date you send the memo

    RE:    The subject of the memo


    Start with your purpose in writing the memo.  Include
    relevant details, or what the recipient must know, and
    close with what the recipient must do.

    Thank the recipient and offer to answer any questions.


    ABC:df
```

A memo usually is not signed at the bottom the way a letter would be. Instead, the sender initials the memo next to his or her name at the top. Sometimes, for security reasons companies require full signatures on memos.

Note the structure of the following sample memo. The opening gets right to the point. Helms recalls that he and Sperry have agreed that there is a potential problem. The memo proposes a solution. For emphasis, the solution is set off — highlighted — in its own paragarph. Other ways to visually emphasize ideas include using numbers, letters, headings, or bullets (black dots) at the left-hand margin. The final two sentences tell the reader what to do.

Note also that job titles appear next to the names. These titles can be omitted in very informal memos. However, memos that will be filed for future reference should have the titles included.

SAMPLE MEMO 1

MEMORANDUM

```
TO:      Janice Sperry, Vice President, Marketing
FROM:    Rob Helms, Purchasing Agent
DATE:    July 10, 1988
RE:      Purchase Agreement #47
```

When we spoke last Thursday, we agreed that the above purchase agreement #47 was vague and could cause problems with the completed job. I propose the following change:

1. Delete lines 4-7.
2. Insert the following in place of lines 2-7:
    "The seller is under no obligation to accept returned merchandise 90 days after delivery."

Let me know by the 15th if you agree with this change or have another suggestion. Thank you.

JS:cd

The following memo is a very informal one between two coworkers. No last names appear in the heading, and without these names, the memo would be almost useless as a record. Mary gets to the point immediately, however, noting co-responsibility for coordinating the company's calendar and letting Pat know the times during the week that she will be available. Mary then tells Pat what to do — that is, to decide on a convenient time to work together.

SAMPLE MEMO 2

```
                        MEMO

        TO:     Pat
        FROM:   Mary
        DATE:   November 3, 1987
        RE:     Company Calendar


        You and I are responsible for coordinating the company
        calendar.  I'm available any morning next week.  Please
        let me know the day and time convenient for you.
```

Now read the following memo. Does it meet all the requirements of a well-written memo? Yes. This short memo gets the job done. The subject is clearly stated in the RE line. In the first sentence, the reader learns the new due date and what has to be done. Sentences 2 and 3 show the writer's concern for Bill Greenway's well being. There is nothing wrong with a personal touch. One improvement would be to include the job titles and/or department names.

SAMPLE MEMO 3

```
FROM THE DESK OF JOHN SMITH:


TO:     Bill Greenway
DATE:   December 10, 1987
RE:     Monthly Report


You should be pleased to know that your December monthly report
will not be due until January 7, 1988.  This extension should
make your vacation a little more relaxing.  Enjoy the holidays.
```

Long Memos

Sometimes you will need to write a longer memo. For example, you may want to provide background information related to the subject, as well as give current information. Read the following memo and note how the need dictates form. In this memo, the introduction explains the background of Dr. Taylor's idea. The first part of the memo tells what the writer intends to do. The memo then asks Martin Atkins, the reader, to do three things: read, select, and estimate. What Martin Atkins has to do is detailed as well. The memo concludes with a due date. It is effective and should result in Dr. Taylor's getting what he wants.

SAMPLE MEMO 4

MEMO

```
TO:      Martin Atkins, Director of Rehabilitation Services
FROM:    Bruce Taylor, M.D., Hospital Administrator
DATE:    June 10, 1988
RE:      Development of a hortitherapy program for patients
```

At the recent Hospital Directors' Round Table, Dr. Seymour Watson of the New England Hortitherapy Council gave a speech on the positive results achieved with hospitalized patients who had been taking care of plants. He further explained the long-term benefits of hortitherapy, especially its continued use after the patient's discharge.

Dr. Watson gave me some guidelines on raising funds for such a project. I am going to survey the board to see how much money could be made available for our own hortitherapy program.

I've attached Dr. Watson's studies, "The Use of Hortitherapy in Geriatric Settings," "Hortitherapy in a Psychiatric Setting," and "Outpatient Programs in Hortitherapy." Please study these and decide which approach we could use at Sunnycrest.

After you decide which patients would benefit most from the program, estimate what personnel and supplies would cost for 20 patients. I'll need your cost estimates by July 16, 1988, so that I can review them before presenting my report to the Board of Directors on July 30.

MA:sz

Disciplinary Memos

If you find it necessary to write a disciplinary memo, bear in mind that a disciplinary memo must:

- document inappropriate or unacceptable behavior
- focus on the serious effect of such behavior
- establish guidelines for future behavior
- state consequences of continued inappropriate behavior
- schedule a follow up review of progress

PRACTICE

III   Directions: Rewrite the memo below to conform with the guidelines for a disciplinary memo.

Memo

```
TO  :  Edna Employee
FROM:  Sandy Supervisor
DATE:  March 25, 1988


We talked today about your being late a lot lately.  This is
not the way we do things around here.  It makes it look like you
don't care about your job, and other people complain about it.

The next time you're late it could be serious.
```

PRACTICE

IV   Directions: Write an appropriate memo for each situation below.

1. From a supervisor in the order department to the inventory control manager, noting a shortage in a recent shipment to a key client.
2. From a supervisor, who plans to be away, to an employee designated to cover that supervisor's duties during that time.

Reports and Proposals

A report is a detailed statement of accomplishments or findings. A proposal is a request for funding or support to solve a recognized problem or to implement a new idea.

Since reports and proposals serve different functions, they take on different forms. Regardless of the format, however, the basics of good writing prevail. You should present your information in a clear, concise style. You need to document your facts, and if you are taking facts from another source, you must give credit to those sources. In a formal report for school, you would use footnotes. For a business report, you would include footnotes where appropriate. Your conclusions should be set off from your facts, so the reader is able to distinguish fact from opinion.

Reports

Most reports have a set form, similar to an outline. For example, a business report may follow this format:

Cover page:	Title, author, date of report
Summary or abstract:	A brief overview of the subject covered and conclusions drawn
Introduction:	A beginning section in which you set the scene, giving relevant background information and/or explaining terminology used in the report
Body:	The information you are sharing, which supports the conclusions you have drawn
Appendix:	All additional relevant data, such as sources of information, additional charts and graphs, and supporting statistics

In preparing reports for business, check for company style by referring to previous reports. If you ask, you may even find a company manual with clear guidelines for report writing. For school reports, ask your teacher what particulars are important to him or her. No one form is correct, but you should use the form preferred.

A lengthy report should have a cover page indicating the purpose of the report, the person or persons to whom it is submitted, the person or persons by whom it is submitted, and the date. The table of contents indicates the scope of the report and the organization of the body of the report. Lengthy reports include a summary at the beginning so that the reader can know at the start the scope and breadth of the report without having to first read the entire report. In the following sample, note the cover page, table of contents, and excerpt from the introduction of a report.

REPORT

OF THE

JOINT STATEWIDE TASK FORCE ON
SOLID WASTE DISPOSAL SITES

Submitted to:

John Doe

Commissioner of Environmental Protection

by:

The Joint Statewide Task Force on Solid Waste Disposal

March, 1988

TABLE OF CONTENTS

I.   INTRODUCTION AND OVERVIEW

The purpose of this report is the assessment of the condition of existing solid waste disposal sites in this state. Faced with the crisis brought about by the closing of landfills while the amount of solid waste produced continues to rise, hard choices to be made by government require an accurate appraisal of those few remaining sites. May they safely continue in use? If so, for how long and under what conditions? It is the purpose of this report to provide answers to those questions.

At the turn of this century, refuse was taken to a nearby "dump," of which there may have been a thousand. The focus was then upon keeping down flies, odor, and avoiding fires. The remedy was the keeping of a "sanitary landfill," which meant nothing more than regularly covering the refuse with layers of soil or sand.

In the intervening years, the nature of the waste stream changed. Many more toxic materials forced their way into those landfills. Often, hazardous waste from manufacturers was accepted along with household waste. Rainwater on the site would come in contact with hazardous waste and be tainted by it, flow into and become part of the groundwater, and contaminate nearby wells. That tainted water was called leachate.

At this time, there are ten landfills that accept household wastes and eighty that accept industrial wastes. All present problems. Their continued use is made necessary because we have yet to come to grips with reduction of the waste stream and alternative technologies that would neutralize that waste. Those aspects are beyond the scope of this report. We start with an assessment of existing landfills.

Proposals

Proposals follow the same general approach as reports, although most proposals have their own form. Among different companies or agencies, the requested format will vary; one typical form follows.

TYPICAL PROPOSAL FORMAT

PROPOSAL ELEMENT	*EXAMPLE*
Background: Describe in one short paragraph the history of the operation you plan to change.	MarketRite has been offering one express lane to customers with ten or fewer items for the past twelve years. The express shopper used to be the exception, but is now the rule. Many working men and women stop in for three or four items on their way home.
Present Conditions: What goes on now? Why is it inadequate?	Express lanes defy the term. The lanes are exceptionally long and customers often choose to forego buying the one or two items to avoid the lines. This is demonstrated by the merchandise left on the magazine racks near the express lanes.
Proposed Solution: What changes will you make? What new equipment will be needed? What personnel changes will be needed? How will other operations be affected?	Open two lanes for express purchases during peak times. In order to maintain regular service in other lines, additional part-time help must be hired. Encourage respecting the item limit for express lanes. Have the store manager periodically check for bottlenecks during assumed "slow times" and reassign someone from a regular line to express. This step will be difficult at first, but will become easier as patterns are noted.
Benefits: What long and short term benefits will result?	MarketRite will attract the new breed of shopper. Working people will find shopping at MarketRite is as convenient, more cost effective, and more versatile than the

convenience stores. We will retain the traditional shopper by continuing to provide quality check-out for them while eliminating the disgruntled "fast shopper" who "just has six items" and would like to cut into the regular line.

Alternatives: What are some possible alternatives?

Do not hire additional part-time help for peak times. This would mean closing a regular register to open the additional express lane and would reduce service to the traditional shopper.

Do not try to monitor during assumed "slow times." Nothing will be gained by not trying.

Hire additional full-time help to keep the extra express lane open. This may not be cost effective. Relieving the problem during peak times may be sufficient.

Essays

Essays, written for school, for publication, or for yourself, present your own ideas, views, or conclusions. Essays, as well as other writing, benefit from careful planning. Follow these steps to good essay writing.

EASY WRITING STEPS

Plan
Establish a controlling idea by defining your topic and major points.

Outline
Think through your writing from beginning to end. A perfect, final outline is not necessary; outlining serves to order your thoughts and ideas and to subordinate supporting details to major points.

Draft
Fast and furious. Get it down on paper. Don't agonize over grammar, structure, and word choice.

Edit

Fine tuning. Now is the time to agonize over organization, grammar, structure, and word choice. Begin with the end. If you want your audience to continue reading, say immediately why you are writing a mystery. Don't keep your audience in suspense.

Follow with relevant details. Include facts that support the point you want to make. If you lead your readers down an unrelated side road, they may not return to the main issue.

Rewrite

The final product. Make sure that editing did not destroy the flow of writing. One change often necessitates others. Follow through. Simplify reading with subheadings, capitalization, underlining, bulleting, and spacing.

Editing and Rewriting

As you begin editing, ask yourself some important questions.

1. Does your letter, memo, report, proposal, or essay follow your original plan? If not, why not? You may have followed your plan but find that the ideas could be arranged more effectively now. Move those misplaced paragraphs or sentences. Don't hesitate to change the order, even though, at the beginning, it seemed the right way to arrange things. On second look, you may have found a better way of saying what you want to get across to the reader.

2. Are your ideas well supported? If not, you may need to expand on an idea and add evidence to your argument. On the other hand, if you've gone beyond the subject matter when you've defended a point, you may need to shorten that paragraph or delete an entire section.

3. Is the tone of your writing appropriate? Some people answer this question by reading the report or letter aloud. You can read to a friend — real or imagined — and ask yourself along the way, "Is this the way I would talk?" "Is my idea stated in a conversational way?" "Is the letter overwritten and stiff?" Remember: informal does not mean substandard, and "substandard" does not mean informal.

4. Have you accomplished your purpose? Find a friend who is not an expert in the subject at hand. Have that person read your letter or report. If your friend is honest, you'll soon know if you've accomplished your purpose for writing.

Checking Your Language

Wordiness

Have you avoided repeating words or thoughts? You can expect your first draft to suffer from wordiness and repetition. Remember, though, that no reader wants to waste time cutting through sentences filled with repetition. When you force your readers to struggle, you try their patience. As you read the examples below, remember to go back and take two or three more words out of every sentence after you've finished editing your work.

Here are some examples of wordiness and repetition with their corrected forms:

No: Today in our modern world we can offer new products at competitive prices.

Yes: Today we can offer new products at competitive prices.

Note that "today" means the same as "modern world."

No: These are the basic essentials of our plan.

Yes: These are the essentials of our plan.

Note that by definition, "essentials" are basic.

PRACTICE

V   **Directions:** In the following sentences, eliminate the words that are not necessary to the meaning of the sentence.

1. Even after the machine stopped, smoke was visible to the eye.
2. We'll rent a conference room midway between our two offices.
3. If you don't understand an abbreviation, refer back to the index.
4. Rewrite the introduction again before you go on.
5. First and foremost, I want to commend your department.
6. Our study group reached a consensus of opinion.
7. Advanced planning was credited with saving the company.
8. Our product is totally unique.
9. The reason is because it would cost too much to replace the old equipment.
10. The battle produced gains that were small in size.

Stilted Phrases

Have you avoided words that writers seem to *save* for letters, memos, and reports? Business letters are frequently filled with legal language as well as archaic words and phrases, even though they add no meaning. Ask yourself, "Would I use this in conversation or at any other time?" If the answer is no, strike that heavy phrase from your work.

Here are some examples of stilted, out-of-date, and overly formal phrases that creep into business and report writing.

Don't Use	Substitute
Due to the fact	Because
Attached herewith	Here is
In receipt of	Have received
In reference to	Concerning
At the present time	Now
Under separate cover	Separately
Thanking you in advance	Thank you

PRACTICE

VI **Directions:** Substitute plain English for the stilted language used in the following sentences.

1. In the process of checking your account, we have found that your bill is overdue.
2. Attached please find my check for $42.37.
3. I will take your plan under advisement.
4. We beg to advise you that our product will be on sale in May.
5. I am in receipt of your letter and its contents are noted.

Clichés and Pretension

Did you use words that everyone has already used many times before? Are those words stilted and stuffy? These pretentious words are popular today, but you'll improve your writing if you choose a simpler, more precise term.

Don't Use	Substitute
Utilize	Use
Maximize	Increase
Finalize	Finish
Prioritize	Rank
Optimize	Cut the cost, improve
Bottom line	Profit
Interface	Meet or work together
Facilitate	Help
Profitwise	Profit

PRACTICE

VII **Directions:** Substitute a precise word or a simpler word for the underlined word or words in each sentence.

1. We need to systematize our files so that we can utilize them easily.
2. Size-wise, these bookcase are a better choice for our office.

3. The way you use your time affects the <u>bottom line</u> figure for the company.
4. A larger sales force will <u>maximize</u> our profits.
5. Absenteeism <u>impacts</u> on production schedules.
6. Your report <u>legitimizes</u> our need for monthly meetings.
7. The personnel and production departments will <u>interface</u> to solve the problem.

Keeping Sexism Out of Your Writing

Follow these guidelines to avoid sexism in your writing.

1. Do not add *ess* to words that do not require that suffix. For example, *actor* means male actor and *actress* means female, *Manager* means male or female *manager.*
2. Where the word is comfortably modified to be unisex, modify it. *Chairperson* sounds as legitimate as *chairman.*
3. Try to avoid situations that require a singular pronoun. For example, instead of the following:

Each member of the management team took his place (or his/her place) at the conference table.

Use:

Members of the management team took their places at the conference table.

Proofreading

Proofreading is an important part of editing what you have written. It assures you that careless errors in grammar, punctuation, and sense have been caught and corrected. Proofreading must be done in several steps:

1. Read through for content. Do not expect to pick up technical errors. Do expect to pick up missing or transposed words or sentences and errors in information.
2. Read for grammar, spelling, punctuation, and sense. Force yourself to read *each* word.
3. Read one more time to ensure that changes did not alter consistency or sense.
4. Have another person proofread your work, after you have proofread it yourself.

SUMMARY OF
STEPS TO SIMPLIFY AND CLARIFY YOUR WRITING

1. Use action verbs. Write so that your nouns act and are not acted upon. (Unless you do not want to assign responsibility.)

   Instead of: A new check-cashing policy will be introduced this spring.
   Use: General Markets will introduce a new check-cashing policy this spring.

2. Limit your use of prepositional phrases.

   Instead of: We scheduled a meeting of supervisors of MIS for January 12.
   Use: We scheduled an MIS supervisors' meeting for January 12.

3. Eliminate unnecessary words and phrases.

   Instead of: When a new spa opens, all of the spas in the Wonder Woman chain take part in the grand opening of that spa.
   Use: All Wonder Woman spas take part in the grand opening of a new spa in the chain.

4. Use nouns rather than pronouns as often as possible.

   Instead of: When he gives the report to him, make sure he understands the ramifications.
   Use: When Tom gives the report to Jason, make sure Jason understands the ramifications.

5. Focus on concrete word choice rather than abstract.

   Instead of: In order to create a holiday atmosphere, we want to encourage spirit and festivity throughout the store.
   Use: In order to create a holiday atmosphere, we want managers to develop special displays, provide holiday music, and remind cashiers to say, "Happy holidays" to customers.

6. Avoid using nouns as verbs.

   Instead of: Please Federal Express the report to Michael.
   Use: Please send the report to Michael by Federal Express.

7. Use positive words; avoid negative words.

Instead of: Only fifty some odd residents turned out for the opening of the Middletown Bank.

Use: Over fifty residents participated in the opening of the Middletown Bank.

PRACTICE VIII

Directions: Please correct each sentence below according to the rules.

1. Use action verbs.

   The order was placed too late.

2. Limit your use of prepositional phrases.

   We arranged a meeting with the manager of data processing at the location in East Brunswick.

3. Eliminate unnecessary words and phrases.

   There are two possible approaches that we are considering.

4. Use nouns rather than pronouns as often as possible.

   When he gives the report to him, make sure he understands the ramifications.

5. Focus on concrete word choice rather than abstract.

   Contributions help many people.

6. Avoid using nouns as verbs.

   Please Federal Express the report to Michael.

7. Use positive words.

   If it's not inconvenient for you now, perhaps we could talk.

Writer's Block

Any adult who has ever had reason to write more than three words at a time has experienced writer's block. What is writer's block? Think of it as the "empty paper syndrome" — the fight between the need to Get Something Down on a blank piece of paper and the desire to Get It Down Correctly on the first try — an impossible task.

To a great extent, writer's block occurs because we refuse to admit — or we haven't been taught — that no one can produce perfect written work on the first try. Stated another way, writer's block results from thinking that you can put an idea on paper AND edit it at the same time. This creates unreasonable pressure. You can't. I can't. Well-known writers can't. You say you need proof? Read on.

Recently, the editors of *Writer's Digest* asked several authors of fiction to write articles using the title, "How I Write My Books." Their articles revealed different approaches to their craft, but one idea remained constant: there are two aspects to writing — creating and revising.

You may be wondering if this applies to you — after all, you don't write fiction — it does. Whether fiction or fact, you are dealing with two things: creating and revising.

What can be done to circumvent writer's block? Without knowing it, you have probably just taken the first step simply by thinking about the idea that creating and revising are two different tasks. If you accept that as a fact, you can go on to attack the first half of the process — creating.

Educators have developed techniques to help the writer get the creator working. Whether called brainstorming, improvisational writing, or clustering, these techniques have one idea in common. They insist that each writer is a combination of creator and editor. Each technique requires that your editor leave the room while your creator works. The creator must work unhampered by concerns of spelling, word choice, and sentence structure. Each technique asks that, as you think about your subject, you jot down your thoughts in single words, phrases, or brief sentences, no matter how or in what order they occur to you. DON'T JUDGE YOUR THOUGHTS. JUST WRITE THEM DOWN. The result will be many related ideas (and a few unrelated, but that doesn't matter) which are not in logical order. That's fine. That proves you are part of the human race in which minds do not work in outline form.

Once you have your thoughts on paper, you can open the door and let the editor in. The editor will help you put your thoughts in order and polish your grammar, structure, and word choice. Finally, the editor will increase the readability of your essay by adding necessary subheadings, listing points where appropriate, and using white space creatively.

SOME TOOLS FOR BETTER WRITING

Chicago Manual of Style, Illinois: University of Chicago Press, 1982.

The Elements of Style, New York: Macmillan Publishing Company, Inc. 1979.

The Merriam-Webster Dictionary, New York: Pocket Books, 1981.

Oxford American Dictionary, New York: Oxford University Press, 1980.

Roget's International Thesaurus, New York: Harper & Row Publishers, Inc., 1979.

20,000 Words, New York: McGraw-Hill Inc., 1985.

Webster's Instant Word Guide, Massachusetts: Merriam-Webster, Inc., 1980.

ANSWER KEY

Chapter 22

Writing Right

Practice I *Page 288.*

1419 Maple Street
Dayton, Ohio 82050
May 20, 1982

Service Manager
Wake-Up Corporation
2042 Main Street
Chicago, Illinois 60791

Dear Service Manager:

I bought the enclosed clock radio at Warren's Department Store in Dayton, Ohio, on May 15, 1982. The alarm did not work properly from the start.

On May 19, I brought the clock radio back to Warren's to exchange for a new model or to have it repaired. The salesman would not accept the clock radio. He insisted on returning it to you. This is a great inconvenience. I never even used this appliance.

Please send me a new clock radio immediately. I also would encourage you to work out a fairer arrangement with your distributors. I know I would never buy a Wake-Up product again because of the inconvenience.

Very truly yours,

Tom Williams

Tom Williams

Practice II *Page 288*

February 10, 1988

Ms. Suzanne Jones
1 Willow Way
Edison, New Jersey 08817

Dear Ms. Jones:

Thank you for informing me about the unfortunate experience
you had at MarketRite last Friday. You clearly understand
the importance of sharing such information with management.
We do want to make our shopping environment pleasant.

There is no excuse for the treatment you received. John Rich
surprised and embarrassed himself by yelling at you. Although
that behavior was not typical, it never should have occurred
at all. Of course, I have spoken with John and extend his
personal apology.

Please accept the enclosed gift certificate as our way of
apologizing and stating that you are a valued customer.
When you are in MarketRite again, please ask for me. I would
like to thank you personally for helping us improve our service.

Sincerely,

Matthew Manager

Matthew Manager
Vice President
Customer Relations

MM:er
enc.

Practice III *Page 293.*

MEMO

```
TO:     Edna Employee
FROM:   Sandy Supervisor
DATE:   March 25, 1987
```

As we discussed in our meeting today, you have been 30 minutes late for work on three occasions in the last two weeks. These incidents follow two earlier discussions we had regarding tardiness.

In our talk today, we went over the Company's policy on tardiness and agreed that when you are late it creates problems for other employees who must cover for you. It also results in late filling of orders, which can affect our customer relations. Repeated tardiness also causes resentment among co-workers who are consistently on time. As we agreed, you will purchase a new alarm clock and get a bus schedule so you have an alternative mode of transportation if your car will not start. As I pointed out, further incidents of tardiness could result in withholding of your upcoming wage increase or, if sustained improvement is not seen, termination.

We will meet again in two weeks to review your record.

Practice IV *Page 293.*

1. TO: Jack Barnes, Inventory Control Manager
   FROM: Sally Farmer, Supervisor, Order Department
   DATE: October 10, 1987
   RE: ORDER #67–8850/October 1, 1987

   Please note that the above order was shipped short of 50 copies of WRITING THE EASY WAY. This customer is one of our key buyers, and expects a replacement shipment within 2 days. Can you look into this and assure me that the shipment will go out immediately via Federal Express?

2. TO: William
   FROM: Rita
   DATE: February 16, 1988
   RE: My upcoming vacation — 2/23–2/30

   Please read the attached outline of duties in its entirety before I leave on Tuesday. I will be available to answer any questions you might have regarding materials, personnel, etc. Please maintain a log of messages, and note which ones will not have been answered. John should be available to assist you when necessary. Thank you for taking on the extra load; I'll be available for same when your vacation comes along.

Practice V *Page 301*

1. Even after the machine stopped, smoke was visible.
2. We'll rent a conference room between our two offices.
3. If you don't understand an abbreviation, refer to the index.
4. Rewrite the introduction before you go on.
5. First I commend your department.
6. Our study group reached a consensus.
7. Planning was credited with saving the company.
8. Our product is unique.
9. It would cost too much to replace the old equipment.
10. The battle produced gains that were small.

Practice VI *Page 302*

1. Checking your account, we have found that your bill is overdue.
2. Here's my check for $42.37.
3. I will consider your plan.
4. We want you to know that our product will be on sale in May.
5. I've received your letter.

Practice VII *Page 302*

1. We need to <u>organize</u> our files so that we can <u>use</u> them easily.
2. These bookcases are a better <u>size</u> for our office.
3. The way you use your time affects our <u>profits</u>.
4. A larger sales force will <u>increase</u> our profits.
5. Absenteeism <u>affects</u> production schedules.
6. Your report <u>demonstrates</u> (shows) our need for monthly meetings.
7. The personnel and production departments will <u>meet</u> (**work together**) to solve the problem.

Practice VIII *Page 305*

1. Henry placed the order too late.
2. We arranged a meeting in East Brunswick with the data processing manager.
3. We are considering two possible approaches.
4. When Ron gives the report to Gary, make sure Gary understands the ramifications.
5. Contributions provide food and clothing for the homeless.
6. Please send the report to Michael by Federal Express.
7. If it's convenient for you now, perhaps we could talk.

23.
Final Review

This review covers all of the concepts presented in *English the Easy Way*, Chapters 1-22.

- Spelling
- Usage
- Effectiveness of Expression
- Punctuation and Capitalization

After completing the Final Review exercises, evaluate your ability on the SUMMARY OF RESULTS chart on page 306. Acceptable scores for each practice are given.

To learn your weaknesses, find the question numbers you answered incorrectly on the SKILLS ANALYSIS table. The table will show which of your skills need improvement and the necessary chapters to review.

Spelling

Directions: Blacken the space beneath the number which corresponds to the number of the incorrectly spelled word in each group. If there is no error, blacken space number 5.

		1	2	3	4	5
1.	1) belief 2) reference 3) caucas 4) changeable 5) No error	‖	‖	‖	‖	‖
2.	1) temperture 2) exceed 3) misspell 4) absence 5) No error	‖	‖	‖	‖	‖
3.	1) quantity 2) probably 3) warrant 4) libary 5) No error	‖	‖	‖	‖	‖
4.	1) subversive 2) lucritive 3) psychology 4) queue 5) No error	‖	‖	‖	‖	‖
5.	1) hygenic 2) currency 3) eczema 4) salient 5) No error	‖	‖	‖	‖	‖

				1	2	3	4	5

6. 1) Wednesday   2) biscuit   3) efemoral
    4) contemptible   5) No error

7. 1) corrugated   2) diphtheria   3) voucher
    4) unecessary   5) No error

8. 1) wierd   2) tuition   3) capital   4) duly
    5) No error

9. 1) illustrative   2) laboratory   3) judiciary
    4) receits   5) No error

10. 1) though   2) simular   3) surgeon
    4) voluntary   5) No error

11. 1) preference   2) economical   3) prefered
    4) deterrent   5) No error

12. 1) psychology   2) cooperation
    3) rationally   4) argument   5) No error

13. 1) generally   2) improbable   3) dispensible
    4) portable   5) No error

14. 1) truely   2) niece   3) neighbor
    4) occurrence   5) No error

15. 1) cunning   2) tomatoes   3) mouthfuls
    4) crushs   5) No error

16. 1) sheep   2) pianos   3) Z's   4) thiefs
    5) No error

17. 1) men-of-war   2) supersede   3) succeed
    4) precede   5) No error

18. 1) misunderstand   2) achevement
    3) condemned   4) cancellation
    5) No error

19. 1) acquire   2) assessment   3) Thrusday
    4) character   5) No error

20. 1) churches   2) wield   3) category
    4) realize   5) No error

Usage-Part A

Directions: Blacken the space beneath the number which corresponds to the number of the error in each sentence. If there is no error, blacken space number 5.

1 2 3 4 5

1. No *two* *cities* in *this* country *is* identical. ‖ ‖ ‖ ‖ ‖
         1   2   3   4

    No error
     5

1 2 3 4 5

2. *Any* of the local merchants *are* *willing* to ‖ ‖ ‖ ‖ ‖
     1   2   3

    support the United Fund. *No error*
     4   5

1 2 3 4 5

3. A carton of cigarettes *has been laying* on this ‖ ‖ ‖ ‖ ‖
                 1   2   3

    counter *all* week. *No error*
          4   5

1 2 3 4 5

4. *Either* of those two congressmen *will vote* ‖ ‖ ‖ ‖ ‖
     1   2   3

    against the President's *proposed* bill. *No error*
                  4   5

1 2 3 4 5

5. *One* of the *necessary* prerequisites for ‖ ‖ ‖ ‖ ‖
     1   2

    change *are* *open-mindedness.* *No error*
         3   4   5

1 2 3 4 5

6. Manuel and *me travel* to *work* together each ‖ ‖ ‖ ‖ ‖
             1   2   3

    week-day morning. *No error*
     4   5

                                                        1 2 3 4 5
7. Taxes and *laughter* *is* always *present* in our   ‖ ‖ ‖ ‖ ‖
              1   2   3

   American way of life. *No error*
       4   5

                                                        1 2 3 4 5
8. Everyone must *realize* *their* own potential   ‖ ‖ ‖ ‖ ‖
                    1   2

   and *try* to *achieve* it. *No error*
       3   4   5

                                                        1 2 3 4 5
9. Mario *is* a much *more* *efficient* bartender   ‖ ‖ ‖ ‖ ‖
          1   2   3

   than *him*. *No error*
         4   5

                                                        1 2 3 4 5
10. Elissa *types* *much* *quicker* *than* any *other* ‖ ‖ ‖ ‖ ‖
             1   2   3   4   4

    woman in the office. *No error*
                             5

                                                        1 2 3 4 5
11. *Each* of the choices *are* *equally* unappealing   ‖ ‖ ‖ ‖ ‖
      1   2   3

    to *me*. *No error*
        4   5

                                                        1 2 3 4 5
12. Before the alarm *had stopped ringing*, Vera   ‖ ‖ ‖ ‖ ‖
                          1   2

    had *pulled* up the shade. *No error*
      3   4   5

                                                        1 2 3 4 5
13. One of *those* women *speak* *as* well *as* a profes- ‖ ‖ ‖ ‖ ‖
             1   2   3   4

    sional lecturer. *No error*
                          5

14. The dishes in the box *is on* sale this week only
    <u>1</u> <u>2</u>

    and will be *sold* for more next week. *No error*
    <u>3</u>   <u>4</u>   <u>5</u>

    1 2 3 4 5
    ‖ ‖ ‖ ‖ ‖

15. The Township Committee *had* not *realized*
    <u>1</u>   <u>2</u>

    that so many residents *were concerned* about
    <u>3</u>   <u>4</u>

    the new zoning law. *No error*
    <u>5</u>

    1 2 3 4 5
    ‖ ‖ ‖ ‖ ‖

16. *Either* the subway or the *buses is crowded* at
    <u>1</u>   <u>2</u> <u>3</u> <u>4</u>

    this time of day. *No error*
    <u>5</u>

    1 2 3 4 5
    ‖ ‖ ‖ ‖ ‖

17. I *noticed* that older women *walk more*
    <u>1</u>   <u>2</u> <u>3</u>

    graceful than teen-age girls. *No error*
    <u>4</u>   <u>5</u>

    1 2 3 4 5
    ‖ ‖ ‖ ‖ ‖

18. *Each* of the contestants *hope* to *win* the
    <u>1</u>   <u>2</u>   <u>3</u>

    grand prize. *No error*
    <u>4</u>   <u>5</u>

    1 2 3 4 5
    ‖ ‖ ‖ ‖ ‖

19. When I must *speak* to a *large* group of peo-
    <u>1</u>   <u>2</u>

    ple, I always speak *too soft*. *No error*
    <u>3</u> <u>4</u>   <u>5</u>

    1 2 3 4 5
    ‖ ‖ ‖ ‖ ‖

20. The mail carriers *each has their* own *personal*
    <u>1</u> <u>2</u> <u>3</u>   <u>4</u>

    gripes. *No error*
    <u>5</u>

    1 2 3 4 5
    ‖ ‖ ‖ ‖ ‖

21. _Any_ of the women in that office _may_ express
    1   2
    their opinion at _any_ time. _No error_
    3   4   5

    1 2 3 4 5
    ‖ ‖ ‖ ‖ ‖

22. Either the executive _or_ members of his staff
                         1
    was _responsible_ for _breaking_ the law. _No error_
    2   3   4   5

    1 2 3 4 5
    ‖ ‖ ‖ ‖ ‖

23. Before they _signed_ the treaty, both parties
                1
    agreed to _uphold_ the terms _provided_. _No error_
    2   3   4   5

    1 2 3 4 5
    ‖ ‖ ‖ ‖ ‖

24. Eisenhower _was_ president before Kennedy
                1
    was, and Nixon _served_ after Kennedy _had_.
    2   3   4
    No error
    5

    1 2 3 4 5
    ‖ ‖ ‖ ‖ ‖

25. Either Charlie or _I_ will _call_ you or _he_ when the
                     1   2   3
    order _is_ ready. _No error_
          4   5

    1 2 3 4 5
    ‖ ‖ ‖ ‖ ‖

26. _Romeo and Juliet are_ one of my favorite
                      1
    plays, but _I've_ never _seen_ _it_ performed.
               2   3   4
    No error
    5

    1 2 3 4 5
    ‖ ‖ ‖ ‖ ‖

27. _Was_ _it_ Mr. Farrar _whom_ _called_ you? _No error_
    1   2   3   4   5

    1 2 3 4 5
    ‖ ‖ ‖ ‖ ‖

28. I *am* *always* at the bus stop *earlier* than *him.*
     1   2   3   4
No error
  5

       1 2 3 4 5
       || || || || ||

29. Eileen and *me* *are* *working* on the night shift
               1 2   3
with *them.* *No error*
     4   5

       1 2 3 4 5
       || || || || ||

30. Fifteen minutes *are* all that I *can* *spare* to lis-
                1   2   3
ten to *your* problems. *No error*
       4   5

       1 2 3 4 5
       || || || || ||

31. The problem of *too* many people *require*
                1   2
immediate attention by world leaders
     3
as well as scientists and environmentalists.
     4
No error
  5

       1 2 3 4 5
       || || || || ||

32. After many months *of* *arguing,* Congress fi-
                 1   2
nally *adapted* the bill *into* law. *No error*
      3   4   5

       1 2 3 4 5
       || || || || ||

33. Because his lawyer *strongly* *adviced* him to do
                   1   2
so, Mr. Rodriguez *offered* his wife a generous
 3
settlement. *No error*
          5

34. The *principle* reason for *my* not borrowing
          1   2

     your credit card is that I'm afraid I'll *lose* it.
      3   4

     No error
      5

1 2 3 4 5 ‖ ‖ ‖ ‖ ‖

35. *Your* supervisor *does* not appreciate *you* walk-
    1   2   3

     ing in *consistently* at 9:10. *No error*
             4   5

1 2 3 4 5 ‖ ‖ ‖ ‖ ‖

Usage-Part B

Directions: Blacken the space beneath the number which corresponds to the number of the error in each sentence. If there is no error, blacken space number 5.

1. My brother *he* never *calls* before *visiting us*.
            1   2   3   4

     No error
      5

1 2 3 4 5 ‖ ‖ ‖ ‖ ‖

2. Great men *throughout* history *hardly never*
              1   2   3

     avoided some minor *scandal. No error*
                4   5

1 2 3 4 5 ‖ ‖ ‖ ‖ ‖

3. If you *had* called ahead *of* time, I could *of been*
        1   2   3 4

     ready when you arrived. *No error*
                   5

1 2 3 4 5 ‖ ‖ ‖ ‖ ‖

4. Lady Bird Johnson *scarcely never missed* an
                 1   2   3

     opportunity to *beautify* America. *No error*
              4   5

1 2 3 4 5 ‖ ‖ ‖ ‖ ‖

5.   The *sightseeing* trip on the sightseeing bus
             1

    was *one of* the highlights of our *much* de-
     2   3   4

    served vacation. *No error*
                   5

    1 2 3 4 5

6.   Manny *was* shocked when Alfred *raised* his
         1   2

    voice; no one had *never spoken* to him in that
                3   4

    tone of voice. *No error*
               5

    1 2 3 4 5

7.   The sun *it* *is* 865,000 miles in diameter and
          1 2

    has a surface temperature of *about* 10,000 ° F.
     3   4

    No error
      5

    1 2 3 4 5

8.   A wise consumer *carefully* *reads* the labels
                1   2

    and doesn't *never* *buy* unmarked products.
            3   4

    No error
      5

    1 2 3 4 5

9.   If you really *had* *wanted* to, you could *of*
             1   2   3

    prevented that misunderstanding. *No error*
     4   5

    1 2 3 4 5

10.   Some scientists *they* believe *that* one of the
            1   2

    long-range *effects* of food additives *is* hyper-
          3   4

    activity in children. *No error*
               5

Effectiveness of Expression—Part A

Directions: Blacken the space beneath the number which corresponds to the number of the correct completion for each sentence below. Choice 1 is always the same as the underlined portion and is sometimes the right answer.

1 2 3 4 5
|| || || || ||

1. In today's all-volunteer U.S. Army, *the recruit he starts* his two-year enlistment in a different atmosphere.

    1. the recruit he starts
    2. the recruit starts
    3. the recruit starting
    4. a recruit he is starting
    5. the recruits they start

1 2 3 4 5
|| || || || ||

2. *The reason that the former soldier would not recognize living conditions in today's army is because* the facilities are more home-like and less barracks-like.

    1. The reason that the former soldier would not recognize living conditions in today's army is because
    2. The reason is that the former soldier would not recognize living conditions in today's army because
    3. The former soldier would not recognize living conditions in today's army because
    4. Being that the former soldier would not recognize living conditions in today's army is because
    5. Because the former soldier would not recognize living conditions in today's army is because

1 2 3 4 5
|| || || || ||

3. Today's soldier enjoys *not only more comfort but also better pay.*

    1. not only more comfort but also better pay.

2. not only more comfort and better pay.

3. no more comfort and also better pay.

4. not only more comfort and, in addition, better pay.

5. not only more comforts and, in addition, better pay.

1 2 3 4 5
|| || || || ||

4. Nowadays the army can afford to be choosy *although the recession has increased* the number and the quality of the applicants.

1. although the recession has increased

2. despite the recession has increased

3. in addition to the recession having increased

4. since the recession has increased

5. but the recession has increased

1 2 3 4 5
|| || || || ||

5. The recruits get *tough, demanding, and training which is useful* under the command of their drill sergeants.

1. tough, demanding, and training which is useful

2. tough, demanding, useful training

3. tough, demanding, usefully training

4. tough, demanding, and usefully trained

5. tough, demanding, and useful in their training

1 2 3 4 5
|| || || || ||

6. Carl Williams is an excellent basketball coach and *he makes friends with the team members.*

1. he makes friends with the team members.

2. a good friend to the team members.

3. the team members are his friend.

4. the team members liking him.

5. liking the team members.

7. Every Thursday night the Morgan family watches TV and *TV dinners are served*.

    1 2 3 4 5

    1. TV dinners are served.
    2. they ate TV dinners.
    3. eats TV dinners.
    4. eat TV dinners.
    5. are eating TV dinners.

8. The City Council meets every Wednesday evening in private and *publicly on Thursdays*.

    1 2 3 4 5

    1. publicly on Thursdays.
    2. Thursdays meets publicly.
    3. every Thursday in public.
    4. also Thursdays in public.
    5. has public meetings on Thursdays.

9. Carlos Battaglia has a good historical perspective *since he understands* current events.

    1 2 3 4 5

    1. since he understands
    2. because he understands
    3. ; however, he understands
    4. ; therefore, he understands
    5. so he doesn't understand

10. I am not in agreement with most of the policies of the present administration, *but I can't change them*.

    1 2 3 4 5

    1. but I can't change them.
    2. so I don't want to change them.
    3. so I can't change them.
    4. since I can't change them.
    5. ; therefore, I can't change them.

Effectiveness of Expression—Part B

Directions: Blacken the space beneath the number which corresponds to the number of the group of words that correctly completes each sentence.

1 2 3 4 5
‖ ‖ ‖ ‖ ‖

1. The boundaries of science have expanded significantly,
    1) and two distinct fields of science have emerged: pure and applied.
    2) even though two distinct fields of science have emerged: pure and applied.
    3) whenever two distinct fields of science have emerged: pure and applied.
    4) and two fields of science, they have emerged: pure and applied.
    5) despite two distinct fields of science have emerged: pure and applied.

1 2 3 4 5
‖ ‖ ‖ ‖ ‖

2. The British pound was devalued
    1) and the reason was because of an inflationary spiral.
    2) and the reason was because of inflation.
    3) and it was because of an inflationary spiral.
    4) because of an inflationary spiral.
    5) and it was when the inflation spiraled.

1 2 3 4 5
‖ ‖ ‖ ‖ ‖

3. The Federal Trade Commission has proposed new rules that would permit pharmacies to advertise prices for prescription drugs,
    1) although it will save consumers millions of dollars a year.

   2) thereby saving consumers millions of dollars a year.

   3) however saving consumers millions of dollars a year.

   4) in addition to saving consumers millions of dollars a year.

   5) and it would save consumers millions of dollars a year.

4.   Many people believed that the recent product "shortages"

   1) were because manufacturers wanted to raise prices.

   2) resulted from manufacturers wanting to raise prices.

   3) happened because of the manufacturers wanted to raise prices.

   4) were because of the manufacturers, they wanted to raise prices.

   5) resulted from manufacturers, they wanted to raise prices.

```
1  2  3  4  5
|| || || || ||
```

5.   Viewers find it difficult to reach agreement on whether

   1) or not television, it encouraged violent behavior.

   2) or not television, it does or doesn't encourage violent behavior.

   3) or not television encourages violent behavior.

   4) television hardly never encourages violent behavior.

   5) or not television encourages violent behavior by viewing television.

```
1  2  3  4  5
|| || || || ||
```

6. One member of the Surgeon General's Scientific Advisory Committee on Television and Social Behavior felt that
    1) there is scarcely no question about whether television has a negative effect on its viewers.
    2) there isn't no question about whether television has a negative effect on its viewers.
    3) there isn't hardly any question about whether television has a negative effect on its viewers.
    4) there is no question about whether television has a negative effect on its viewers.
    5) there really isn't no question about whether television has a negative effect on its viewers.

1 2 3 4 5

7. Some TV viewers express their resentment toward anyone else censoring their viewing choices,
    1) saying it's their job to censor the TV programs their children see.
    2) saying it's the parents' job to censor the TV programs their children see on television programs.
    3) saying it's the parents' job to censor the TV programs their children see.
    4) saying parents, they should censor the TV programs their children see.
    5) saying TV it should be censored by no one but parents.

1 2 3 4 5

8. An environmental protection agency should
    1) set automobile pollution standards,

1 2 3 4 5

oversee stripmining, and prohibit dumping in public waterways.

2) set automobile pollution standards, oversee stripmining, and they will prohibit dumping in public waterways.

3) set automobile pollution standards, do the overseeing of stripmining, and they will prohibit dumping in private waterways.

4) set automobile pollution standards, overseeing stripmining, and prohibiting dumping in private waterways.

5) set automobile pollution standards, and they will oversee stripmining, and prohibit dumping in private waterways.

9. Many people who formerly drove to work are now taking buses

$$\begin{array}{ccccc}1 & 2 & 3 & 4 & 5\\ \| & \| & \| & \| & \|\end{array}$$

1) in order to conserve gas, preventing air pollution, and saving money.

2) and by the way, they conserve gas, prevent air pollution, and they're saving money.

3) in order to conserve gas, and they'll be preventing air pollution, and to save money.

4) in order to conserve gas, to prevent air pollution, and to save money.

5) in order to conserve gas, do air pollution prevention, and save money.

10. In order to encourage the commuter not to drive to work, some communities have installed park-and-ride facilities

$$\begin{array}{ccccc}1 & 2 & 3 & 4 & 5\\ \| & \| & \| & \| & \|\end{array}$$

1) where the commuter can leave his car and board a bus for the trip to work.

2) where they can leave his car and board
a bus for the trip to work.

3) where they can leave their cars and
board a bus for the trip to work.

4) and then they can leave their car and
board a bus for the trip to work.

5) so that they can leave their car and
board a bus for the trip to work.

1 2 3 4 5
‖ ‖ ‖ ‖ ‖

11. American flags are usually produced at the
rate of 500,000 a year;

1) although sales are up 10 to 15 percent
due to Bicentennial celebrations.

2) despite the fact that sales are up due to
Bicentennial Year celebrations.

3) however, sales are up 10 to 15 percent
due to the Bicentennial Year celebrations.

4) even if sales are up 10 to 15 percent due
to the Bicentennial Year celebrations.

5) so sales are up 10 to 15 percent due to
the Bicentennial Year celebrations.

1 2 3 4 5
‖ ‖ ‖ ‖ ‖

12. The year 1985 showed a marked decline in
Americans traveling abroad

1) in spite of the recession and inflation.

2) inasmuch as there was a recession and
inflation.

3) due to the recession and inflation.

4) because it was a recession and inflation.

5) even though there was a recession and
inflation.

1 2 3 4 5
‖ ‖ ‖ ‖ ‖

13. The French Revolution did not occur when
the peasants had no rights whatsoever;

1) rather, the Revolution occurred when

the peasants began to taste the better life.

2) but it happened when they began to taste the better life.

3) so it did when they got some rights.

4) rather, the Revolution occurred when the peasants, they began to taste the better life.

5) instead they made the Revolution when they became rich.

                                                1 2 3 4 5

14.   Modern China has eliminated serious contagious diseases

1) because they use trained non-professionals to aid their country's limited number of doctors.

2) since using trained non-professionals to aid their limited number of doctors.

3) therefore it uses trained non-professionals to aid the country's limited number of doctors.

4) by using trained non-professionals to aid the country's limited number of doctors.

5) for using trained non-professionals to aid the country's limited number of doctors.

                                                1 2 3 4 5

15.   During the first half of the eighteenth century, the Carter family built a mansion at Williamsburg where the family

1) it grew its own food, rode to hounds on horses from their own stables, and shipped its tobacco to England from its private dock.

2) they grew their own food, rode to the hounds on horses from their own sta-

bles, made equipment in their own craft shops, and shipped their tobacco to England from their private dock.

3) grew its own food, rode to the hounds on horses from its own stables, made equipment in its own craft shops, and shipped its tobacco to England from its private dock.

4) grew its own food, rode to the hounds on horses from their own stables, made equipment in its own craft shop, and shipped their tobacco to England from its private dock.

5) grew their own food, rode to the hounds on horses from their own stables, made equipment in their own craft shop, and shipping tobacco from their own private dock.

Punctuation and Capitalization

Directions: Blacken the space beneath the number which corresponds to the number of the error in each sentence. If there is no error, blacken space number 5.

1. According to historians, when the people in
   power cannot keep the governed content,
   revolution is a possibility. *No error*

   1   2   3   4   5

2. The *Declaration of Independence* states,
   ". . . that all men are created equal, that they
   are endowed by their Creator with certain

   1   2   3   4   5

inalienable rights; that among these are Life,

$$\overline{3}$$

Liberty, and the pursuit of Happiness ".

$$\overline{4}$$

$$\frac{No\ error}{5}$$

3. Great literature, as well as great art is a part
$$\overline{1} \qquad \overline{2}$$
of the <u>American</u> <u>tradition</u>. <u>No error</u>
$$\overline{3} \qquad \overline{4} \qquad \overline{5}$$

1	2	3	4	5
‖	‖	‖	‖	‖

4. The pioneers were a hardy brave group of
$$\overline{1}$$
people who would look in disbelief on the
$$\overline{2}$$
comforts of today's middle class. <u>No error</u>
$$\overline{3} \qquad\qquad \overline{4} \quad \overline{5}$$

1	2	3	4	5
‖	‖	‖	‖	‖

5. During their first few years on the American

continent, the pioneers lived off the animals
$$\overline{1} \qquad \overline{2}$$
in the woods, and stole corn from the natives.
$$\overline{3} \qquad\qquad \overline{4}$$
$$\frac{No\ error}{5}$$

1	2	3	4	5
‖	‖	‖	‖	‖

6. They traveled with the bare necessities; food,
$$\overline{1} \quad \overline{2}$$
water, warm clothing, tools, and weapons.
$$\overline{3} \qquad\qquad \overline{4}$$
$$\frac{No\ error}{5}$$

1	2	3	4	5
‖	‖	‖	‖	‖

7. The V<u>i</u>rginians needed their own leader,
     —
     1

Jefferson<u>,</u> <u>S</u>am Adams was not their type.
      — —
      3 4

No error
—
5

1	2	3	4	5
‖	‖	‖	‖	‖

8. Many say George Washington was a compe-

tent general, and a good president; however,
     —   —   —
     1   2   3

some historians would disagree. *No error*
   —   —
   4   5

1	2	3	4	5
‖	‖	‖	‖	‖

9. There are those who would say that "John
                             —
                             1

Kennedy was the greatest president to date,
                   —   —
                   2   3

and others would say that he has been ide-

alized. *No error*
—   —
4   5

1	2	3	4	5
‖	‖	‖	‖	‖

10. A flower consists of a calyx, a corolla, a stamen
          —   —   —   —
          1   2   3   4

and pistils. *No error*
          —
          5

1	2	3	4	5
‖	‖	‖	‖	‖

SUMMARY OF RESULTS

After reviewing the Answer Key on page 335, chart your scores below for each practice exercise.

Skill	Your Number Right	Your Number Wrong (Including Omissions)	Acceptable Score
Spelling			15 Correct
Usage—Part A			26 Correct
Usage—Part B			7 Correct
Effectiveness of Expression Part A			7 Correct
Effectiveness of Expression Part B			11 Correct
Punctuation and Capitalization			7 Correct

SKILLS ANALYSIS

To discover your weak areas, locate the question numbers you got wrong and circle them on this Skills Analysis chart. Refer back to those chapters where you got questions wrong.

Skill	Question Number	Chapter Reference
Spelling	1 to 20	*See Chapter* 18
Usage: Part A Agreement of Subject and Linking Word	1, 7, 14, 26, 30	7

Skill	Question Number	Chapter Reference
		See Chapter
Agreement: Special Problems	2, 4, 5, 11, 16, 18, 20, 22	8
Correct Form of Irregular Action Word	3	1
Correct Use of Pronouns	6, 8, 9, 21, 25, 27, 28, 29, 35	10
Time: Special Problems	12, 15, 23, 24	9
Agreement of Performer and Action Word	13, 31	2
Word Usage	32, 33, 34	20
Correct Use of Descriptive Words: -ly ending	10, 17, 19	3
Usage: Part B Repetition	1, 5, 7, 10	15
Double Negative	2, 4, 6, 8	15
Word Choice	3, 9	20
Effectiveness of Expression Part A Repetition	1	15
Wordiness	2	15
Coordination of Ideas	4, 9, 10	15
Balance	5, 6, 7, 8	12
Effectiveness of Expression Part B Coordination of Ideas	1, 3, 11, 12, 13, 14	15
Wordiness	2, 4, 5	15
Double Negative	6	15
Unclear Pronoun Reference	7, 10	15
Balance	8, 9, 15	12

Skill	Question Number	Chapter Reference
		See Chapter
Punctuation and Capitalization		
Quotation Marks	2, 9	16
Comma	3, 4, 5, 8, 10	13
Semi-colon	7	13
Colon	6	16

ANSWER KEY

Chapter 23

Final Review

Spelling *Page 311.*

1. (3) caucus
2. (1) temperature
3. (4) library
4. (2) lucrative
5. (1) hygienic
6. (3) ephemeral
7. (4) unnecessary
8. (1) weird
9. (4) receipts
10. (2) similar
11. (3) preferred
12. (5) No error
13. (3) dispensable
14. (1) truly
15. (4) crushes
16. (4) thieves
17. (5) No error
18. (2) achievement
19. (3) Thursday
20. (5) No error

Usage—Part A *Page 313.*

1. (4) No two cities in this country *are* identical. See Chapter 7.
2. (2) Any of the local merchants *is* willing to support the United Fund. See Chapter 8.
3. (3) A carton of cigarettes has been *lying* on this counter all week. See Chapter 1.
4. (5) No error. See Chapter 8.
5. (3) One of the necessary prerequisites for change *is* open-mindedness. See Chapter 8.
6. (1) Manuel and *I* travel to work together each week-day morning. See Chapter 10.
7. (2) Taxes and laughter *are* always present in our American way of life. See Chapter 7.
8. (2) Everyone must realize *his* own potential and try to achieve it. See Chapter 10.
9. (4) Mario is a much more efficient bartender than *he.* See Chapter 10.
10. (2) Elissa types much *more quickly* than any other woman in the office. See Chapter 4.
11. (2) Each of the choices *is* equally unappealing to me. See Chapter 8.
12. (1) Before the alarm *stopped* ringing, Vera had pulled up the shade. See Chapter 9.
13. (2) One of those women *speaks* as well as a professional lecturer. See Chapter 8.
14. (1) The dishes in the box *are* on sale this week only but will be sold for more next week. See Chapter 7.
15. (5) No error. See Chapter 9.
16. (3) Either the subway or the buses *are* crowded at this time of day. See Chapter 8.
17. (4) I noticed that older women walk more *gracefully* than teen-age girls. See Chapter 4.
18. (2) Each of the contestants *hopes* to win the grand prize. See Chapter 8.
19. (4) When I must speak to a large group of people, I always speak too *softly.* See Chapter 4.
20. (2) The mail carriers each *have* their own personal gripes. See Chapter 8.
21. (3) Any of the women in that office may express *her* opinion at any time. See Chapter 10.

22. (2) Either the executive or members of his staff *were* responsible for breaking the law. See Chapter 8.
23. (2) Before they signed the treaty, both parties *had agreed* to uphold the terms provided. See Chapter 9.
24. (1) Eisenhower *had been* president before Kennedy was, and Nixon served after Kennedy had. See Chapter 9.
25. (3) Either Charlie or I will call you or *him* when the order is ready. See Chapter 10.
26. (1) Romeo and Juliet *is* one of my favorite plays, but I've never seen it performed. See Chapter 7.
27. (3) Was it Mr. Farrar *who* called you? See Chapter 10.
28. (4) I am always at the bus stop earlier than *he*. See Chapter 10.
29. (1) Eileen and *I* are working on the night shift with them. See Chapter 10.
30. (1) Fifteen minutes *is* all that I can spare to listen to your problems. See Chapter 7.
31. (2) The problem of too many people *requires* immediate attention by world leaders as well as scientists and environmentalists. See Chapter 2.
32. (3) After many months of arguing, Congress finally *adopted* the bill into law. See Chapter 20.
33. (2) Because his lawyer strongly *advised* him to do so, Mr. Rodriguez offered his wife a generous settlement. See Chapter 20.
34. (1) The *principal* reason for not borrowing your credit card is that I'm afraid I'll lose it. See Chapter 20.
35. (3) Your supervisor does not appreciate *your* walking in consistently at 9:10. See Chapter 10.

Usage—Part B *Page 318.*

1. (1) My *brother never* calls before visiting us.
2. (3) Great men throughout history *hardly ever* avoided some minor scandal.
3. (3) If you had called ahead of time, I could *have* been ready when you arrived.
4. (2) Lady Bird Johnson *scarcely ever* missed an opportunity to beautify America.
5. (1) The trip on the *sightseeing* bus was one of the highlights of our much deserved vacation.
6. (3) Manny was shocked when Alfred raised his voice; no one had *ever* spoken to him in that tone of voice.
7. (1) The *sun is* 865,000 miles in diameter and has a surface temperature of about 10,000° F.
8. (3) A wise consumer carefully reads the labels and *doesn't buy* unmarked products.
9. (3) If you really had wanted to, you could *have* prevented that misunderstanding.
10. (1) Some *scientists believe* that one of the long-range effects of food additives is hyperactivity in children.

Effectiveness of Expression—Part A *Page 320.*

1. (2) In today's all volunteer U.S. Army, *the recruit starts* his two-year enlistment in a different atmosphere.
2. (3) *The former soldier would not recognize living conditions in today's army because* the facilities are more home-like and less barracks-like.
3. (1) Today's soldier enjoys *not only more comfort but also better pay.*
4. (4) Nowadays the army can afford to be choosy *since the recession has increased* the number and the quality of the applicants.
5. (2) The recruits get *tough, demanding, useful training* under the command of their drill sergeants.
6. (2) Carl Williams is an excellent basketball coach and *a good friend to the team members.*
7. (3) Every Thursday night the Morgan family watches TV and *eats TV dinners.*
8. (3) The City Council meets every Wednesday evening in private and *every Thursday in public.*
9. (4) Carlos Battaglia has a good historical perspective; *therefore, he understands current events.*
10. (1) I am not in agreement with most of the policies of the present administration, *but I can't change them.*

Effectiveness of Expression—Part B *Page 323.*

1. (1) The boundaries of science have expanded significantly, *and two distinct fields of science have emerged: pure and applied.*

2. (4) The British pound was devalued *because of an inflationary spiral.*

3. (2) The Federal Trade Commission has proposed new rules that would permit pharmacies to advertise prices for prescription drugs, *thereby saving consumers millions of dollars a year.*

4. (2) Many people believed that the recent product "shortages" *resulted from manufacturers wanting to raise prices.*

5. (3) Viewers find it difficult to reach agreement on whether *or not television encourages violent behavior.*

6. (4) One member of the Surgeon General's Scientific Advisory Committee on Television and Social Behavior felt that *there is no question about whether television has a negative effect on its viewers.*

7. (3) Some TV viewers express their resentment toward anyone else censoring their viewing choices, *saying it's the parents' job to censor the TV programs their children see.*

8. (1) An environmental protection agency should *set automobile pollution standards, oversee strip-mining, and prohibit dumping in public waterways.*

9. (4) Many people who formerly drove to work are now taking buses *in order to conserve gas, to prevent air pollution, and to save money.*

10. (1) In order to encourage the commuter not to drive to work, some communities have installed park-and-ride facilities *where the commuter can leave his car and board a bus for the trip to work.*

11. (3) American flags are usually produced at the rate of 500,000 a year; *however, sales are up 10 to 15 percent due to the Bicentennial Year celebrations.*

12. (3) The year 1985 showed a marked decline in Americans' traveling abroad *due to the recession and inflation.*

13. (1) The French Revolution did not occur when the peasants had no rights whatsoever; *rather, the Revolution occurred when the peasants began to taste the better life.*

14. (4) Modern China has eliminated serious contagious diseases *by using trained nonprofessionals to aid the country's limited number of doctors.*

15. (3) During the first half of the eighteenth century, the Carter family built a mansion at Williamsburg where the family *grew its own food, rode to the hounds on horses from its own stables, made equipment in its own craft shops, and shipped its tobacco to England from its private dock.*

Punctuation and Capitalization *Page 329.*

1. (5) No error

2. (4) The *Declaration of Independence* states ". . . that all men are created equal, that they are endowed by their Creator with certain inalienable rights; that among these are Life, Liberty, and the pursuit of Happiness."

3. (2) Great literature, as well as great art, is a part of the American tradition.

4. (1) The pioneers were a hardy, brave group of people who would look in disbelief on the comforts of today's middle class.

5. (3) During their first few years on the American continent, the pioneers lived off the animals in the woods and stole corn from the natives.

6. (1) They traveled with the bare necessities: food, water, warm clothing, tools, and weapons.

7. (3) The Virginians needed their own leader, Jefferson; Sam Adams was not their type.
8. (1) Many say George Washington was a competent general and a good president; however, some historians would disagree.
9. (1) There are those who would say that John Kennedy was the greatest president to date, and others would say that he has been idealized.
10. (4) A flower consists of a calyx, a corolla, a stamen, and pistils.

MOVE TO THE HEAD OF YOUR CLASS

THE EASY WAY!

Barron's presents THE EASY WAY SERIES—specially prepared by top educators, it maximizes effective learning, while minimizing the time and effort it takes to raise your grades, brush up on the basics, and build your confidence. Comprehensive and full of clear review examples, **THE EASY WAY SERIES** is your best bet for better grades, quickly! Each book is $9.95, Can. $13.95 unless otherwise noted below.

4187-9	**Accounting the Easy Way, 2nd Ed.**
4194-1	**Algebra the Easy Way, 2nd Ed.**
4625-0	**American History the Easy Way—$9.95, Can. $12.95**
4197-6	**Arithmetic the Easy Way, 2nd Ed.**
4286-7	**Biology the Easy Way, 2nd Ed.**
4371-5	**Bookkeeping the Easy Way, 2nd Ed.**
4626-9	**Business Letters the Easy Way, 2nd Ed.**
4627-7	**Business Mathematics the Easy Way, 2nd Ed.**
4078-3	**Calculus the Easy Way, 2nd Ed.**
4198-4	**Chemistry the Easy Way, 2nd Ed.**
4253-0	**Computer Programming In Basic the Easy Way, 2nd Ed.**
2800-7	**Computer Programming In Fortran the Easy Way**
2799-X	**Computer Programming in Pascal the Easy Way— $11.95, Can. $15.95**
4081-3	**Electronics the Easy Way, 2nd Ed.**
3347-7	**English the Easy Way, 2nd Ed.**
4205-0	**French the Easy Way, 2nd Ed.**
4287-5	**Geometry the Easy Way, 2nd Ed.**
2719-1	**German the Easy Way**
3830-4	**Italian the Easy Way**
4079-1	**Mathematics the Easy Way, 2nd Ed.**
4390-1	**Physics the Easy Way, 2nd Ed.**
4204-2	**Spanish the Easy Way, 2nd Ed.**
3346-9	**Spelling the Easy Way, 2nd Ed.**
4196-8	**Statistics the Easy Way, 2nd Ed.**
4389-8	**Trigonometry the Easy Way, 2nd Ed.**
4080-5	**Typing the Easy Way, 2nd Ed.—$10.95, Can. $14.95**
4615-3	**Writing the Easy Way, 2nd Ed.**

BARRON'S EDUCATIONAL SERIES
250 Wireless Boulevard • Hauppauge, New York 11788
In Canada: Georgetown Book Warehouse • 34 Armstrong Avenue
Georgetown, Ontario L7G 4R9

Prices subject to change without notice. Books may be purchased at your local bookstore, or by mail from Barron's. Enclose check or money order for total amount plus sales tax where applicable and 10% for postage and handling (minimum charge $1.75, Canada $2.00). All books are paperback editions.
ISBN Prefix 0-8120

Notes

Notes

Notes

Notes